A MENTOR BOOK

MW1182
$1.50

Walter A. Fairservis, Jr.

THE ANCIENT KINGDOMS OF THE NILE

AND THE DOOMED MONUMENTS OF NUBIA

ILLUSTRATED WITH DIAGRAMS, MAPS AND PHOTOGRAPHS

A DISTINGUISHED ARCHAEOLOGIST STUDIES THE CULTURAL AND POLITICAL HISTORY OF NUBIA, EGYPT, AND THE SUDAN... CRADLE OF THE WORLD'S EARLIEST CIVILIZATIONS, A RECORD OF WHICH STILL SURVIVES IN MAGNIFICENT RUINS DESTINED TO BE ENGULFED BY THE NILE WHEN THE NEW HIGH DAM IS BUILT

PHARAOHS' BIRTHPLACE

Dr. Fairservis brings to life a fascinating land as he tells of the dawn of civilization in the Nile Valley. Using geology, geography, paleontology, archaeology, and history to re-create the past, he describes prehistoric man in Africa; the first empires of Sudan, Nubia, and Kush; the rise of the pharaohs; the monuments of Ramses II; the fall of Egyptian civilization and the emergence of Christian Nubia; the slave trade; and the rule of the British Empire in the Sudan . . . including the eye-witness accounts of some of the first Europeans to view the ancient remains of the great Nile civilizations.

At the present day the monuments of Nubia, among the most imposing ever created by man, are doomed to be engulfed by the surging waters of the Nile when the Saad-el-Aali dam is built. This necessary reservoir will cover the great temples of Ramses and Nefertari, and numberless other inscriptions, tombs, cemeteries. Dr. Fairservis urges both governments and individuals to offer help in saving these age-old edifces of history.

Also included in this volume are a chronology, notes, appendices, glossary, bibliography, and index, as well as diagrams, maps, and photographs—all of which help bring alive an ancient historical region.

MENTOR and SIGNET Titles
of Special Interest

The Ancient Kingdoms Of The Nile

And the Doomed Monuments of Nubia

by

Walter A. Fairservis, Jr.

A MENTOR BOOK from,

NEW AMERICAN LIBRARY

TIMES MIRROR

New York and Scarborough, Ontario

The New English Library Limited, London

Acknowledgments

Acknowledgment is made to the following copyright holders for permission
to reprint copyrighted material:

Cambridge University Press for *A History of the Arabs in the Sudan*,
Vol. I, by H. A. MacMichael.

R. E. Cheesman and Macmillan & Co., Ltd., London, for *Lake Tana and
the Blue Nile* by R. E. Cheesman, copyright 1936.

Gustavo Colonnetti for the adaption of the Abu Simbel illustration.

J. B. Lippincott Company for *The Egyptian Sudan* by E. A. T. W. Budge.

Luzac and Company Ltd., London, for *The Religion of Ancient Egypt* by
S. A. B. Mercer.

Macmillan & Co., Ltd., London; The Macmillan Co. of Canada, Ltd., and
St. Martin's Press, Inc., for *Sudan Days and Ways* by H. C. Jackson, by
permission of the publishers.

Peabody Museum of Harvard University for *Excavations at Kerma* by G. A.
Reisner, copyright 1923 by the Peabody Museum of Harvard University.

Underwood & Underwood for *Egypt Through the Stereoscope* by James
H. Breasted, copyright 1905 by Underwood & Underwood, New York.

University of Chicago Press for *Palaeolithic Man and the Nile Valley in
Nubia and Upper Egypt* by K. S. Sandford and W. J. Arkell, copyright 1933
by the University of Chicago.

The Viking Press, Inc. for *Never to Die* by Josephine Mayer and Tom
Prideaux, copyright 1938 by Josephine Mayer and Tom Prideaux, by permission
of The Viking Press, Inc.

MENTOR TRADEMARK REG. U.S. PAT. OFF. AND FOREIGN COUNTRIES
REGISTERED TRADEMARK—MARCA REGISTRADA
HECHO EN CHICAGO, U.S.A.

SIGNET, SIGNET CLASSICS, SIGNETTE, MENTOR AND PLUME BOOKS
are published *in the United States* by
The New American Library, Inc.,
1301 Avenue of the Americas, New York, New York 10019,
in Canada by The New American Library of Canada Limited,
81 Mack Avenue, Scarborough, 704, Ontario,
in the United Kingdom by The New English Library Limited,
Barnard's Inn, Holborn, London, E.C. 1, England

FIRST PRINTING, OCTOBER, 1962

PRINTED IN THE UNITED STATES OF AMERICA

Contents

v

List of Figures

List of Plates

(PLATES 1-13 APPEAR BETWEEN
PAGES 64 AND 65)

(PLATES 51-62 APPEAR BETWEEN
PAGES 208 AND 209)

And so Nubia, from the days of antiquity, has stood as an example and a token of what man can achieve when his toil and ingenuity are pitted against the elements and an unfriendly climate.—ANDRÉ BERNAND-FRENCH, National Council for Scientific Research, and ABDULLALIF AHMED ALY, Professor, Faculty of Letters, Cairo University (*The UNESCO Courier,* February, 1960)

Prologue

A miracle is to happen in a truly antique land—a miracle that may in its way revive the glories of the pharaohs. For a great dam is being built on the borders of Nubia, ancient gateway to Africa, a dam that will dwarf all dams that seek to chain the waters of the Nile. Not since the Pleistocene have the mud-laden waters of Africa's mightiest river met such a barrier. Neither the granite-toothed cataracts that impede the river road to Khartoum nor the great desert cliffs of the Nubian plateau have offered the challenge to the river's might that this new man-created, all-controlling High Dam hurls at the water gods. The vast floods that pour from the hills far to the south will find escape to the Mediterranean only by means of sluices opened at man's convenience. The waters await their turn, a turn that comes when the drying soil of Egypt requires a moist renewal. Thus the thwarted Nile will swell back upon itself and for nearly two hundred miles its rising waters will flood the land of Nubia.

Nubia is a dry land, a land of black rocks and endless sand, a land of heat and thirst. It is also a land of history, creating by its environmental extremes the desperate heroes and villains who shape the course of stern events. "He who holds Egypt holds the key to India"; "He who holds Nubia and the Sudan holds Africa." How the deadly slogans of strategy ring about the valley of the Nile, ringing today as they have rung for thousands of years. There is a mighty lesson to be learned in the narrow, water-worn Nile Valley that splits the desiccated land of Nubia. Buhen, Semna, fortresses of ancient Egypt's Middle Kingdom; Abu Simbel, temple complex of Egypt's most vainglorious pharaoh; Philae, seat of beauty and ritual; and so many temples, churches, forts, and villages; even Wadi Halfa, river port of the Sudan, famous as the jump-off point for Kitchener's army of conquest—all these represent pages from an epic story which in its fashion reflects the whole tale of mankind itself.

The lure of Nubia and the Sudan is sufficient warrant for any book, but the desperate need to interest people at large in the peculiar and necessary fate of Nubia is a spur to anyone who knows something of the land and its history. Nubia is the gateway to the Sudan. It is the bridgeland between the Arabized Africa of the north and the country of the Negroes on the south. The Arabs in fact named the Sudan "Bilad-es Sudan," country of the blacks. It is said that during the Roman period Emperor Diocletian moved the Noba tribe, a group of Negroes, from the Kharga Oasis to the Upper Nile Valley and afterward, in Arab days at least, the country was known as Nubia. Even the ancient Egyptians realized that there was a boundary in the Nile Valley between truly Egyptian peoples and those of Nubia. This boundary was generally at the First Cataract of the Nile near the island of Elephantine. South of this was the land of Wawat, what came to be called Nubia. Both the Aswan Dam and the new High Dam are constructed on this ancient border in involuntary homage to tradition. Beyond this point the desert and the valley stretch into the distance fading into dusty haze—a haze out of which caravans and boats have come with the hides, foods, woods, and raw metals that tell of other regions, of great forests and exotic beasts, of teeming rivers and pungent flowers, of silhouette peaks and endless abyss, of dwarf men and giants; in short, of Africa, seat of high adventure and imperial treasure. Thus for all men Nubia has been the gate and the bridge to the Sudan and beyond.

We cannot hope to write in any thorough manner of the story that is Nubia. For Nubia is at once Egypt and the Sudan. It is of the Mediterranean world and of Africa. It is both simple and complex in one paradoxical lump. That is the reason for its timeless lure. Its horizons offer and its deserts and cataracts bar the way and only he who never weakens wins to the goals beyond its borders. Ancient Egypt may have gained a portion of its greatness because of the dream lure and eternal stress of Nubia. So indeed one might suspect that both men and nations need a Nubia to draw hopes and offer challenges by which to express the greatness that is inherent in them. It is no small contribution which this land of drowned temples and man-made lakes-to-be makes to all men.

If there is a note of urgency, even at times of bitterness, cropping up here and there on the following pages, there is

reason for it. It has been over a year since the first major
appeal was made by UNESCO for concrete help in saving
the monuments of Nubia from the waters which are bound
to engulf them when the new dam, Sadd-el-Aali, is built. In
that time scholars, institutions, and many private organizations have responded nobly to the challenge. At this time
the valley of the Nile is alive with archaeological enterprise
as men face up to what is in reality an overwhelming task:
several dozen major temples to save, thousands of inscriptions and graffiti to record, untold numbers of cemeteries,
town mounds, and crumbled churches to excavate, acres to
map archaeologically. Each problem solved only reveals more
problems wanting answers. What will scholars want to know
ten, twenty, or one hundred years from now? What is important to preserve? What has to be sacrificed for the sake
of time? Tantalizing, oftimes agonizing decisions have to
be made. The fact that this is being done so efficiently is
a tribute to everyone concerned.

The United Arab Republic, the beneficiary of the desperately needed dam, is so well aware of its responsibilities
to the world that it has already donated men and over ten
million dollars from a not-too-ample treasury to record and
preserve the treasures of Nubia. The Republic of the Sudan is
also contributing concretely to salvage what can be salvaged
in Upper Nubia. Both governments offer more than fair
shares in the recovered antiquities and in concessions
elsewhere in their territories. The U.A.R. even permits the
moving of some of the temples to foreign soil.

With one or two exceptions the governments of the
world, especially those that possess the lion's share of the
resources on both sides of the iron curtain, have contributed
a mere trickle of urgently needed money or none at all.
James Henry Breasted, first of America's historians of the
ancient world, pointed out long ago that an age of character
was bound to arise out of the evolving ideas of the ancient
world. The Nubian salvage is an expression of human
character international in scope, as I have tried to outline in
this writing. It has an intensely practical aspect, not only
for nations but for thinking individuals.

It is strange that in an age when knowledge of our place
in the universe has taken such an awesome form, when our
obvious need is for that age Breasted predicted, we seem
to be able only to repeat our centuries-old somber actions. It
is passing strange that on one side of the iron curtain the

political doctrine emphasizes the rightness of the masses, and on the other side the majority opinion is what counts; yet it remains that the only ones who really labor and sacrifice are in the minority. The hypocrisy of both sides is apparent historically. It is apparent now as money and raw material mount annually into the billions for weapons of war, for increased pleasure, for falsehood, while so many worthwhile things are kept alive only by the devotion of a few. Nubia represents a neutral field for international co-operation on a huge scale; it represents a mirror of history in which men can see themselves as they actually are and take heed; it represents a chance for men to prove that humanness means so much more than feelings of the flesh alone. For such a purpose a trickle of funds should become a torrent. The devoted few should be inundated with material help comparable in every way to the rising waters of the High Dam.

This book is an attempt to explain something of the wonderful story of Nubia and the adjacent lands of Egypt and the Sudan. To the layman some of this may be complex; to the professional I am vulnerable both for what is omitted and for what is said. Nevertheless, it is an attempt to provide some solid ground for an understanding of just why Nubia was important in the past and why it remains so in the present. In the appendixes are some vital facts about the dam and some addresses for those who want to send material support to the archaeological projects. Whatever my writing, there should be no excuse for any individual who believes he is individual not to send some help. For as with all human action, the proof of a man's responsibility and right to manhood depends on his selflessness.

1

The Birthland
of the Nile

*For the Nile is the only river on our globe which rises in
the tropics and flows northward to penetrate for nearly 700
miles into the climatic belt where the first great national organi-
sations of men arose.*—JAMES HENRY BREASTED

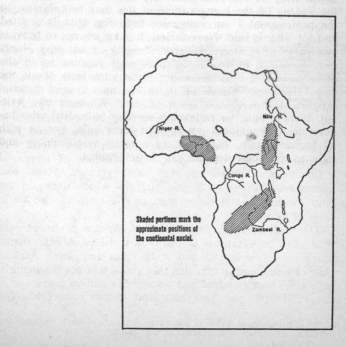

Shaded portions mark the
approximate positions of
the continental nuclei.

Nubia is not simply a gateway to the vast reaches of interior Africa, it is also a mirror to the remote past of the entire continent. For he who would understand the particular mode of Africa must envision the immense prospect of its geological history.* This is not a simple matter, for geologists, like astronomers, speak in mighty dimensions and almost infinite measures of years. These standards mark the depth of the roots of the land, and their physical manifestations have directed the course of life from the one-celled to the emancipated Homo sapiens of new Africa.

Most Ancient Beginnings

In contrast to the other continents where orogeny has created still youthful and colossal mountain ranges such as the Rockies, Alps, and Himalaya, Africa is a stable plateau land founded on a basement complex of often perceptible old rock formations, ancient even by geological standards. Some three thousand million years ago the whole earth was undergoing the final stages of transition from being a viscous amalgam of chemical compounds to a stratified stable globe of lands and waters. Volcanic action laid down the basic lavas and pegmatities along the arcs where the thickening earth's crust remained disjointed. In time, patches of hardened volcanic rocks appeared here and there over the earth. These became the nuclei about which the continents were formed. Africa's birth took place, it appears, in three areas: West Africa, where Liberia and Ghana now flourish; South Africa in the region of Southern Rhodesia and Transvaal; and East Africa in roughly the Kenya-Uganda territories. Here were continental nuclei which grew with additions of terrestrial sediments and intrusions of igneous granites. Here, too, quartz veins shone with gold deposits which drew, in far later times, the acquisitive men of the earth to the birthlands of a continent.

The characteristic shape of the African continent was created by an extension of the West and East African nuclei along an east-west axis and of the East and South African centers north and south. But that shape was not distinguishable some four hundred and seventy-five million years ago in the Palaeozoic era; for great land masses connected Asia

---

* A chronological table is placed at the end of each chapter and pertains to the particular material of that chapter.

and Africa—some geologists would include Australia and
South America as well. But whereas during the Palaeozoic
and the succeeding Mesozoic (Age of Reptiles) these adjacent
land areas underwent great tensions and as a result were
warped into heights and depressions, the ancient plateau of
Africa remained stable, though traces of eruptive volcanoes
and subterranean intrusions into the older formations indicate that the earth's crust even there was barely able to
restrain the fluid magma beneath. Metamorphosis of the
granites and the sediments of the plateau was a continuing
process and helped in the building of the land.

There is still some discussion over the causes of the separation of continents by seas and oceans. Wegener's theory of
the drifting apart of continental masses is probably the
most famous explanation advanced. His idea derived from
the apparent fit of the Americas into the western side of
Africa. Thus as the continents floated apart on the yielding
strata beneath the earth's crust, the waters of the Atlantic
entered the space vacated; Africa remained the relatively
unmoved heartland, while as the Americas drifted westward
the stresses along the front of the moving continents were
of sufficient dimension to crumble that portion of the continental shelves, thus forming the high ranges of the Andes
and Rockies. Wegener's theory, however, is becoming less and
less accepted with greater understanding of earth processes.

More plausible theories derive from continuing studies of
the earth's structure and the stresses and strains inherent in
its physical character. One theory gaining general acceptance
depicts the earth as a cooling globe, whose interior main-
tains enormous amounts of heat energy and whose dense
structure remains constant. In contrast, the outer portion of
the globe has cooled and solidified to form a crust. The
section between the crust and the heated interior, over
250 miles in thickness, is cooling and as a result is
contracting. This contraction cannot have expression toward the interior of the earth because the interior is constant
in volume. Thus only along the boundary between the crust
and the cooling zone are contractions possible. The crust,
nicely shaped to the underlying earth zone, is accordingly
subjected to great tensions, particularly along the horizontal
plane. Portions of the crust give under the strain and thus
mountains shoot up and depressions curve down. In this way
the relief features of the earth's surface are created. The
process still continues.

With the rise and fall of the land, the sea waters ebb and flow in and out of the landscape. The marvelous and inevitable process of erosion brings the debris of the mountains to the sea, and there the deposition of sediments paradoxically weights the sea-bottoms down while building them up. The horizontal tensions inherent in the crust push hard on the edges of any deepening zone (geosyncline), forcing it still farther down until at last the deepest sediments, perhaps thirty thousand feet down, yield to pressure and high temperature. Slowly they bend and the result is an upward thrusting along the sides of the depression and with this an uplift of the flat central area to form a plateau.

The magnitude and complexity of these earth processes is very great indeed: weaker strata yielding, stronger rocks resisting, the faulting of enormous areas, volcanism at points of weakness, and above all the continual assertion and reassertion of wind, ice, and rain, the eroding factors which painstakingly reduce the highest mountains to stubs in the geologically short span of a few million years. From none of these geological factors is Africa divorced. But remarkably, much of Africa seems least, of all the earth, subject to them.

At the end of Mesozoic time the tensions of the earth's surface separated Africa almost entirely from the great Eurasian land mass of the north. The Atlantic Ocean in its deep bed lay between Africa and the Americas, while far to the south, a vast shallow sea covered an old land-bridge to Antarctica. To the east the Indian Ocean stretched for hundreds of phosphorescent miles to the root-lands of India and Australasia. On the north the Tethys Sea, mighty ancestor of the Mediterranean, lay in a wide shallow sheet from the Atlantic to the reaches of Central Asia. But the ancient plateau of Africa sprawled about the equator, retaining in its vast interior the plant and animal life which reflected its former connection with the lands north and east.

The Tertiary, or Age of Mammals, began some sixty million years ago. By its conclusion, much of what we consider the modern features of the earth were formed. The seas gradually retreated toward their present beds, the young mountains of the earth shot up along their present lines, and the familiar forms of the continents emerged. For Africa this meant a gradual division into a low plateau area in the north, subject to flooding where the Sahara and Sudan regions are today; and a high plateau in the south—the area between being a long inclined plain of great significance to human history.

The Pleistocene, which began perhaps one million years ago, added another land area. This was the lowlands which served as deltas for those rivers which, flowing out of their basins in the interior of high Africa, tumbled over the bounds of the plateau to meander to the sea in a maze of swamps and marshes. These became the "white man's graveyard" in the nineteenth century, as they were the source of virulent fevers and pestilences that killed the careful and the unwary alike.

One of the most stupendous events in recent geological time occurred in East Africa during the Pleistocene. Here the earth's tensional forces caused great blocks to fault along a north-south line. The shearing thrust great walls of ancient rock upward, usually parallel to each other, while the land between was pressed downward, forming enormous valleys, known as rifts. The Great Rift Valley of East Africa is a mighty symbol of the ever-restless qualities of our earth manifested even on the solid plateau of Africa. The African rift is practically coincident with the location of the great East African lakes, almost all but Lake Victoria being located in rift valleys. In turn, the rifts cross the Abyssinian Highlands to the Red Sea, which is itself in a rift. This links the African rifts to those of Syria and Palestine (the Gulf of Aqaba and the Jordan Valley).

The great mountain volcanoes, Kenya and Kilimanjaro, are apparently by-products of the disturbances accompanying the formation of the rifts, and even today active volcanoes and steam jets remind the East African of the newness of his mountains and valleys.

Thus we find the African continent in the twentieth century sticking like a vast peninsula out of the land masses of the Northern Hemisphere. On the east and west low coastlands neatly outlined by a monotonous ribbon of sand beaches and bars are continually beaten by the waves of the open sea. Beyond are swamps and alluvial mudlands, and yet farther beyond, the plateau rims that mark truly ancient Africa. Here are found the basins of the great tropical rivers, Niger, Zambesi, and Congo. Here too, far to the east, are the sources of the Nile, the "Giver of Life." Thus Egypt and Nubia owe their existence to High Africa and to geographical features far from their borders.

The Origin of the Nile

Theories on the origin of the Nile Valley differ, but the most accepted idea is that during the Tertiary period the formation of the Red Sea hills that lay between the present Nile Valley and the Red Sea caused a small down-warping of the plateau just to the west. This created a trough into which an arm of the Tethys Sea was pushed. The small streams of the area concentrated their flow into the southern, unsubmerged portion of the trough and in so doing cut farther into the bedrock. This was accelerated by the uplift of a part of the African plateau just north of the area where today Khartoum is located. Those were days in which rainfall was plentiful on the slopes of the surrounding hills. As a result the Nile of Nubia and Egypt was a mighty river several hundred feet higher than today and spread far beyond the few-mile widths which measure the present Nile Valley.

South of Nubia proper there existed a vast lake, Lake Sudd, whose traces still survive in the great swamps of the Bahr-el-Jebel and other branches of the White Nile. This lake received the drainage from the great lake regions of Central Africa and from the Ethiopian Highlands via the ancestors of the White and Blue Niles. The flatness of the country in the area of what is now known as the Southern Sudan is striking, the fall of the Nile bed being only some twenty feet in five hundred miles. About twenty-five thousand years ago Lake Sudd was separated from the headwaters of the ancient Nile Valley by an east-west running ridge. This formation, known as the Sabluka Ridge, helped keep Lake Sudd confined to its great basin in Northeastern Africa. Although the lake therefore remained without any outlet, the rate of evaporation was so high that overflow did not occur initially. However, the silts deposited in the lake by the streams of the East African and Ethiopian Highlands gradually built up the lake bottom, at once causing the water level to rise and imbuing the Sudan with a rich black alluvial soil, the foundation for the republic's present-day cotton wealth.

The rise of the lake made it possible for the Nile tributaries to capture the overflow waters. Eventually a gorge was cut through the Sabluka ridge and the northward drainage of Lake Sudd began. Thus the modern Nile came into being.

The Marvelous Course of the Nile

The Nile is a mighty river, 4,160 miles long. Its basin includes over one million square miles of jungle, swamp, desert, and valley. If one considers the vast expanse of Lake Victoria and its tributaries, the Nile begins below the equator in the Southern Hemisphere and flows over some thirty degrees of latitude through the Northern before emptying into the Mediterranean. I must admit a continuing feeling of awe and wonderment at the incredible Nile and all that it represents. For one thing, the true source of the Nile is the South Atlantic Ocean over two thousand miles to the west. Here rain clouds gather and are swept by cyclonic winds eastward. From March to August much of Equatorial Africa is bathed in an intense rainfall, in places exceeding sixty inches. Like the moonsoons of the Indian Ocean, these rainstorms are often spectacular. Heavy thunder, brilliant lightning, and an awesome crash of water are regular and commonplace.

The geologist Bailey Willis describes a storm on the Ruwenzori, the fabled mountains of the moon.

Ruwenzori is a mountain of many moods. Nowhere else have I seen sunshine and storm pursue each other so swiftly. On this hand is brilliant landscape, all green, golden and violet; on the other, in the shadow of a cloud, the tones are subdued and even. The cloud advances. As it passes swiftly overhead its ragged front is seen torn by conflicting currents. The cold down draft struggles with the rising hot air. Now the storm is on. The forested slopes turn a dark blue. They vanish in torrents of rain. Lightning flashes and thunder rolls.[1] *

In an Africa already bizarre to the Occidental by reason of its flourishing strange fauna and flora, and the characteristic adaptations to environment of its indigenous human cultures, the great storms are a final touch to the canvas, a master stroke to complete a picture already teeming.

* For numbered footnotes, see pages 237-241.

The drain-off after these storms is also spectacular. It begins thousands of feet above sea level where a spring relieves the stress of a saturated ground table or where tiny rivulets converge. The slopes of extinct volcanoes or eroded fault-blocks accelerate the process of turning rivulets to streams, and streams to rivers—a familiar story, but in East Africa the great rifts make it a magnificent one. For

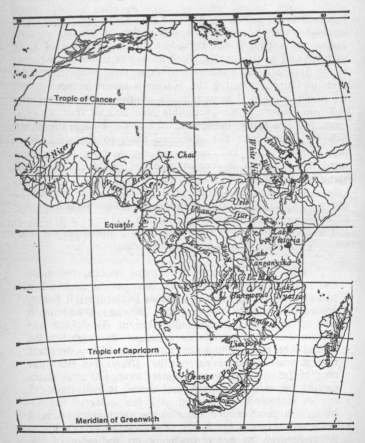

MAP OF THE DRAINAGE PATTERN OF THE AFRICAN CONTINENT. The Nile is the only African river to cross northern Africa to the Mediterranean Sea. (*The American Museum of Natural History*)

the rift valleys and volcanic slopes are too new and water has not had time to abrade and wear and so reduce the sharpness of the landscape. Waterfalls and rapids are the rivers' response to the young landscape and its tough, ancient rocks.

The White Nile has its true source in Lake Victoria. This lake is really a sea. It covers some twenty-six thousand square miles, second only to Lake Superior among world lakes. It is subject to violent storms which make navigation among its islands and jutting points of land frequently hazardous. Surprisingly, in a country of rifts Lake Victoria is simply the deepest part of the Nyanza plateau and as such is broad and shallow. In this it is comparable to the situation of Lake Sudd. The outlet for Lake Victoria is at Jinja on the northeast where the Ripon Falls cataract (now largely dammed) runs through a gap some three hundred yards wide. The altitude here is something over 3,700 feet above sea level. The Victoria Nile runs along a relatively narrow and picturesque channel at considerable speed for about seventy miles where it empties into another shallow marshy lake, Lake Kioga. Here other rivers empty their contents and the augmented stream flows westward into the Albert or Western Rift in which lies Lake Albert. The descent of the Nile is very rapid and this descent is effectively symbolized by the lovely and dramatic Murchison Falls. Here the river is pressed into a gap in the bedrock only some 18 feet in width but falling over 125 feet:

As we proceeded the river gradually narrowed to about 180 yards, and when the paddles ceased working we could distinctly hear the roar of water. I had heard this on waking in the morning, but at the time I had imagined it to proceed from distant thunder. By ten o'clock the current had so increased as we proceeded, that it was distinctly perceptible, although weak. The roar of the waterfall was extremely loud, and after sharp pulling for a couple of hours, during which time the stream increased, we arrived at a few deserted fishing-huts, at a point where the river made a slight turn. I never saw such an extraordinary show of crocodiles as were exposed on every sandbank on the sides of the river; they lay like logs of timber close together, and upon one bank we counted twenty-seven, of large size; every basking place was crowded in a similar manner. From the time we had fairly entered the river, it had been confined by heights somewhat precipitous on either side, rising to about 180 feet. At this point the cliffs were still higher, and exceedingly abrupt. From the roar of the water, I was sure that the fall would be in sight if we turned the corner at the bend of the river; accordingly I ordered the boatmen to row as far as they could; to this they at first objected, as they wished to stop at the deserted fishing village, which they explained was to be the limit of the journey, farther progress being impossible.

However, I explained that I merely wished to see the fall, and they rowed immediately up the stream, which was now strong against us. Upon rounding the corner, a magnificent sight burst suddenly upon us. On either side of the river were beautifully wooded cliffs rising abruptly to a height of about 300 feet; rocks were jutting out from the intensely green foliage; and rushing through a gap that cleft the rock exactly before us, the river, contracted from a grand stream, was pent up in a narrow gorge of scarcely fifty yards in width; roaring furiously through the rock-bound pass, it plunged in one leap of about 120 feet perpendicular into a dark abyss below.

The fall of water was snow-white, which had a superb effect as it contrasted with the dark cliffs that walled the river, while graceful palms of the tropics and wild plantains perfected the beauty of the view. This was the greatest waterfall of the Nile, and, in honour of the distinguished President of the Royal Geographical Society, I named it the Murchison Falls, as the most important object throughout the entire course of the river.[2]

The Nile flows slowly into Lake Albert after its dramatic descent over Murchison Falls, having reached the floor of the rift. It meanders into a wide delta providing a basis for a luxuriant vegetation and effective homeland for hippopotami, crocodiles, and great flocks of birds.

Lake Albert lies in a magnificent setting with high mountains to east and west and fine forests along each bank. Water draining over the abrupt cliffs and hurtling through canyons falls in beautiful cascades some of which appear to vanish into the carpets of trees at the foot of the rock walls. The mountains rise into awesome peaks whose silhouettes, in the form of cones and sharp-angled edges, recall in the changing light the primitive timelessness which will always make these portions of Africa unique.

The Nile is of course the draining river for Lake Albert. The outlet, somewhat surprisingly perhaps, is only about five miles from the Victoria Nile inlet. Between Lake Albert and the beginning of the great swamp area near Juba in the Sudan the river wanders leisurely along the floor of the rift valley coming very near to the watershed of the river Congo. At last the mountain walls close in and the river, cutting across the heights of upwarped strata, descends in an eighty-mile stretch of rapids. The Fola Falls at the beginning of the descent are the most spectacular of these rapids. Here the Nile, squeezed into a sixty-foot-wide canyon, roars through a gorge about the length of an American football field and then drops into a deep depression to emerge and race on until some eighty miles later the mountains vanish and the slow drift to the north begins again.

The White Nile, here called the Bahr-el-Jebel, enters a clay plain that stretches hundreds of miles to the north. A large portion of this area is marshy land, the remains of ancient Lake Sudd. But broad grasslands provide good nutrient for cattle-raising people like the Dinka, Nuer, and Shilluk, and in the Khartoum area, the Gezira, a region lying in the triangle between the Blue and White Niles, is the center of cotton cultivation in the modern Sudan.

Many rivers drain into this shallow basin that makes up huge portions of the provinces of Equatoria and the Upper Nile, the southernmost provinces of the Sudan. But their waters do little to augment that of the White Nile. The vast swamps transpire moisture to the air on such a great scale that only a fraction of the total water that enters the region escapes into the Nile Valley beyond. The swamps themselves provide their own flood-control mechanism.

Along the White Nile two zones are demarcated. The first is the marginal land which is seasonally inundated. This is called "toich" locally and on its sandy surface grow the tall grasses which provide cattle fodder. It is a matter of wonderful adaptation that some of the tallest people of Africa, the Nilotes, live on toich soil where grow the tallest grasses. These people move to high ground only during flood periods. Trees, by the way, can exist here only as long as they remain clear of the stunting waters. It is astonishing to see the landscape of the normally treeless toich broken by the triumphant silhouette of a tree poised precariously on a termite nest!

The second zone is the pure swampland of permanent flooding. This is the home of the ever-graceful papyrus, the tall flowering reeds, bulrushes, water-lettuce, and lovely white water lilies. Here too grow the water grasses (*Vossia cuspidata*), floating beds of sharp leaves. At first this vegetation occurs only along the banks of the river but as the stream meanders along, going slower as the gradient flattens out, the floral world closes in. The river world becomes a sedge, a dense, all-obscuring endless morass of blind lagoons, impenetrable green walls, and snaking channels. Reeds tower into the air as much as twenty feet and, thin as their stalks are, their structure is tough and en masse indestructible. Though the channels of the Nile are distinguishable, experience in the past has shown how readily they can be blocked. The floating and standing vegetation combine to create enormous sudd dams which resist with stubborn success the power of steam-driven boats. Dynamite is needed to blast the channel clear. In modern times every effort is made to prevent these "log jams" that prevent navigation, but vigilance can never be relaxed.

The sudd swamps were the great barriers to Nile explorers seeking the sources of that great river from the north. They have remained so from great antiquity, forcing would-be travelers far to the east and west on circuitous routes to the fabled country of Lake Albert and the Ruwenzori. Efforts to cross the sudd swamps by river often met with disastrous failure. There are horrible cases on record of boats trapped in the swamp, the crew and passengers unable to reach land, and finally dying of starvation, mosquitoes, all-pervading moist heat, and worst of all a melancholia induced by a closed green world. Sir Samuel Baker's diary account of his trip through the sudd in 1869–1873 with a fleet of boats, some steam-driven, exemplifies one excellent reason why the sources of the Nile remained a secret for so many centuries:

January 17   Made about 300 yards of heavy cutting through rafts of vegetation. The lake of last year nearly choked up; about 100 acres of rafts having completely destroyed it.

January 20   At 7 A.M. I took the dingy, and with much

difficulty pushed about a mile through the grass until
I found the whole country closed by vegetation. I
think the river has opened a new channel, and that
the passage of yesterday will take us to nearly the
same spot above the sudd that we reached by another
route last year.

January 25 The men cut about 300 yards.

January 26 We again accomplished about 300 yards,
and pushed the vessels within the channel.

January 30 The fleet joined in sections during last
night and today. Set to work with the long-handled
hoes, and cut a channel through the shallows for fifty
yards, and took the vessels forward.

January 31 Cut a channel through the shallows, but we
could not get the steamer along.

February 1 About 1,200 men at work cutting a channel and towing the steamer and noggurs through. The
diahbeeah and two noggurs passed ahead for about a
mile. We then stopped to await the steamer and other
vessels that were delayed by the powerful current.

February 6 I took the diahbeeah a mile and a quarter
ahead to a sudd, passing over several shallows of only
two feet eight inches, and three feet, which will
again cause great delay and labour. I returned to the
fleet, and assisted in the tedious work of dragging the
vessels over the shallows. In the evening I returned
to the diahbeeah, and having dragged the dingy across
the sudd, I explored the channel ahead for an hour,
for about three miles; passed over distressing shallows
for a space of a quarter of a mile ahead of the diahbeeah, after which I entered a deep, narrow channel
with very rapid current.

It is quite impossible to say where we are, as the
professed guides seem to know nothing of this horrible chaos, which changes its appearance constantly.
It is most harassing.

February 7 I unpacked and served out a hundred
spades for digging channels; and I have ordered them
to commence tomorrow morning, and dig out a

straight passage for the thirty-one vessels that still remain in the shallows.

February 8 This is the date of departure last year from Khartoum; an inconceivable madness, had any one known the character of the river. All hands as usual tugging, hauling, and deepening the river with spades and hoes; but the more we dig, the faster the water runs out of the bed, which threatens to leave us high and dry.

February 9 The work as usual. All hands thoroughly disgusted. I am obliged to lighten the vessels by discharging cargo in the mud. Our waggons make excellent platforms for the luggage. Even with this assistance we only drew seven vessels through the shallows into the true river channel.

To-morrow we must discharge more cargo.

The anxiety of leading 1,600 men, and fifty-eight vessels with heavy cargoes, through this horrible country is very distressing.

When I shall have succeeded in dragging the vessels into the true channel, I shall construct a dam in the rear, so as to retain the water at a higher level. I have no doubt that a series of such dams will be required to enable us to reach the Nile. Should it be impossible to proceed with the heavy vessels, I shall leave them thatched over as floating stores, with a small guard, until the next wet season shall raise the river level.

March 9 From Feb. 11 to this date we had toiled through every species of difficulty. The men had cut one straight line of canal through a stiff clay for a distance of 600 yards. Many were sick, some had died; there appeared to be no hope. It was in vain that I endeavoured to cheer both officers and men with tales and assurances of the promised land before them, should they only reach the Nile. They had worked like slaves in these fetid marshes until their spirits were entirely broken,—the Egyptians had ceased to care whether they lived or died.[3]

The sudd region has a profound effect upon the waters of the White Nile, for so great is the transpiration as the water lies in shallow lagoons or under beds of river flora that about one-half of the amount present downstream of Lake

Albert is lost. The final lagoon encountered in the northern-most portion of the sudd area is known as Lake No and it is important only in that it is the junction with the Bahr-el-Ghazal (River of Giraffes) which drains the western country up to the watershed of Lake Chad, the vanishing great lake of West Africa north of the Congo basin, a token of the vastness of the Nile system.

The White Nile flows sharply eastward out of Lake No in one of those characteristic bends by which a mature river seeks its level, is this case a detour around the Nuba mountains just to the north. Some fifty miles east of Lake No as the river again bends northward the abundant flow of the river Sobat revives the life of the stream. The Sobat drains out of the westernmost portion of the Ethiopian Highlands and readily doubles the water of the White Nile so that it again encompasses its pre-sudd volume.

South of Malakal and the junction with the Sobat, the aspect of the country changes. The swamp vegetation still exists along the shores of the Nile but more palms can be seen, and beyond, the country is forested and plains of acacia and meadow grass are the home of the swift un-gulates like the antelope, the buffalo, the giraffe, and of course the great feline predators, the lions and leopards. West of the Nile, however, the Nuba mountains stand in their granite firmness and by their elevation retain survi-vals of the High Africa the river has left. Here grow the northernmost bamboos, the baobab, and the ebony. The Nuba tribes are, like their Negro relatives south and west of the sudd swamps, primarily agriculturists. Thus they are an isolated pocket in the midst of a land of cattle raisers and nomads.

The White Nile channel is a broad one and it carries the river majestically and serenely with little meander north-ward. Until well past the Sobat junction annual rainfall has been so abundant that men and animals have had little con-cern for their sources of moisture. But as the White Nile flows into the north the rain shadow becomes increasingly lighter. From sixty inches annually in the sudd country the rainfall rapidly decreases. Khartoum has about eight months of drought and less than twelve inches the rest of the year while Nubia on the borders of Egypt receives practically no rain at all. The vast Sudan thus encompasses two extremes— on the south almost absolute saturation, on the north an all-parching dryness. For contrast there is nothing so dramatic as these comments by two British travelers, one the anthropologist E. E. Evans-Pritchard in the Nuer country of Equatoria, the other by the journalist G. W. Steevens with Kitchener's force in 1898 in the north.

It is part of the comprehensive uselessness of this country that its one priceless production can never be exported. If the Sudan thirst could be sent home in capsules, like the new soda-water sparklets, it would make any man's fortune in an evening. The irony of it is, that there is so much thirst here—such a limitless thirst as might supply the world's whole population richly: on the other side there are millions of our fellow-creatures, surrounded by every liquor that art can devise and patience perfect, but wanting the thirst to drink withal. Gentlemen in England now abed will call themselves accursed they were not here. And even the few white men who vainly strive to do justice to these stupendous depths and intensities, these vast areas and periods of thirst—how utterly and pitiably inadequate we are to our high opportunity.

I wonder if you ever were thirsty? Probably not. I never had been till I came to the Sudan, and that is why I came again. If you have been really thirsty, and often, you will be able to distinguish variations of the phenomenon. The sand-storm thirst I hardly count. It is caused by light soil forming in the gullet; wash the soil away and the thirst goes with it; this can be done with water, which you do not even need to swallow.

The desert thirst is more legitimately so called; it arises from the grilling sun on the sand, from the dancing glare, and from hard riding therein. This is not an unpleasant thirst; the sweat evaporates on your face in the wind of your own galloping, and thereby produces a grateful coolness without, while throat and gullet are white-hot within. The desert thirst consists in this contrast; it can be satisfied by a gulp or two of really cool water which has also been evaporating through a canvas bottle slung on your saddle.

But in so far as it can be satisfied, it is no true Sudan thirst. The true Sudan thirst is insatiable. The true Sudan thirst—which, to be sure, may be found in combination with either or both of the others, and generally is—is born of sheer heat and sheer sweat. Till you have felt it, you have not thirsted. Every drop of liquid is wrung out of your body; you could swim in your clothes; but, inside, your muscle shrinks to dry sponge, your bones to dry pith. All your strength, your substance, your self is draining out of you; you are conscious of a perpetual liquefaction and evaporation of good solid you. You must be wetted till you soften and swell to life again.

You are wetted. You pour in wet, and your self sucks it in and swells—and then instantly it gushes out again at every pore, and the self contracts and wilts. You swill in more, and out it bubbles before you even feel your inside take it up. More—and your pores swish in spate like the very Atbara. Useless; you must give it up, and let the goodness sluice out of you. There is nothing of you left; you are a mere vacuum of thirst. And that goes on from three hours after sunrise till an hour before sundown.[4]

On a tour of Western Nuerland in October of 1936, a fairly dry year, we walked almost continuously in several inches of water for seventeen days. . . .[5]

At Khartoum, the modern capital of the Sudan, some fourteen hundred miles from the Mediterranean Sea, the Blue Nile (Bahr-el-Azrak) joins the White Nile (Bahr-el-Abiad). In flood season (July to September) the Blue Nile's flood is double that of the White Nile and it contributes the major portion of the Nile waters annually even though its flood drops below that of the White Nile in the dry season. The Blue Nile is a magnificent stream that begins over nine thousand feet above sea level in the Ethiopian Highlands south of Lake Tana. The real source is a sacred spring described by Major R. E. Cheesman, formerly British consul in Ethiopia:

The Church of St. Michael and Zarabruk stands on the top of a ridge half a mile from the source of the Blue Nile. Its priests are in charge of the spring, and no one else is allowed to draw its waters. They say that if anyone attempted to dip an unhallowed vessel in it, spirits would snatch it away, and it is certain that the pilgrims are too superstitious to put this to the test. I asked to be allowed to drink from it, and the priest arrived in his vestments, accompanied by a church boy-student who is called a deacon, who held an umbrella over him, while another deacon carried a brass cross mounted on a staff. When the priest heard that I had already eaten, although he gave me the water he insisted that it should be kept till the next day and drunk before breakfast. Not only does the water lose its curative power if taken after food, but it can be very deadly, and instances were given of men who, ignoring this warning, had swallowed the water after a meal and had died.

In 1933 my wife and I were at Gish Abbai together, and the priest took her across the bridge of branches to the spring. The small crowd of pilgrims that were waiting near and hoped to be healed of their maladies by the magic balm of the water next day, raised no voice of protest, but when she touched the water with the end of a long stick they called out to the priest, "Don't let her touch it. She is a woman," and of course their wishes were respected. She turned to the priest and asked what evil would befall if she were to bathe in the spring, and he replied very seriously, "You would die." [6]

Some seventy miles from the spring is Lake Tana, the major catch basin for the plateau waters.

Flowing out of Lake Tana the river (called locally the Abbai) makes an imposing turn southeast, south, west, and at last to the northwest and the Sudan. In the process it hurtles into immense gorges, races through cataracts, and pours over rapids in a tumultuous descent that slows only when the river is tamed by the flat plain of the Sudan. At Roseires near the Ethiopian frontier a station is established where engineers in the late spring have watched their water meters eagerly; for as the Blue Nile goes so goes the Egyptian Nile. Just when water resources are lowest in the northern country, word is telegraphed that the water is rising at Roseires and Egypt's crop is safe for another year. How eagerly men have waited that word!

North of Khartoum the deserts encroach on either side. This is the true beginning of Nubia, though in ancient times this land below Wadi Halfa was often called "Kush." This is a region of desolation except for the ribbon of green that marks vegetation along the banks of the river. Even the Atbara, last tributary of the Nile, is dry much of the year though at flood time it is a considerable stream. It always seems that flood time is too short, and the dry river course with its occasional tepid pools—all too familiar!

The Nile has cut deep canyons in the sedimentary plateau

of the Nubian Desert and in the process reached to the old basement rocks whose unerodable granite casements, protruding here and there in the channel, cause cataracts. There are six of these barriers to navigation and at low Nile boat passage is made almost impossible by some of them. The stretches between the cataracts are smooth and generally, except for the monotony of the landscape, excellent for travel. Thus the cataracts are frustrating; for otherwise men might have been able to journey from the Mediterranean to the swamp country without ever leaving their boats. This has been virtually impossible no matter how desirable or necessary. The cataracts have in their own way directed the course of history. Listen, for example, to Lieutenant Colonel F. C. Denison, commander of the Canadian Voyageurs contingent sent to aid the Gordon relief force in 1884 to ascend the cataracts and save General Gordon at Khartoum. This attempt was unsuccessful and part of the blame can be put on the delays caused by the treacherous cataracts.

The Nile boat or whaler as they were called is from 30 to 32 feet long, 6 or 7 beam. From 8 to 12 soldiers were told off to each boat, and one voyageur. The boats were then packed, the voyageur superintending and helping, with 100 days' reserve rations. This was no easy job with some of the boats, that were very pointed in the bow and stern. In that case it was packed above the gunwhale of the stern 2 or 3 feet.

As a usual thing six men pulled. The voyageur took the rudder, sometimes the bow. When the boat came to a strong current, the men would pull their best, and with a good way on would get up; but if they failed and were carried back, I have seen them make the attempt a second and third time, straining every nerve, and then succeed. If it was impossible to row up, all the crew but the bowman and the man at the rudder would disembark, get out their tracking line, put it over their shoulders, and walk along the bank, tracking the boat, until they reached smooth water again. When they came to a bad rapid, instead of having one crew on the rope 3, 4, or 5 crews, according to the rush of water, would be put on. This was avoided as much as possible, as it took 5 times as long. When it became necessary to place 30 or 40 men on the line it was generally necessary also to unload the arms, and perhaps part of the load. In these cases a voyageur was put in the bow, another in the stern. Great care had to be exercised to see that there should not be any slack rope, so that on the Nile you would hear the words from morning until night, "Pull up the slack," "Haul away." Then the men were on the line and when all was ready the word would be given, "Shove off." If there was too much slack rope, the current would catch the boat, running her out into the stream broadside on, and sometimes filling the boat. She would turn over, throwing the voyageurs into the water, unless they were smart enough to climb over one side as she went under at the other, and then cling to the bottom, until taken off.

I saw one boat upset in this way, in the worst rapid on the Nile. The men, two smart active boatmen, coolly climbed over on the upturned boat. I immediately manned another boat with voyageurs, pulled off for them in an anxious frame of mind; but before we had got half way there, I noticed the men seize a floating box, and pull it on to the bottom of the boat, and by the time we reached them they had four or five rescued boxes on the upturned boat. I was very much pleased with this, not at their saving the stores, for that was of no special moment, but at the coolness of the voyageurs, while standing on the bottom of a boat, thinking of saving stores instead of being terrified & afraid for their own safety.

I might mention that all the stores were done up in tin boxes with an outside casing of pinewood. The biscuit box, containing 35 lbs or 100 lbs according to size, being water tight and enclosing some air inside, would float a man easily, so that many a good life was saved on the Nile by a biscuit box.[7]

The Nile makes a great *S* turn in the cataract country. At Abu Hamed it reaches 19° 30′ north, but turns southwest and then flows almost due south to the eighteenth parallel before beginning its northern course again. The cataracts and the narrowness of the valley, which also hinders land movement, caused the creation of a caravan route over the desert from Abu Hamed in Sudan to Korosko in Egypt near the twenty-third parallel above Abu Simbel.

This is an agonizing route of 230 miles now largely traversed by Sudan Railways. Midway on the journey brackish water is to be had at Murrat Wells but this is the sum of it.

Again that indefatigable English pioneer of the Sudan, Sir Samuel Baker, traversed the route in May, 1861.

A few hours from Korosko the misery of the scene surpassed description. Glowing like a furnace, the vast extent of yellow sand stretched to the horizon. Rows of broken hills, all of volcanic origin, broke the flat plain. Conical tumuli of volcanic slag here and there rose to the height of several hundred feet, and in the far distance resembled the pyramids of Lower Egypt—doubtless they were the models for that ancient and everlasting architecture; hills of black basalt jutted out from the barren base of sand, and the molten air quivered on the overheated surface of the fearful desert. 114° Fahr. in the shade under the water-skins; 137° in the sun. Noiselessly the spongy tread of the camels crept along the sand—the only sound was the rattle of some loosely secured baggage of their packs. The Arab camel drivers followed silently at intervals and hour by hour we struck deeper into the solitude of the Nubian desert.

We entered a dead level plain of orange-coloured sand, surrounded by pyramidical hills: the surface was strewn with objects resembling cannon shot and grape of all sizes from a 32-pounder downwards—the spot looked like the old battle-field of some infernal region; rocks glowing with heat—not a vestige of vegetation—barren, withering desolation. —The slow rocking step of the camels was most irksome, and despite the heat, I dismounted to examine the Satanic bombs and cannon shot. Many of them were as perfectly round as though cast in a mould, others were egg-shaped, and all were hollow. With some difficulty I broke them, and found them to contain a bright red sand: they were, in fact, volcanic bombs that had been formed by the ejection of molten lava to a great height from active volcanoes; these had become globular in falling, and, having cooled before they reached the earth, they retained their forms as hard spherical bodies, precisely resembling cannon shot. The exterior was brown, and appeared to be rich in iron. The smaller specimens were the more perfect spheres, as they had cooled quickly, but many of the heavier masses had evidently reached the earth when only half solidified, and had collapsed upon falling. The sandy plain was covered with such vestiges of volcanic action, and the infernal bombs lay as imperishable relics of a hail-storm such as may have destroyed Sodom and Gomorrah.

Passing through this wretched solitude we entered upon a scene of surpassing desolation. Far as the eye could reach were waves like a stormy sea, grey cool-looking waves in the burning heat; but no drop of water; it appeared as though a sudden curse had turned a raging sea to stone. The simoom blew over this horrible wilderness, and drifted the hot sand into the crevices of the rocks, and the camels drooped their heads before the suffocating wind; but still the caravan noiselessly crept along over the rocky undulations, until the stormy sea was passed; once more we were upon a boundless plain of sand and pebbles.[8]

This is nomad country where the camel, horse, and goat are dominant. The people are of a variety of racial stocks: Arab, Negro, and Mediterranean Egyptian occur in mixed and comparatively pure form. Restlessness is the rule in spite of the intense heat. The country is fly filled and its aridity demands movement except in the valley itself where the rise and fall of the river provides a pale reflection of Egypt ahead.

This is also a land of history, for in spite of the hopelessness of the barrier lands and the usually too narrow valley, this Nubian alchemy of cataracts and sand is a lodestone for many things. Gold in the hills to the east and a rich trade with lands of the south and west: these are the reasons for the Egyptian fortresses like those of Buhen and Semna, for Kerma and Abu Simbel. There are early Christian churches here and strange Afro-Arabian mosques. The maps are studded with the crossed swords of famous battlefields, especially those that marked the savage wars during the Mahdist period when such names as Gordon, Kitchener, Wingate, Slatin, and Burnaby gained a reputation and made a beginning or an end. Even before the Egyptians came, when the climate was better, prehistoric men made their villages and pitched their camps by the banks of a far wider river Nile. The traces of these men will largely disappear forever when the great High Dam at last arises.

Nubia is the cataract country, the first or last of the great Nile barriers, depending on your route. It is out of Nubia that the Nile comes at last, moving among the islands of Aswan where once was the First Cataract but where now a great dam has stood for sixty years and another will stand in five. Here are the submerged islands of Philae, favorites of the Ptolemies and many a tourist. Here too is the island of Elephantine, which marks the true border of old Egypt and indeed of many an empire since.

Beyond, the Nile Valley fluctuates between being a narrow canyon with high walls and fading back into huge bays whose rich alluvium furnished the economic basis for ancient civilization. Egypt is a more open country than Nubia. The valley is wider and the belts of soil thicker and far more luxuriant. Here too is contrast, for to the east the barren hills of the Red Sea never have looked more desolate, and to the west the Libyan Desert is a far-flung eternally sandy waste that has forced men and cultures away from West Africa for millennia.

The Nile in Egypt is usually a brown color that knows no term. It can be light or dark with seasons but it always sets off the brilliant green of the fields, the yellow bunches of dates, and the white cotton dress of the fellahin in a way that marks Egypt as distinctly as the pyramids.

Cairo, capital of modern Egypt and ancient center of the Moslem world, is at the apex of the fan-shaped Nile delta. Here the river begins to break into various channels that wander through marshes and feed irrigation canals until they merge with the waters of the Mediterranean. Here they mark the sea waters with the African silt which tells the sailor, even before Alexandria rises whitely on the horizon, that the land of Amun-Re is near.

It is obvious to anyone reading these passages that the whole system of the control of the Nile waters is very complex. Greatest of all the problems is, of course, the right distribution of water at the right time. In the centuries before dam control, the populace living in the Nile Valley could not be certain that there would be a sufficient supply of water available to irrigate crops during the dry season. Storage of an abundant harvest would carry people over a poor harvest caused by low Nile flooding. But in the days when much of the productive land is taken up for commercial crops such as cotton and sugar cane the land must be used fully even during the dry season. The obvious answer is storage of water and its gradual release during the season of low flooding. This is a complicated matter in which politics as well as economics have a stern role.

Mussolini's conquest of Ethiopia in 1936 set forth a series of fearful speculations that the Italians would divert the flow of the Blue Nile to irrigate the more arid portions of Ethiopia. This turned out to be an unwarranted fear. But during the British rule of the Sudan, projects to dam various parts of the Nile, especially at Sennar on the Blue Nile in order to channel waters to the Gezira, caused a good deal of alarm in Egypt. Any diminution of the Nile waters would naturally affect Egyptian prosperity. Accordingly, treaties have been drawn up which strictly regulate the amounts of water stored by these dams, the time of release, and the utilization of the sluices during flood. An elaborate system of water gauges is maintained by international agreement all the way from Lakes Tana and Albert to Aswan and beyond. These are reported on regularly and the information distributed by law-bound agreement. Meteorological observations, silt-content of waters, evaporation rates, and the like are all a part of a full system of measurements and scientific observations that make the Nile system one of the most thorough in the world. Such systems have to be, for failure of water is a never-ending possibility. For Egypt it has been always said that "the Nile is life." Thus there is abiding and good reason for Gamel Nasser's determination to add another giant advance in the control of the Nile. The precedent of millennia of concern is motivation enough.

Principal Periods of Geological Time [9]

Age of the earth: *ca.* 3,350 million years

MILLIONS OF YEARS AGO	PERIOD		DURATION
2,100–550	pre-Cambrian	*ca.*	1,500 million years
520–185	Palaeozoic	*ca.*	335 million years
185– 60	Mesozoic	*ca.*	125 million years
60– 1	Tertiary:	*ca.*	59 million years
60– 40	Eocene	*ca.*	20 million years
40– 28	Oligocene	*ca.*	12 million years
28– 12	Miocene	*ca.*	16 million years
12– 1	Pliocene	*ca.*	11 million years
1– 0	Quaternary:	*ca.*	1 million years
	Pleistocene	*ca.*	1 million years
	Holocene	*ca.*	10,000 years

2

Prologue to Civilization

*Among the ruins . . . which will be engulfed by the waters
. . . special mention must be made of prehistoric sites, both
Neolithic and Palaeolithic.*—J. VERCOUTTER, Directory of the
Antiquities Service, Republic of the Sudan (*The UNESCO
Courier*, February, 1960)

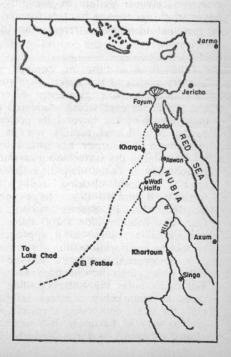

One of the more farsighted and successful archaeological field studies of the twentieth century was carried out in the 1920's and early 1930's by the geologists K. S. Sandford and W. J. Arkell. Under the auspices of the Oriental Institute of the University of Chicago the two scientists undertook a survey of the prehistoric Nile Valley from the Mediterranean to a point in Upper Nubia some forty miles south of Wadi Halfa. This was a complete and extraordinarily important survey which was continued under considerable difficulties and not a little hazard. They utilized the motorcars of the 1920's, camels, boats, and especially their feet to visit and study over seven hundred miles of the Nile Valley. They plotted and explored ancient river beds, old beaches, exposed gravel deposits, sandstone outcrops, and the like and in so doing gathered river pebbles, rock samples, shells, and above all the flint tools of ancient men.

The result of this more than six years of painstaking research was the revelation of an Egypt infinitely older than even the classical writers of antiquity had envisioned: an Egypt where Stone Age hunters roamed the shores of a Nile so vast that the modern river is an insignificant stream in comparison.

[This] was a time of copious rainfall in Egypt. The dry wadies of the desert were running streams, and the landscape was pleasantly diversified with forest and grassland, over which wandered troops of wild animals. Reaching far beyond its present bounds, the ancestral Nile flowed rapidly over a pebbly bed, augmented on its journey northward by a host of tributaries draining the surrounding country. The Nile of the present day is but a dwindled shadow of the original river. Constantly choking itself with fine silt where formerly it hurried down large pebbles, and winding languidly through deserts without receiving additions from any tributary for 1,200 miles from its mouth, it diminishes in volume as it approaches the sea, owing to loss by evaporation and absorption.

. . . Of greatest interest . . . are the traces of the mighty Nile which then flowed high above its present level. For many miles the hills bounding the valley are terraced at remarkably constant heights. In the frequent cliffs the strata composing them can be seen to undulate and to vary in hardness, but nevertheless they are all planed off evenly at about 50 feet, 100 feet, 150 feet or greater heights above the present valley floor. Often these abandoned Nile beds are still, like their smaller counterparts in the tributary wadies, covered by the gravels brought there by the river; and rolled among them may be found also the stone implements of Man.[1]

The Shores of the Ancient Nile

The fact that man's traces are found in the gravel of the river terraces indicates, of course, that men were living on the shores of the river which the terrace represents. This is a vital fact in the study of ancient man. Similar terrace systems marked by Palaeolithic tools are found along many river valleys in the Old World and their exploration and the study of their relation to other fluvial systems is a continuing process.

During the Pliocene period, that is, the latest period before the coming of the Ice Age (Pleistocene), it has been noted that an arm of the ancient Mediterranean protruded along the Nile Valley. This arm or gulf reached almost to the present dam at Aswan, or at least four hundred miles along the present Nile Valley, and it was well over five hundred feet above the present sea level. During this period heavy rainfall caused all the surrounding streams that fed into the proto-Nile Valley to empty there vast quantities of gravels and silts which were the erosional produce of the Red Sea hills to the east, and the plateau of Lower Africa on the west and south. Above Aswan in Upper Nubia the ancient Nile has not been clearly traced so far but there is a suggestion that its size was probably no greater than some of its tributaries of those days. The gulf filled with erosional deposits and this caused a retreat of the sea arm. (This may have been helped by a fall of the sea as the Mediterranean found its modern bed.) Then the Nile, luxuriantly fed by the rainfall of the time, flowed over the gulf-filling deposits, and the river began to cut the channel of the modern Nile Valley. This process began when the Nile was at least three hundred feet higher than today, at the beginning of the Pleistocene period. River terraces have been traced at 300, 200, 150, 100, 50, 30, and 10 feet above present level, each indicating an old bed of the Nile. The present Nile is then but a vestige of its

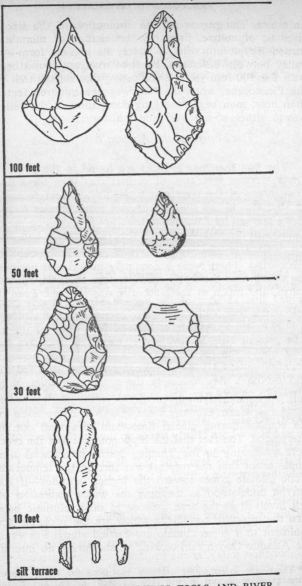

100 feet

50 feet

30 feet

10 feet

silt terrace

SEQUENCE OF PALAEOLITHIC TOOLS AND RIVER
TERRACES in the Nile Valley.

ancestors. The reason for the diminution of the size of the river is, of course, primarily the change of climate which turned Egypt into what is largely its present form—a river valley between deserts.* Traces of man are found beginning with the 100-foot terrace, indicating that during that part of the Pleistocene, when the Nile was one hundred feet higher than now, man began the long occupation of the valley that was to witness so much of human history.

The Heritage of the Ice Age

The Pleistocene and the so-called Ice Age are practically synonymous. The period began perhaps one million years ago and ended around 10,000 B.C. Study of glaciation in Europe and North America has determined that there were at least four major glaciations of the Northern Hemisphere during this period. There were accordingly interglacial periods during which time the world's temperature rose, the climate was warm, and much of the land area was ice-free. Even during glacial times there were phases of ice advance and retreat as the climate fluctuated. The interstadials and oscillations of the last glaciation of Europe are particularly well known in this regard. Such phases of fluctuation serve to complicate what is already a complex affair.

It is obvious that general temperature fall and with it the advance of the ice sheets bring about climatic change not only to the areas lying in proximity to the glaciers but to the world as a whole. Climatic zones tend to be compressed toward the equator during glacial times and to spread out during interglacial. The fact that the hippopotamus and the crocodile were swimming in the Thames during interglacial times is ample proof that the tropical was forcing the temperate and arctic climate zones toward the higher latitudes—if forcing can be understood as meaning the widest extension of the belt involved at the area expense of other climatic belts. In turn the moisture conditions which are the probable accompaniment to a given climate are carried along. For example, the Atlantic Ocean rain-bearing winds during an interglacial

* There are intermediate terraces but none of these appears to represent as important a Nile level as these above. The correlation of terrace and river platform remnants in disparate parts of the river system is a major task of the geologist.

are able to bring rain to more northerly latitudes, since the high pressures of the cold zones have retreated. The reverse is also true and it is likely, though not altogether proven, that maximum glaciation in Europe was indicated by maximum rainfall in the equatorial latitudes. Such a rainfall is called a pluvial and it has its drier component, the interpluvial. The main terraces of the river systems far south of the glaciated areas mark maximum floods of the river and are probably the marks of greatest rainfall and thus of a pluvial. The Nile terraces ought, therefore, to be equated with the known glaciations of the north—would that it were as easy as it sounds!

In addition to the Nile terraces there is other evidence for climatic change. This is furnished by the Fayum area just south of Cairo. The Fayum is a watered depression of great fertility that juts westward from the Nile Valley. Numerous prehistoric cultures have been identified there. These represent the ancient men who lived along the shores of lakes built up by local drainage and Nile floods which poured into the depression. As the climate grew wetter or dryer the shore lines fluctuated. In a fashion similar to that in the Nile Valley a succession of ever-contracting shore lines were built up there which have been correlated to the equivalent terraces of the Nile Valley. At the present time the lake is but a vestige of its former self.

South of the Fayum there is another depression entirely cut off from the Nile Valley. This is the oasis of Kharga, a depression in the Egyptian desert almost due west of Luxor, the site of ancient Thebes. The depression was largely cut in the desert plateau by eroding winds. So deep was the cut that in places the water table was reached and springs came forth to provide moisture in the midst of one of the most desolate regions of the earth. Here too the tools of ancient men have been found, some of them associated with gravel deposits lying along the beds of bone-dry wadies. These wadies mark the course of ancient streams built up by ample rainfall which flowed out of the desert into the depression. The old springs also fluctuated with the climate and their deposits of porous tufa stone mark water in plenty. There appear to have been two great pluvial periods at Kharga—the earlier a time before Stone Age men arrived and a later when the faunal advantages of the watered hundred-mile-long depression were utilized to the full by Palaeolithic hunters. Between the moist periods there were dry periods, the whole sequence evolving toward the arid conditions of today.

All this evidence points to profound climatic changes of tremendous significance. Much of the Sahara Desert area exhibits traces of a more prosperous past. Far to the west ancient watercourses are found in large number. Not only are the tools of Stone Age men found associated with these extinct streams but the fossil remains of aquatic mammals, reptiles, and Mollusca are conclusive evidence for a more humid past.

One area, however, seems to have been least affected by moisture conditions. This is the Libyan Desert area west of the Kharga depression, extending far south of the coastal region, where many of the battles between the British Eighth Army and Rommel's Afrika Korps were fought in World War II. This region is often known as the Great Sand Sea. Here, for hundreds of miles, is a shifting sea of sand called an *erg*. The sand is packed in dunes frequently running in regular order in parallel ridges, broken only now and again by areas of blackish gravel and sullen bare rock. This sand sea has been a formidable barrier for thousands of years, diverting men either west along the narrow strip of the North African coast or south along the Nile Valley. Like a great rock in the midst of a river, the sand sea has divided the channel of movement and sent men and their cultures on prescribed courses. This again points up the miracle of the Nile, which flows along the eastern margin of the sand sea, providing a gateway to the South.

Another striking phenomenon of the Ice Age was the rise and fall of sea level. A basic requirement of glaciers is abundant moisture. During glacial times much of the world's rainfall is turned into ice which returns little to the sea until melting occurs. As a consequence the world sea level sank perhaps as much as three hundred feet during the height of a glaciation. Rivers emptying into the sea were thus accorded a steeper gradient and this enabled them to cut into their channels with greater expedition. However, with the return to warm climate sea levels rose and rivers were so slowed in their flow by the fall in gradient and the flooding of their deltas that they deposited their load of erosional gravels and silts in their valleys, readily filling the channels. Thus these rivers built up their beds in their lower reaches and cut into their beds in the upper reaches where the gradient was steep. In both cases, terraces were eventually created. The problem of the geologist and his compatriot, the prehistorian, is to determine how these terrace systems relate to the old sea beaches that mark the shore lines of ancient seas. If this could be done on a world-wide scale the correlation of glaciations, sea levels, river terraces, and related human cultures would be brought about and we would know a great deal more of our earth and men at the dawn of human existence. The problems are exceedingly great, and at present they absorb the waking hours of a large number of devoted scientists, and not a few of their slumbers.

It is clear, in any case, that the Africa of the Pleistocene was, with the rest of the continents, the scene of natural events of great significance to mankind: the formation of the rift valleys, the gradual desiccation of Low Africa, the creation of the plateau lakes, the subsequent drainage to the sea where shores rose and fell, the pluvial floods and interpluvial aridities. These had a direct bearing upon all resident life; we are impressed with a dynamic changing world. But in comparison with the ice-battered continents to the north, Africa was apparently far more suitable for life survival than most regions. Accordingly, the flourishing old and energetic new were brought together in the creation of a distinct African entity. This is apparent in the traces of the Stone Age remaining lo these many millennia!

Old Stone Age Africa

The Stone Age tools made by the men who lived on the shores marked by the 100-foot terraces of the Nile Valley were characterized by crudely flaked flint handaxes familiar in the high terraces of West European river valleys. These bifacially flaked tools are known in Europe as Chellean or Abbevillian handaxes. These, and the large stone cores and broad angular flakes associated with them, are found in a heavily patinated and often much water-worn condition. The handaxes are also found on the 50-foot terraces but they are more refined at this level and are called Acheulian handaxes after exactly similar ones found in Europe and the Near East. The Acheulian forms were of long duration, for they are again found along the 30-foot Nile terraces. Here they tend to be smaller and their edges and points more apparent. Crude tools made from flakes occur here also. These are of special interest because they indicate the appearance in Egypt of a technique of flake-tool manufacture known widely as the

Levalloisian. The Levalloisian comes into full usage in the period represented by the 10-foot terrace (3-4 m.) and the handax traditions almost disappear.

The Nile Valley had about reached its present physical dimensions after the time of the 10-foot terraces. The climate from now on appears to have become increasingly drier. The Nile tributaries, one by one, ceased to flow until for almost a thousand miles, from the Mediterranean to beyond the borders of Nubia, there was no local addition to the main river. Such an event had consequences of important moment. The Nile of Egypt and Nubia, its flow diminished by evaporation, and receiving no near reinforcement, deposited the fine silts brought from its sources into its Egyptian bed. Thus the Nile Valley was filled with silt rising higher with each annual flood.

The bringing of new soil to refertilize the cultivated earth is, of course, the familiar action of the Nile of ancient and modern Egypt. But the Nile of the so-called silt stage of perhaps twenty thousand years ago was a larger river than at present, and, as it choked itself with silt, it rose higher in Upper Egypt and Nubia until in some places it rose to the level of the 100-foot gravel terraces which marked man's first appearance in the region! This is one reason why archaeologists have to keep their wits about them; for obviously the human artifacts of the silt terraces found at the same level as those of the gravel terraces are not as old—far from it. In other words, mere height above the present Nile level has little bearing on antiquity unless one knows one's terraces. And one must remember that when the sea level was lower than at present the Nile flowed into the Mediterranean at a lower level. Thus, in Lower Egypt the old silt beaches go *below* the level of the modern silt deposits in exactly the *reverse* situation!

The geological status of these silt formations is most important, for associated with some of them is a human industry, sometimes called the Sebilian, which seems to be a very refined Levalloisian flake-tool industry with a tendency toward increasing smallness of tool types from early to late. There are even tools made of small flint blades highly suggestive of the flake-blade forms of the Late Stone Age in Palestine and Europe. The industries also occur in the lower lake levels in the Fayum (22 meters).

The Old Stone Age in the Sudan

In the Sudan nothing comparable to this Egyptian sequence of Stone Age tool industries was known until quite recently. However, principally through the discoveries of A. J. Arkell (not the Arkell of the Egyptian researches) a Sudanese sequence is being formulated. These new Sudanese finds are proof that Stone Age men found that land favorable for the hunting which was the basis of their livelihood. Arkell found the earlier (Abbevillian) and the later (Acheulian) hand-axes in the gravel at several places near Khartoum. The most important site was Khor Abu Anga at Omdurman, capital of Mahdist Sudan, opposite Khartoum. These finds were made not far above the level reached by the present high Nile flood. Though the geological situation is uncertain here, the fact that the ancient tools were found on an eroded surface of the local limestone, in some cases only a few feet under deposited gravels, indicates that a dry climate in that region of the Sudan was of very long duration. Arkell believes this puts grave doubt on the theory of a great Pleistocene lake being in that area as recently as ten thousand years ago.[2]

Other handaxes of Abbevillian and Acheulian affinities have been found in the Sudan, especially in the terraces of the Atbara River, last tributary of the Nile (Khor Hudi, Sarsareib).

Pebble tools, which are older in origin even than the handaxes, though frequently found contemporary, were located in gravels over 150 feet above the present Nile near the Fourth Cataract (Nuri), and both pebble tools and hand-axes occur here and there in Upper Nubia. Probably not all of these tools are of the oldest periods but some certainly represent survivals of older traditions.

In 1924, the English Governor of Fung Province in the Sudan had his house near the Blue Nile at Singa. He found in the river bed a fossilized human skull which is now generally accepted as representing a proto-Bushman. Not directly associated with this skull but deriving from a strata of apparently equivalent age some thirty miles away (Abu Hugar) are a body of stone tools collected by Arkell. These tools, though primitive, are not as old as the handax–pebble tool industries but seem to be related to one of the aspects of the Levalloisian flake-tool tradition, especially as that tradition is expressed in East Africa.

Representations of a later Levalloisian, proof of a developing technology, were found by Arkell in the northern Sudan right to Nubia (Tangasi, Abu Tabari). These industries all probably date to the last great African pluvial (Gamblian).

Though the Sudan has representations of the Stone Age industries of Egypt there are gaps in the sequence and there are forms such as the pebble tools of the Atbara and the crude Levalloisian flakes of Singa that indicate different influences were at work. This seems to be in keeping with the historic role of the country as a gateway to the south.

Ancient Primates of Africa

The progress of African prehistoric research has been remarkable these past several decades. Startling discoveries of fossil hominids in South and East Africa and the development of firmly supported sequences of Stone Age industries in places such as the Transvaal, the Rhodesias, Kenya, and Tanganyika, have placed Africa in an extremely significant position in our understanding of the origin of mankind and the development of archaic cultures.

Though made far south of the Sudan, the discoveries of primate forms ancestral to modern man, at least in certain features, are worth mentioning here. On Rusinga Island near the eastern shore of Lake Victoria the bones of fossil monkeylike animals have been found in Miocene context. These date back perhaps twenty-five million years. One of these animals is called Proconsul and because of an over-all refinement of limb size and the absence of certain ape features is now regarded as in the evolutionary line both toward man and the great apes.

A later step in the hominid story is illustrated by the recovery of a series of related primates in South Africa, especially in the Transvaal. These creatures are known collectively as the Australopithecinae or "the southern apes." The Australopithecinae, though presenting an apelike visage, were in reality man-apes. This means that while they possessed certain apelike characteristics such as the jutting jaw (prognathism) and a small brain case relative to that jaw, they did walk upright, had manlike teeth, and perhaps most important of all, had a cranial capacity not far below that of man (700 cc.) or at any rate much above that of great apes. In recent years evidence has come to the fore that suggests that "the southern apes" lived together in bands and probably used very rough pebble tools. The making of tools is an essentially human characteristic and if this evidence is clearly confirmed the Australopithecinae will take their place as the earliest men.[3]

Whereas the Australopithecinae as tool users probably never developed stone tools more advanced than pebbles with a few flakes battered off here and there, the men who appear to have followed after, at least as is known in North Africa (Algeria), were makers of handaxes. The handax is of course as definite and purposeful a tool as is a hammer or a chisel. It is as indicative of the presence of early man as finding his footprints—perhaps more so.

At Palikao in Oran Province, Algeria, three human mandibles were uncovered toward the bottom of a gravel pit. These jaws were found in association with Acheulean handaxes and fauna like the saber-tooth tiger and now extinct forms of the rhino, hippo, and buffalo. The fauna indicate that these men were living during the early portion of the Middle Pleistocene and were, in time at least, somewhere intermediate between the Australopithecinae and the late Stone Age. Detailed studies of these jaws proved that they represent individuals of a human form known previously only from Java and China. These are the Pithecanthropids best known to the public as Java Man and Peking Man (or Woman), details of whose anatomy can be obtained elsewhere. Sufficient to note that they were perfectly human though not as advanced in feature as modern man (Homo sapiens). They had a stone tool kit which in its Asian form was larger than that found with its North African representatives (*Atlanthropus mauritanicus*). The discovery of Pithecanthropids so far to the west of where they were known previously would seem to indicate that they stand somewhere intermediate toward modern man, but whether in the direct line or merely as an offshoot of the evolutionary process is still to be determined.

In Kenya, however, at both Kanam and Kanjera, Professor L. B. Leakey has recovered fragments of jaws and skulls which evidence that longheaded men of modern type were makers of both pebble tools and crude handaxes at least as early, and perhaps earlier, than Atlanthropus. However, there is still a problem of dating, primarily because the geology is so complicated in this area of volcanoes, rifts, and shifting lake beds.

Probably the most important sequence of Stone Age cultures in all Africa exists near the Kenya findspots. This is Oldwai Gorge in Northern Tanganyika, again found by Dr. Leakey and his associates. The sequence is important not only because it demonstrates the evolution of a culture trait, i.e., the handax, of the remote past but because it indicates so many details of that evolution that many prehistorians have come to the view that the originating place of the handax traditions was Africa and very likely East Africa. Since handaxes of equivalent type are found abundantly from the Bay of Bengal to England it would appear that areas such as the Sudan and Egypt were on the direct route to the north and east, disseminators of a truly African culture. The problem of just who the primitive hunters were who carried these archaic cultures which the handaxes represent is still to be solved, but it is sufficient to note that for all intents and purposes the handax was far superior to the pebble tool which it succeeds at Oldwai. Its efficiency as an unspecialized implement useful for a hundred purposes made it a tool worth having and thus its spread was assured. For thousands upon thousands of years it served man, and in that time it became more and more efficient and was very probably used in more specialized ways. This seems to be a characteristically human phenomenon that insists on change—a dissatisfaction, as it were, with the status quo; so that one efficiency gained leads to another no matter how long it may take. This is the relentless, endless pursuit to which man's superior mind dedicated his body. To this all of man's accomplishments are due now as then. If the handax can be called the oldest true tool it would appear that in this sense at least Africa is the real cradle of mankind.

Ancestral Races of Africa

Whatever or wherever the evolution of modern mankind, we find at the end of the Palaeolithic, perhaps some 10,000–12,000 years ago in the Mesolithic period, that there were at least four racial groups existing on the continent.

The short-statured peppercorn-haired Bushman stock (to which the Hottentots belong) hunted through East and Southern Africa including the Ethiopian Highlands and a part of the Southern Sudan. Today these people live in a small fraction of their former range and can be found principally in the rigorous vastness of the Kalahari Desert. Pygmies inhabited the Congo Basin but on a much wider scale than they do today. Along the shores of the Mediterranean, the Red Sea, and at least a part of the Nile Valley were the longheaded, medium-height, slender-limbed, brown-skinned, and dark-haired Mediterranean people—ancestors of the modern Egyptians and usually listed by anthropologists as a subrace of the Caucasoids. The most important group, which with the Caucasoids was destined to gradually expand its range and which today best symbolizes Africa among the races of mankind is of course the Negroids. These are a dark-skinned people with kinky hair, broad noses, and a tendency to be tall. In earliest times apparently, they inhabited regions just north of the equator, especially in the Western Sudan and West African coast areas.

These early men of Africa were all hunters and gatherers, and during the last oscillations of the last pluvial phases the fantastic herds of animals which have been until recently a characteristic feature of Africa were existent almost everywhere. All these were fair prey for skillful hunters with their specialized hunting cultures: lances, bows and arrows for the chase, gouges, axes, scrapers and burins for the preparation of tools and skins; red ocher, ostrich skull beads, and bone needles for the adornment of the body and the sewing of leather are but a part of the tool repertory available to Mesolithic men. Many of these tools had been inherited from the cultures of the last phases of the Old Stone Age so that the types of blades and projectile points were of long tradition. Nonetheless the men of *ca.* 10000 B.C. were supreme hunters, the triumphant heirs of the Stone Age. Neither the ponderous hippo, the enraged lion, nor the swift antelope appear to have escaped their culture-won advantage, though our evidence is all on the side of man! In any case Africa has always been beneficial to hunters, more perhaps than any other region on earth, and it appears very likely that sizable populations flourished in the best game areas of East, West, and Northern Africa.

Though we cannot say for sure that the Sahara Desert was ever a land of great fruitfulness, it was at least in those days much better than it is now. Except for the Great Sand Sea there appear to have been grassy plains extending west from the sudd of the Eastern Sudan to beyond the waters of Lake Chad northward to Algeria. This was apparently a kind of open veldt country which supported hoofed beasts and their parasites the great cats and man. Here too, elephants and rhinos gave variety to the scene and with them the buffalo and wild cattle. The whole recalls the open plains of Kenya and Tanganyika.

For reasons still not quite clear but certainly having something to do with the shift of the storm belts after the last glacial retreats, the Sahara region was subjected to a continuing decrease of rainfall. This caused the waning of rivers and lakes and, coupled with a high rate of evaporation, the water supplies became dearer. This was not a sudden phenomenon but one that lasted for thousands of years and is still going on. Certainly there were times when the rainfall situation ameliorated and the veldt, hovering on the verge of becoming desert, was revived. But these moisture periods became progressively rarer.

The effect of increasing aridity upon the fauna is not always as clear as it might seem, for whereas some animals gradually adapt to the situation and survive even under bone-dry conditions others retreat or find refuge in places where a familiar environment is still maintained no matter how limited. Thus crocodiles were found in pools of water in the 1920's in the Central Sahara, and there have been recorded on numerous occasions, even within the last few centuries, reports of elephants, rhinos, hippos, and giraffes caught in remote pockets of water and vegetation in the midst of the desert and surviving until man destroyed them. Of interest is the fact that the Negro hunters who roamed the pastures of the Sahara appear to have retreated to the south with the game leaving a kind of vacuum to be filled later by the nomadic Caucasoids.

Earliest Farming and Herding

This dry cycle was underway at a critical time in the story of mankind. Some time between 10000 B.C. and 7000 B.C. two important accomplishments were achieved. The first was the cultivation of grain, i.e., the development of farming, and the second, the domestication of certain animals. Recent studies are throwing a great deal of light on these critical steps in human progress, but we are still a long way from a definite conclusion. We do know that the first successful farming took place somewhere along the bounds of, or within, the so-called Fertile Crescent countries of the Near East. I say "successful" because we cannot rule out the possibility that attempts at farming with other plants were not carried out elsewhere or even within the Fertile Crescent.

Older theories considered the drying up of the Sahara and other regions of the desert belt of North Africa and Western Asia as a motivation for men and animals to descend into the perennial river valleys such as that of the Nile. These prehistoric men enjoyed the taste of wild grain, and watching it grow in the same places year after year, they put two and two together and "Eureka" it was done! Similarly, animal domestication took place as the result of the concentration of men and animals during which time wild hoofed beasts in particular, becoming used to the presence of men, became tame. This intimacy was too much for observant man and he took over the leadership duties of ram and billy and brought about his own herds and flocks.

These older assumptions have been critically examined not only by skeptical archaeologists but by trained animal and plant experts. Due to their labors we now know that wild grain was probably not found in the river valleys but was native to the slopes of the foothills that surround the Fertile Crescent, especially in its Western Asiatic area. Charles Reed, a leading mammalogist, has indicated that in the event of desiccation the habits of wild goats and sheep would tend to cause them to climb higher to the ecological zones to which they were habituated rather than down to the foreign environment of the river valleys. As a consequence, ancient man would have found the higher slopes flanking the Fertile Crescent a more familiar ground than the frequently marshy and often jungled flood plains of the rivers. In any case there seems no doubt that the hunters of the last phases of the Stone Age were on intimate terms with both the wild ancestors of sheep and goats, and the grains as well. This intimacy appears to have been the bridge between a roving and a settled life. What took place to bring about this change is still debated.

At Mount Carmel in Northern Palestine in a series of

caves, archaeologists have found a succession of Stone Age cultures climaxed in its final stage by the Natufian culture representative of a hunting people who inserted flint blades in a haft and used it as a sickle for the cutting of wild grain. What is of greatest importance is that the lowest levels of the great mound at Jericho, Tell-es-Sultan, contain this Natufian culture. This culture appears here as representative of a settled community living near a great spring—the real reason for the importance of Jericho to the prehistoric villagers as it was to the wandering Hebrews of much later time. The probable date for these Natufians is the eighth millennium B.C. Since they are the first occupants of the site at Jericho they are at the bottom of an almost continuous succession of developing villages and towns that span the years from Stone Age to Biblical times. Yet Jericho is only one site among others of this kind.

In the foothill country of Kurdistan in Northeastern Iraq and Western Iran, extensive field work, especially by R. J. Braidwood and his associates of the Oriental Institute of the University of Chicago, and by Ralph Solecki of Columbia University and the Smithsonian Institute, has revealed a number of sites that would appear to bridge at least part of the gap in our knowledge of what happened when man left the cave home which served him as a hunter and built the village which became his home as a farmer. The Kurdish Hills and adjacent high land areas were apparently the native environment for the wild grains, wheat and barley, and for wild goats and sheep. Here the hunters were in such intimate daily contact with these wild forms that knowledge of their habits led to domestication in a manner still not quite clear.[4] In the case of the animals Arkell has pointed to the experiences in modern times that men have had in the Sudan when in times of drought, normally wild animals gather near human habitation in search of food. Men can tame these beasts by offering food. The animals thus exchange their wild habits for tame ones as a means of survival. Reed and Braidwood suggest that man's tendency to make pets, coupled with the process of "imprinting" (newborn animal following the living thing which nourishes or otherwise impresses it) among other similar events in the relationships of men and animals, led to domestication. Similarly, in the case of plants, men knew "good things when they saw them" (or ate them) and the wild grains gained favor. The reproduction of grain plants from seeds was an easily observable process which, apparently, men seized upon, and through sowing of seed determined the placement of the seed and thus the locale of the living plants. Thus the grain could be cared for within the limits of man's cultivation of the proper soil.

Phases of these processes have been found in the Kurdish Hills. Sites such as those of Braidwood in Iran and Iraq, as well as Solecki's Zawi Chemi Shanidar in the same region, evidence cultures comparable to the Natufian in Palestine in that they represent roughly contemporary cave and village habitation. In some cases the caves and villages appear to have been occupied alternately, perhaps as a seasonal expression. The most important fact is that at all these sites grinding and pounding stone artifacts have been recorded. These are, of course, probably indicative of the grinding of grain. In a way this grinding process is more significant than the domestication or potential domestication of grain that it indicates. A factor often overlooked in the interpretation of man's place in nature is man's ability to take intermediate steps toward a final goal. For example, the process of making flour involves harvesting, separation of the grain kernels from the plant, preparation of grinding equipment, grinding the kernels, sifting the resultant flour, mixing the flour with a liquid, construction of some receptacle or place for baking, making a fire, and the final baking. It is one thing to state that grain was domesticated because it was good, and another to realize why it was good. Fruit, nuts, herbs, meat, fish, can be eaten with very little preparation except the peeling and skinning necessary to reach the edible parts. But breadmaking requires time-consuming and relatively elaborate processing. Without putting undue emphasis on this processing, we must point out that men were ready to undertake these processes some ten thousand or so years ago. In this regard perhaps the greatest value of the large number of tools which have survived from the last phases of the Old Stone Age is that they indicate man's ability to take a number of intermediate steps in making a product.

At sites of somewhat later date (post-7000 B.C.), for example at Jarmo and Tepe Sarab in Kurdistan, and prepottery Jericho in Palestine, the record of the transition to full village life has been retained. Grain and other plants were cultivated, and goats and sheep roamed close by in flocks, subject to man's plans for breeding, growing, and eating. Adobe or boulder walls made up the houses, which were grouped in small clusters. Late in these early village occupations, clay and other materials supersede stone for numerous articles of daily use. Pottery appears after 5000 B.C. and even before that time clay figurines indicate probable fertility rituals. Objects that indicate sporadic overland trade, for example shells from the Persian Gulf, have been found.

The Beginnings of Civilization

Thus we have in Western Asia the start of village life, that stable mode of existence which forms the basis of civilization, the economic and social nucleus in which complex ideas become complex realities. The actual rise to civilization is demonstrated by a remarkably complete record existing in Mesopotamia where high points of the development of villages to towns and towns to cities can be traced. Monumental building, state religion, the wheel, metallurgy, social hierarchy, writing, early law, even nationalism erupt out of the Tigris-Euphrates area, seemingly the first in the story of civilization. Obviously the small farming villages of the hills perfected their means of livelihood and moved after a millennium or so down into the fertile alluvial plains of the river valleys. Here soil and flood-made crops flourish and surplus increased to the point where not everyone needed to work in the fields or watch the flocks.

The appearance of such specialists as the potter, metalsmith, and perhaps even the "beggarman and thief" was the direct result of better times and better control of resources. With some rapidity it appears that the attempts to control the good but formidable environment of Southern Iraq (Sumer) led to group efforts to establish irrigation systems and control flooding; and out of this, perhaps, arose irrigation experts—the first engineers. Priesthood may have evolved from village shamans who interpreted the unknown—the unknown which grew more complex and important to life with a greater world knowledge and consciousness. Soldiers, kings, slaves, nobles, scribes, and the like appeared as the final phase of urbanizing villages at the climax of early agricultural and technological development. They are indicative of intense competition for limited resources—a competition which required strong control at home and success abroad. Thus civilization, as we in the West know it, began.

This is, of course, a very brief summation of what is a

complex and important chapter in man's history. It was certainly a complicated and painful process about which we are only just able to perceive the major signposts in these early stages of research. An important and quite natural by-product of these studies of the past are the areal shifts in emphasis. During the nineteenth century Egypt was regarded as the homeland of man's civilization, oldest in the world. Anthropologists such as G. Eliot Smith saw Egypt as the center from which many of the world's cultures derived eventually. James Henry Breasted, one of the greatest of America's historians, was a firm champion of Egypt as the earliest civilization. Now the pendulum has swung to Mesopotamia primarily because the accumulating evidence for priority gathered from a remarkable series of excavations there seems to place Egypt as the recipient rather than the originator of an overwhelming number of traits important to civilization. Agriculture, animal domestication, earliest metallurgy, the wheel, writing, etc., are all considered to have come to the Nile Valley diffused from their points of origin in Western Asia.

Africa's Civilized Beginnings

Without prejudicing one's ideas by assuming there presently exist sides to join in the matter, it seems clear that there has been understandable tendency to play down the African, and especially the early Egyptian, contributions. For one thing, except for the sudd regions of Southern Sudan, there are no grassy slopes fringing the Nile Valley upon which wild goats and sheep frolicked and untamed barley and wheat flourished. To put it bluntly, there seem to have been no ancestors to these essentials of village life in Africa. Nevertheless it is not unlikely that there were experiments in early post–Ice Age Africa that contributed to the development of man's settled life. A well-known American anthropologist, G. P. Murdock, for example, has championed the theory that agriculture had another and independent origin in West Africa, not too long after its beginnings (ca. 5000 B.C.) in Western Asia (ca. 8000 B.C.). The basis of his argument is primarily linguistic, since archaeological evidence is lacking for the present at least, and there is general absence of Southwest Asian crops in the Western Sudan even today.

We should expect the particular people who first advanced from a hunting and gathering economy to an agricultural one to have multiplied in number and to have expanded geographically at the expense of their more backward neighbors, with the result that the group of languages which they spoke should have spread over an unusually wide expanse of territory. . . . Our criteria are fully satisfied . . . in the Western Sudan by the far-flung Nigritic stock and particularly by its Mande subfamily, which centers on the upper Niger River. Not only do the speakers of Mande exhibit Negro agriculture in its fullest and most developed form, but their distribution demonstrates that they have spread in all directions at the expense of their immediate neighbors . . .[5]

Murdock's list of plants indigenous to, and first domesticated in, West Africa includes sorghum, Guinea yams, okra, calabash, watermelon, tamarind, cotton, and sesame along with varieties of cereal grains, peas, beans, and potatoes. This is an important list containing as it does a number of plants used all over the modern world. If Murdock's idea can be proved it places Africa in a far more important position in the ancient world than hitherto thought.

The trouble is that the evidence is still not of great strength. For instance, if cotton were first cultivated in West Africa several thousand years B.C. it would have had to jump Egypt en route to India and then return somewhere around 550 B.C.—a not inconceivable event, but at least one that can be regarded as unlikely. Nevertheless, the theory stands on some logical facts, and, accordingly, we have to admit its possible contributions. For one thing, the processing of sorghum is not dissimilar to that of wheat or barley and it may well be that improvements on the Western Asiatic grinding and baking techniques derived from Africa. The widespread use of sesame seed as a source of oil essential in the economy of the ancient world may have been a significant factor in the story of civilization. If so, West Africa's importance in ancient times can not be underrated.

Thus Egypt and Nubia may have been between two great farming developments by about 5000 B.C. But so far in archaeological studies of the prehistoric cultures, the Asian contribution appears strong and the West African very faint indeed.

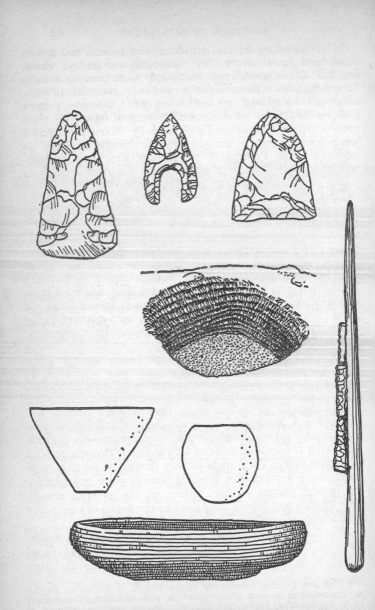

OBJECTS OF THE "A" CULTURE OF THE PREHISTORIC FAYUM.
On the right is a reconstructed sickle, in the center a silo.

In the Egyptian Fayum, settlements of hunters and fishers have been found. Here they also cultivated barley, wheat, and flax. Goats, sheep, pigs, and cattle were possibly domesticated, and the elaboration of arrowheads, groundstone axes, bone harpoons, and the possession of handmade pottery indicate that these people were advancing rapidly in their control of their environment. Bifacially flaked flint blades were inserted into a straight wooden handle to form an effective sickle. Perhaps of most importance were the subterranean silos lined with basketry for the storage of grain —the obvious preparation for that nonrainy day.*

On the western edge of the Nile delta in Lower Egypt the site of Merimdeh is illustrative of a culture comparable in time and status to those of the Fayum (4500 B.C. and later). Here three phases of occupation indicate that construction of huts progressed from slight structures of reeds and poles, perhaps dabbed with mud, to strong, oval constructions surrounded by adobelike walls. Textiles were made—very likely from local plant fibers—and ivory, shell, and bone ornaments were probably used by men and women alike Of great interest are the graves with their eastward-facing occupants flexed in what some like to call the "embryonic position." The fact that these graves were found among the houses of the villages indicates perhaps some belief in a spirit life after death where participation in the activities of the living could take place. It is suggestive of the historical Egyptian idea of an afterlife similar to the present life.

In Upper Egypt the site of El Tasa provides material evidence for a hunting-fishing group with limited grain agriculture and animal domestication. This culture was perhaps somewhat cruder than those of Lower Egypt (though perhaps of earlier date). They made pottery though, some of it quite handsomely decorated by pressing whitish paste into geometric incised designs on the surface of the sacklike vessels. The Tasians also buried their dead in the flexed or contracted position.

Whereas the people of these sites, insofar as we now know, were of the longheaded, rather slight Mediterranean racial stock, it is of interest that the people of the Badarian

* This first farming community in the Fayum is known as Fayum A. Fayum B is a later phase which is a hybrid culture composed of a degenerating Fayum A blended with the hunting cultures of the pre-Fayum A type (back blades, etc.). Fayum A is dated by radiocarbon as 4300–4000 B.C.

culture, which is more or less an elaboration of that of El Tasa and later in time, exhibit Negroid features. Was this because of African cultural contacts still not clearly defined? we might ask. There is no answer as yet except that the Badarian people appear to have been traders as well as hunters, fishers, and farmers. Copper ores like malachite may well have been imported from Nubia; ivory too may have had to come from the south as the supply of elephants and hippos diminished in the immediate Nile Valley. Wooden boomerangs may be of African derivation also. Of greatest importance, however, are the pottery models of boats which indicate an ability to maneuver up and down the Nile with more than a little dexterity. Excellent pottery, especially ripple-decorated ware, reveals a competence of craftsmanship undeniably derived from an exchange of ideas due to widening horizons. How wide those horizons were is tantalizingly suggested by the appearance of a similar pottery in the Sudan (Khartoum Mesolithic) and even west, across the Sahara, to the vicinity of Nigeria. The dating of these distant cultures, especially in the case of the Sahara, is completely uncertain but associations of artifacts with the pottery indicate a time not too distant from that of the Badarian.[6] Again Murdock's theory confronts us, for such evidence can indicate influences moving eastward as well as vice versa. For the moment at least we have no response!

In the Sudan, A. J. Arkell, leading archaeologist of the Sudan, has revealed two significant cultural entities both of which were apparently carried by Negroid peoples. The first of these has been labeled the "Khartoum Mesolithic culture." The type site is a low mound located northeast of the Khartoum central railway station. In ancient times this was the seat of a fishing settlement, though an ample number of swamp-living animals were also killed and eaten along with their aquatic companions the hippo and river turtle. The inhabitants had a stone tool repertory of various kinds of small-blade tools including backed blades, trapezoids, crescents, etc., usually found among Mesolithic bow-and-arrow hunters (or even Upper Palaeolithic—i.e., Caspian). On the other hand they possessed grinding stones (probably for ocher), rubbing and polishing implements and a variety of pottery, some decorated with wavy lines not too unlike the later rippled ware found at Badari—which place the culture in a post-Mesolithic time context. Elaborations of bone harpoons, fishhooks, awls, and the like confirm

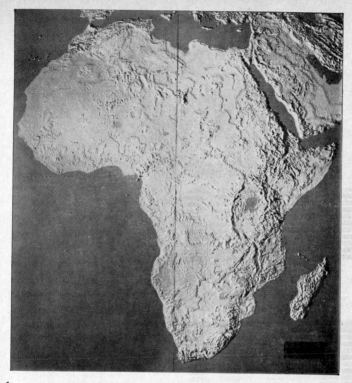

1. RELIEF MAP OF AFRICA. The rifts and lakes of East Africa are strikingly revealed.
(The American Museum of Natural History)

2. RIVER STATION. Bahr-el-Jabel, Southern Sudan.
(The American Museum of Natural History)

3. MORU DINKA, AMADI.
The Dinka are cattle
herders who live in the
sudd region of the South-
ern Sudan.
*(The American Museum
of Natural History)*

4. SHILLUK OF THE SUDAN. The Shilluk live in the northern portion
of the sudd region. They are a kingdom whose monarch is given
divine qualities much perhaps as the pharaohs.
(The American Museum of Natural History)

5. STEAMER. These steamers ply the waters of the White Nile, bringing produce of the Southern Sudan to Khartoum and other Nile ports.
(*The American Museum of Natural History*)

6. THE ASWAN DAM. First of the great dams on the Nile.
(*The American Museum of Natural History*)

7. SYMBOL OF FRUIT-FULNESS of the Nile Valley in Egypt are these bunches of succulent dates growing near a village.
(*W. Fairservis*)

8. EGYPTIAN POTTERY jar decorated with boats, human figures, and ostriches. Middle Prednastic Period.
(*Courtesy of The Metropolitan Museum of Art, Rogers Fund, 1920*)

9. REPRODUCTION OF PALETTE OF KING NARMER, slate. Dynasty I.
Original, Cairo Museum.
(Courtesy of The Metropolitan Museum of Art, Dodge Fund, 1931)

10. PHARAOH CHEPHREN (KHAFRA), builder of
the Second Pyramid at Giza.
(Cairo Museum)

11. MAP OF THE ISLAND OF ELEPHANTINE drawn by one of Napoleon's officers. This island ofttimes marked the frontier between Egypt and Nubia.
(From Description de l'Egypte, Paris, 1820)

12. BLACK GRANITE STATUE OF KING SEN-WOSRET III. Dynasty XII.
(Courtesy of The Metropolitan Museum of Art, Rogers Fund, 1945)

13. WOODEN FUNERARY MODEL OF A GRANARY. From the tomb of Meketre, Thebes. Dynasty XI.
(Courtesy of The Metropolitan Museum of Art, Museum Excavations, 1919-1920; Rogers Fund, Contribution of Edward S. Harkness.)

this later affiliation. Direct indications of animal domestication and agriculture are nonexistent. However, grooved stones are evidence that they had nets or at least fishline, convincing proof of an advanced knowledge of fishing—the probable major basis of their economy. Woven impressions in pottery and in hard mud, the latter probably a remnant of wattle and daub house walls, are signs of an ability to plait and weave. As at Merimdeh, the dead were buried in the settlement in a contracted position but with no particular orientation and apparently without funerary equipment.

OBJECTS OF THE KHARTOUM MESOLITHIC CULTURE (*after Arkell*).

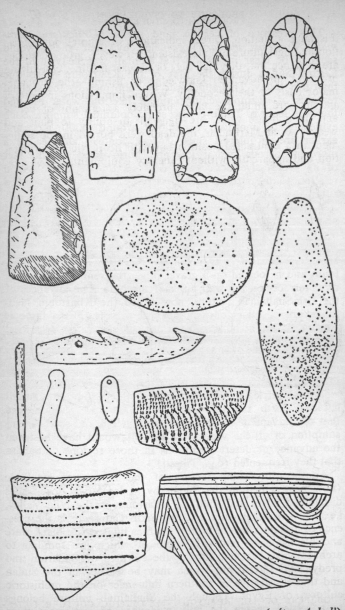

OBJECTS OF THE ESH-SHAHEINAB CULTURE (*after Arkell*).

The presence of certain land snails (*Umicolaria flam-mata, Zootecus insularis*) revealed by their shells would seem to be clear indication that rainfall was heavier in the Central Sudan during the time of the Khartoum Mesolithic than it is today. This appears to be confirmed by the skeletal remains of swamp-dwelling animals like the water rat and the Nile lechwe. There is also some botanical support. Such evidences of moisture conditions around 4000 B.C. and earlier are of interest since it does confirm an idea of a more prosperous land in late prehistoric times and the fact of its progressive desiccation with all that that implies in relation to the stresses and strains on nomadic and settled cultures.

A hunting-fishing culture with many of the tools and weapons of the Khartoum Mesolithic but with additions indicating an advancement in over-all technological progress was revealed by Arkell at the site of Esh Shaheinab. This ancient settlement is only some thirty miles north of Khartoum and is located on a gravel ridge, the remnant of an old river terrace, on the west bank of the Nile. The advances of the Esh-Shaheinab culture, now called the Khartoum Neolithic, are peculiar for a number of reasons.[7] First there is the fact of the domestication of goats, the form being a kind of dwarf goat whose living descendant exists only in Algeria. Algeria, in fact, may have been the homeland of this goat and if so it again would indicate a west-to-east influx of ideas; though in this case the idea of domestication probably spread via North Africa to Western Africa first. In any case, Arkell has put forth the interesting and certainly feasible idea that the advent of herds of goats with their inexorable consumption of all the vegetation in sight would have hastened the advance of desert conditions in those regions of Sahara that they frequented (e.g., Tibesti).

Another interesting feature of the Khartoum Neolithic (now represented in the Sudan by at least two dozen sites distributed north and south of Khartoum in the Nile Valley, i.e., between Jebel Aulia and the Sixth Cataract) is the presence of certain kinds of pottery such as incised-rim black ware and black-topped red ware, both of which are familiar to archaeologists working among the cultures of Badarian and predynastic Egypt, but which may be earlier in the Sudan and thus illustrative of southern influences on the prehistoric cultures of Egypt. Though the Shaheinab culture belongs to a settled people the only evidences of settlement were the hearths and cooking holes. No reed shelters or adobe-walled huts were found and there were no graves anywhere to help to identify the inhabitants of the place, though the cultural similarities with the older Mesolithic culture suggest a basic Negro stock. Stone lip plugs also suggest an African current flowing steadily within the culture. Agriculture may or may not have been practiced—there simply is no evidence for it at the type site. However, Arkell places a point of tantalizing interest before us in view of Murdock's theories on West Africa as a place of origins. In one of the hearths he found:

> a carbonized fragment of the shell of the West African oil-palm Elaeis quineensis, identified at the Royal Botanic Gardens at Kew, whose Director calls attention to the possibility that the fruits, being important economically . . . may have been carried outside the natural habitat of the palm by human agency. It is known that the natural habitat of this palm is in West Africa. . . . No stress is, however, laid on this point; it is just mentioned as being of interest.[8]

Most remarkable of all the features of the Khartoum Neolithic are the close and important parallels with the Fayum Neolithic far to the north. Arkell lists these as:

> use of fireholes and very flimsy habitations
> disposal of the dead outside the settlement, by a method other than burial
> the domestication of animals
> the flaked and partly polished stone celt and stone gouge
> the burnishing of pottery, and
> the manufacture of beads from microline feldspar (amazon stone) [9]

When this evidence of things shared with the Neolithic of Lower Egypt is put alongside the evidence for the Fayum's undeniable sharing of many of its stone tool and weapon types with prehistoric cultures in the Sahara, it would certainly seem as if both Lower Egypt and the Central Sudan owe their Neolithic cultures in large part to areas to the west of the Nile Valley. As Arkell points out, even the bone harpoons of Shaheinab are more similar to those of the

Southern Sahara region (Wadi Azaouak) than to those of the Nile Valley.

This idea of a western homeland for the early cultures of Egypt and the Sudan is a very important one, but unfortunately evidence from the Sahara is only suggestive and not conclusive. To the layman reading thus far, the mysterious ways of archaeology may still seem mysterious, but as a science archaeology is as experimental as chemistry or physics. The proof for theories such as these can only come from more excavation, more study, and the testing of more theories. In this case the Central Sahara and the Nile Valley are the obvious places of concentration. This serves to point up the desperate need to carry on field work in Nubia where the High Dam floods will bury the sites of prehistoric times. Even the date for the Khartoum Neolithic, based as it is on carbon 14 dating, is under fire. For the date of Esh Shaheinab is *ca.* 3500–3000 B.C.,* which is much later than Fayum A. Arkeil disputes these dates in view of the clear parallels between the cultures: "But there are too many archaeological connexions between the Fayum Neolithic and the Khartoum Neolithic for it to seem reasonable to accept a difference of 800 years between the two cultures." [10]

The difficulties involved in assessing the validity of a carbon 14 sample have been shown in recent years to be multifold. It is not therefore unlikely that the Khartoum Neolithic is more nearly comparable in time to its Fayum counterpart.

But even with all the problems of dating and the scant evidence for origins, the outlines of a remarkable story are coming into full perception. The Old Stone Age hunting cultures of the Sahara were in contact with the early farmers who brought grain agriculture from Western Asia. In the Fayum and at Merimdeh we have tangible traces of the hybrid cultures that resulted from this early mixture of Africa and Asia. Far to the south along the Nile Valley in stretches of Nubia and the Central Sudan optimum hunting and fishing provided the basis for a settled existence almost as secure as that of farming. Pottery makes its appearance here and causes some archaeologists to feel that these early ceramics of the Khartoum Mesolithic were the earliest in the world. This early Sudanese settled culture looks to be

*Carbon 14 ages: sample C-753 5060 ± 450; sample C-754 5446 ± 380.

almost purely African—the bulk of its tools and weapons derived from earlier and more westerly cultures and its pottery from local or more southerly cultures. The Khartoum Neolithic, with the Fayum, owes much to earlier cultures and much to the cultures around it. But what per cent is of Asia and what of Africa escapes us for the present. However, in view of the absence of good and ample evidence most archaeologists are inclined to consider the Nile Valley as the highway down which the advances of early Asiatic farming cultures found their way to Africa. C. B. M. McBurney, a profound student of the archaeology of Northern Africa, summarizes the general consensus of opinion:

> Virtually nothing is known as yet of the neolithic in that region [Central Sahara] and in view of the evidence . . . the simplest working theory . . . is a general north-to-south process of diffusion and migration starting some time in the fifth millennium B.C. and ultimately originating in the Levantine coastal region.[11]

Whatever the origin of these cultures, progression from a simple to a more elaborate standard of living is manifest. Men were adapting to the environment not by moving about but by creating new means to control it. In the Nile Valley the simple settlements like Tasa and Badari were located on desert spurs protruding into the fertile alluvium. Though hunting was still a major pursuit, the richness of the annually flooded land became more and more apparent. Perhaps more and more individuals devoted themselves to the soil instead of hunting, the change-over occurring at first slowly but then more rapidly. Probably an influx of brown-skinned Mediterraneans from the north brought about the final conversion to a way of life that still endures, but which after 4000 B.C. was to create one of the splendors of the past —the civilization of ancient Egypt.

Early Stone Age Cultures of Egypt

8000–6000 B.C.	Sebilian III
12000–8000 B.C.	Sebilian II
25000 B.C.	Upper Palaeolithic Sebilian I (silt terraces)
100000 B.C.	Middle Palaeolithic—handaxes—Levalloisian flakes (10′ Nile terrace)
250000 + B.C.	Lower Palaeolithic—handaxes—(100′– 50′ Nile terrace)

Cultures of Prehistoric Egypt and the Sudan

	LOWER (NORTH) EGYPT	UPPER (SOUTH) EGYPT	SUDAN
3200 B.C.	Menes (Narmer) founds	1st Dynasty	
3400-3200 B.C.	Late Predynastic (Gerzean)	Late Predynastic (Gerzean)	
3500-3400 B.C.	Middle Predynastic (Gerzean)	Middle Predynastic (Amratian-Gerzean)	
3600 B.C.	Early Predynastic (Gerzean?)	Early Predynastic (Amratian)	
3800 B.C.	Fayum B	Badarian Culture	Shaheinab
4000 B.C.	Helwan (El Omari) Merimdeh	Tasian Culture	Khartoum Mesolithic
4400 B.C.	Fayum A		

3

Pyramid Kings and Dwarfs

Egypt is the cradle of Mediterranean civilization and the archaeologist's living book of history. Its scattered pages, discovered one by one, were pieced together and read with patience and devotion. . . . despite the wealth of material found, many pages are still missing. . . . No effort should therefore be spared to find and preserve all the vestiges which may throw light on the history of our forbears, for was this not the crucible in which the basic elements of Western civilization were forged?— CHRISTIANE DESROCHES-NOBLECOURT, Curator, Department of Egyptian Antiquities, Musée du Louvre, Paris (*The UNESCO Courier*, February, 1960)

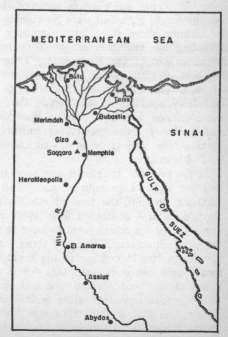

Some 2,670 years before the birth of Christ, Pharaoh Snefru, founder of Egypt's pyramid dynasty, the fourth, carried on a military campaign in Lower Nubia. His success was written in stone: "I brought back seven thousand prisoners, and two hundred thousand cattle, large and small." [1]

Though these figures may be somewhat of an exaggeration, the event nonetheless is of great importance. It is obvious that for Nubia to furnish so large a booty there must have been some prosperity in that land. It is cattle especially that symbolize the kind of prosperity it was. Cattle require grass in some quantity and when grassland is utilized for cultivation man has to supply fodder to maintain his cattle. Cattle, of course, have multifold uses, but one of the most important is as a draft animal. For these early agriculturists cattle supplied the energy resources that enabled them to bring all fertile land under cultivation and probably by means of cattle-motivated water wheels to irrigate normally arid lands. In any case it would appear that by the time of Egypt's Old Kingdom (ca. 2680 B.C.–2258 B.C.) the narrow valley of Nubia and perhaps some of the watered places on the surrounding plateau were flourishing agricultural regions. In addition there were large numbers of pastoral nomads including the ancestors of the Beja peoples of the desert countries east of the Nile Valley. These nomads kept great numbers of cattle, sheep, and goats and moved from place to place with the seasons. A hardy lot living off the meat and dairy products of their herds, they were a considerably more difficult people to subdue than their more vulnerable and probably more pacific agricultural neighbors of the Nubian Nile Valley; or as it was known in those days, the land of Wawat.

In the previous chapter it was seen that in general Nubia and the Sudan kept cultural pace with Egypt up to about 3800 B.C. or until the time of the Badarian culture. But as Egypt's cultures continued their evolvement toward civilization those of the Sudan seem to have remained at a comparatively primitive stage. For one thing, agriculture appears to have been late in coming to the region. The American anthropologist Murdock feels that when agriculture did come it was of the West African type and that this was integrated with Egyptian-type agriculture in the Sudan. One fact seems certain and that is that there was little Egyptian influence on the Sudan for about eight hundred years. This was the more remarkable because those years cover the astounding developments of predynastic Egypt.

Early Predynastic Egypt (ca. 4000–3500 B.C.)

Apparently deriving directly out of the older Badarian cultures, the first of the developmental steps of predynastic Egypt was the Amratian. This period witnessed the spread of grain and flax farming on a wide scale along the Nile Valley. Hunting was still continued as a supplement to the economy, however—almost as if there were a reluctance to give up ancestral ways of life or perhaps more because the early agriculture was still rife with uncertainties. However, the advances made in this period were considerable. Copper was sought for and pounded into needles and fishhooks. Fine flint was mined outside the grounds of the valley and even such luxury materials as gold and alabaster were brought from considerable distances. Slate was cut and smoothed into palettes on which malachite was ground into cosmetic powder. Some of these palettes were charmingly shaped into forms of fish and other animals. Most attractive of all perhaps were the carved ivories among which were combs topped with the forms of goats, giraffes, and birds. Animal drawing and painting was in great vogue in predynastic Egypt. On Amratian pottery scenes of elephants, sheep, giraffes, and hippopotami occur either scratched into the vessel surface or painted in cursive strokes with white paint. These drawings suggest relationships with the rock paintings and drawings found in the Sahara or even those of Eastern Spain.

Two features of the Amratian are already symptomatic of certain culture features of the Egypt to come. One of these is the depiction of boats by the Amratian artists. These vessels were made of lashed bundles of papyrus and were propelled by oars: the sail, apparently, was unknown. No cataracts interrupt the Nile channel in Egypt and the development of boats made accessible the whole stretch of the river from Aswan to the Mediterranean. The increased use of the Nile as a highway anticipated the unity of cultural feature which was to make Egypt unique in the ancient world.

A second feature of great importance is the obvious emphasis which the Amratians placed upon funerary custom. The cemeteries, which supply the greatest archaeological evidence for the period, attest the firm belief in an afterlife which is so profoundly Egyptian. In simple oval-shaped pits the body was interred in a contracted position surrounded by the objects of daily life. The harpoons, knives, sickles, maces, razors, arrows, beads, hooks, pins, and pottery which the deceased familiarly used in his everyday enterprises were placed with him in his grave, eloquent testimony to a simple but evolving way of life. Probably the objects were endowed with magical properties in order that they might continue their functions in the next world. There are even ivory or clay figurines representing servants and probably loved ones emphasizing by their presence the immortality of the wish that things might go on as they always did in spite of death.

Late Predynastic Egypt (ca. 3500–3200 B.C.)

The Gerzean period, which follows the Amratian, demonstrates at once an elaboration on the earlier culture and the influx of new traditions, some of which were certainly Asian. Trade accelerates in this period not only along the river but overland: the latter probably because of increased use of the donkey, the true beast of burden. Not only was copper in great demand because of improved technology (including casting), but lead, silver, malachite, flint, ivory, lapis lazuli, and fine stone for vases were also required. The valley was by now largely under cultivation, though it appears that the marshy delta area was perhaps somewhat unevenly settled and was the seat for localized cultures. Towns grew out of some of the older villages and their mud buildings were well-made structures in which wood framing for doors and windows was relatively commonplace. These towns were the places where much of the nonfarming activity of the surrounding area was centered. Probably the specialized crafts such as those of metallurgy, ivory carving, shipbuilding, and the like, had their headquarters there. The support for such specialists derived from contributions made by the local farmers. At first it appears that these contributions were voluntary, but as society became more elaborate and the annual productivity of the land more certain and fruitful, controls tended to pass from the hands of individual farmers into those who held the political and thus the economic control

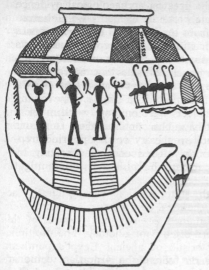

GERZEAN DECORATED
VESSEL with depiction
of Nile boat. "Standard"
is attached to the right
superstructure.

of the towns. It appears obvious that as the individual farmers
grew more dependent on the town specialists for their tools
and luxuries, they also gave up a share of their independence
in order to pay for them. The somber paradox of freedom-
loving man caught in a materialistic world casts its shadow
even in those remote days. Contributions turned into taxes,
and what had been voluntary became enforced.

Whatever the reasons for the change, and admittedly
we are speculating on some of these problems, it appears
that the Gerzean was a time that witnessed both the expansion
of trade and cultivation, and the acceleration of the centralization of Egyptian society.

It is notable that on the paint-decorated vases of the
Gerzean period the scenes depict—besides animals, humans,
and plants—boats of considerable size. These boats were
usually marked by a standard. Set on an upright pole, which
is fixed to one of the cabins, is an emblem such as a pair
of horns, a harpoon, or an animal or bird effigy. Some of
these emblems were used in historical times as representative
of various deities or in some cases as a kind of heraldic
image of an administrative district or nome. Whereas it seems
unlikely that predynastic Egypt was divided up into nomes,
the ship standards may well indicate totems about which a

body of traditions and beliefs had already gathered. That there were regions in which totemic elements were shared in common seems obvious from the historical evidence. In other words, it would appear that these early Egyptians were aware of beliefs that they shared with neighboring villages but which were different from those held outside that portion of the valley or delta in which those villages were gathered. Each region had its town and this was the center not only for trade and news but apparently for the common worship of the local deities. There must have been in those days at least the beginnings of a priesthood in these towns, supported by the village farmers along with the other specialists. The extraordinary formal religion of ancient Egypt has its beginnings in this regionalization.

In later time, though state religion was generally acknowledged everywhere, the local deities and ceremonies were also recognized and maintained, even though features of this kind of dual worship were often contradictory. The multiplicity of deities so characteristic of ancient Egypt's pantheon owes its origin to this early "totemic" division, it would appear. Probably a certain family, clan, or even tribe had as its emblem a beast or bird whose unique powers were accredited to the social unit. Such designations as "the lion people," "the hippo people," and "the harpoon people" were probably used to identify these units. It appears as if at least some of these emblems were carried over from an early hunting tradition where, by sympathetic magic, animal qualities of strength, speed, and cunning were bestowed on the hunter. Perhaps it was during Gerzean times, when agriculture became the dominating pursuit of most of Egypt's people, that these emblems were given their more sedentary qualities familiar to history in such forms as Anubis, the jackal-headed god of embalming; Sekhmet, the warlike lioness goddess; or Thoth, ibis-headed god of wisdom.

The village rule in those ancient days was very probably in the hands of a chief whose post was hereditary, harking back to some totemic ancestor. Again, his chieftainship may have been a carry-over from hunting days. In predynastic times the chief very likely directed the communal activities, which included flood control and irrigation, village law, worship, and possibly the determination of the right time for planting and harvesting. It must be remembered that timing in the Nile Valley is a matter of considerable concern. The anticipation of the Nile flood and with it the measurement of the rise and fall of the river very early became the duties of a select group whose functions were closely entwined with religion. It is no surprise then, that in pharaonic Egypt we find both the god-kings and priests involved in annual ceremonies in which river gauges play a major role. The early chiefs very speedily must have delegated such functions to others, which again anticipates the pharaonic court with its host of officials, each of whom was responsible for some function.

It is unfortunate that we know so little about the Gerzean period. Much of the evidence may be buried irretrievably under the mud of the Nile delta. A large percentage of our information has to come from remains in the Nile Valley, that is, Upper Egypt. Nonetheless, we are aware that considerable activity was going on in the delta. The rich alluvium there must have attracted farmers from afar in spite of the marshes. Closer contact with Palestine and Sinai may have brought West Asian advances earlier than into the Valley itself. In any case some of the most important towns in Egypt's history were early located in the delta: Buto, Tanis, Bubastis, and Sais, among others. Significantly, the patron deity of the town of Behedit, Horus the falcon-god, who later became one of the chief gods of all Egypt, appears to have moved from his delta home to Hierakanopolis in Upper Egypt during the Gerzean period. Perhaps this movement is indicative of the true dawn of civilization.

Character of Early Civilization

It is common in the Western world to regard the achievement of civilization as the ultima Thule for all mankind. Surprisingly, when one, in Diogenes fashion, asks individuals what civilization really is, the answers generally resolve themselves into the axiom, "If you have material comfort you have civilization." For some, the greater the distance one stands from physical labor, the greater the degree of civilization. In effect this means that the civilized man has little to do with the production of his daily bread, the construction of his house, or the weaving of his clothes. He is said to supply services in other ways with which to compensate those who so fulfill his daily physical requirements. Thus the potter makes vessels used by the farmer, who is glad to give bread to the potter in exchange. In modern civilizations a man may be involved in nonessential services which service other nonessential services which in turn service still others, ad infinitum, until at last one reaches the farmer whose produce makes the whole thing tick. Civilization, by definition, has to do with city life and city-influenced culture. The city is, of course, the parasite which feeds upon the food producers' surplus; and in turn the food producer receives city-manufactured articles, increased demands for more "surplus" (which frequently means reducing one's own essential larder), political control, and even involvement in war.

The city caused the intimate interaction of many people. In such a setting, idea exchange produced the remarkable progress of technology. This is particularly apparent in Early Mesopotamia where such progress is more neatly recorded than in Egypt. But the rise of urban communities created the demon of demand whose voice still shrieks in the twentieth-century air. Whereas in earlier times the villager was generally content with the fruits of his own labors, supplemented by articles obtained through barter, the civilized men who were being created by the banks of the Nile and contemporaneously in the valley of the Tigris-Euphrates required far more than the surrounding area could provide. More copper, ivory, lapis, carnelian, gold, silver, lead, better stone, firewood, fragrant plants; this was the waxing cry. Cattle and wheat were not only essentials of living but the media of wealth. Men sought more cattle, bigger silos, more land, and of course, more men to till the soil and herd the cattle. The rich land of Egypt was simply not rich enough to support the demands of an increasingly complex civilized society. Certainly each district found itself lacking in at least some of those materials which had now become essential. Growing populations augmented the problem. At the very dawn of history (ca. 3200 B.C.) civilization moves into the scene accompanied by the sounds of battle. Faintly marked, but nonetheless definite, the last phases of predynastic Egypt are marked by wars between districts: conquests, defeats, alliances, and disruptions. It appears that at one time the districts of the delta (Lower Egypt) united by force into one kingdom, ruled over much of the Nile Valley. The falcon-god Horus may well have reached Upper Egypt as a result of this early conquest. Then Upper Egypt gained the ascendancy and conquered the delta, uniting its white crown with the

red crown of Lower Egypt, and the unification was complete.
However, Egypt was known as the Land of the Two Kingdoms ever afterward in recognition of this ancient division.
Traditionally, the unification was supposed to have taken
place under Narmer (probably Menes), a warrior king of
Upper Egypt. A commemorative slate palette of this king is
in the Cairo Museum, and as the first conquest document of
its kind it is of considerable interest. It is a dismal document
recording the conquest of a portion of the delta. Here at the
very beginning of civilization we have graven on slate the
corpse-strewn battlefield, the maimed, the headless, the un-
utterable agony of war. Here is the victorious general in triumph—bringer of civilization to the misbegotten. Broken into
its essentials, this simple document merely indicates that the
Upper Egyptians wanted something the Lower Egyptians had:
perhaps ease of passage to the copper of Sinai, the possession
of their cattle and fields, or the shores of the Mediterranean.
Flavor these desires with grievances for earlier conquests
and raids, plus personal ambition and the like; and the now
hoary tale begins. The Egypt that first appears on the stage
of history is a nation united by war. It was a rich agricultural
nation but woefully short in certain metals, semiprecious
stones, ivory, and other exotica. Egypt, as one of the world's
first civilizations, provides an illustration for all civilizations.
Rich in some things, poor in others, its economy and social
order labored to stay in balance. Civilization was and is a
hot coal that needed to be juggled to keep a people's
hands from burning.

It may be no coincidence, then, that the period of these
early troubles was that during which Nubia was most
heavily settled by the so-called "A" people. These farmers
and cattle-herders were Mediterraneans identical in racial form
with the Egyptians. Their traces are wide-spread in Nubia.
Archaeologists who have excavated some of their sites find
evidence for peaceful settlement and a fine degree of prosperity. One of the losses caused by the new High Dam must be
the inundation of numerous settlements of these people, thus
preventing a fuller understanding of their life and contribution to Africa as a whole and in turn what Africa's contribution was to them.

There is something suspicious about this settlement of
Nubia in the days when Egyptians were killing Egyptians. It
is almost as if people were saying "The hell with it" and moving south out of harm's way. This is reading into our slender

body of facts more than is warranted, but nonetheless, we can be quite sure that population pressure at least was not a constant motivating force in those remote days.

Archaic Egypt (3200–2680 B.C.)

The unification of Egypt began the First Dynasty. It also marks the beginning of history, for from now on hieroglyphic writing was the writing form of Egypt (*ca.* 3100 B.C.) The first two dynasties are still poorly known. Hazy figures of kings appear in the records. Kings Jer and Hor-Aha of the First Dynasty, and Khasekhemuwy of the Second Dynasty, maintained the war record by raids into Nubia. None of these efforts were large-scale or resulted in permanent conquest, but they are indicative of a desire for the wealth of Nubia; though in all justice the nomads of the desert may have raided Egypt and were accordingly attacked as a police action.

However, in spite of the turbulent origin, the later days of Egypt's earliest history mark a gradual abatement of internal turmoil as Egyptian civilization emerged from its embryonic form.

The impression of chaos one receives from the records of Egypt's historic beginnings is in marked contrast to the steadfast, unchanging, and generally harmonious Egypt one is familiar with in history. Not only in political matters but in the whole range of early Egyptian culture there was an intense activity of experiment and change. The archaeologist working among the remains of the Archaic Period (Dynasties I-III) is struck by the vitality and ingenuity symbolized in a host of recovered objects. The carving of hard stone was so perfected that as one archaeologist remarks, the artist "played with the hard stone as though it were clay." [2] Ivory carving, fine woodwork, pottery, metallurgy, carpentry, even styles of dress exhibit variety and obvious enjoyment in creating new and better results. Mastery of tools and knowledge of materials produced an exquisite decorative art where naturalistic design was spread in loving detail over the surfaces of wood, stone, and metal. Architecture obviously evolves from apparently simple structures of wood, reeds, and mud to larger, more complex buildings of brick and later of stone. Here the traditions of wood structures have a strong influence on those of brick and stone. Mat and reed are imitated on many stone walls giving a distinctly Egyptian character to the architecture.

In the later stages of this age of exuberant inventiveness and increasing political control one feels a stability setting in. This is best symbolized by a building complex that many regard as the triumph of the Archaic Period. This is the wonderful step pyramid and surrounding structures built at Saqqara by the architect Imhotep as a funerary center for King Zoser of the Third Dynasty.

The central building is a pyramid built in six levels by superimposing six square mastaba tomb-like structures up to a height of two hundred feet. The pyramid is set in the midst of an enormous walled compound in which are located the ceremonial structures, storage areas, and subsidiary tombs, the whole resembling the original royal court. Façades made of blocks of white limestone, broken here and there by fluted pillars resembling bundles of papyrus stalks, capped with papyrus capitals, are overwhelming in their aesthetic impact. Delicately embossed hieroglyphs, panels of blue-green tile, and repeats of rows of niches create eye-moving vistas that fully confirm Imhotep as the first great architect of the world's history.

But as Saqqara is the triumph of the Archaic Period it is also symptomatic of a new Egypt. The rulers of the period, in the early phases at least, are depicted as supermen, even demigods, but most probably they were more realistically regarded by many of their subjects as warrior-chiefs who possessed the favor of their patron deities. The Zoser monument is in its way the climax of a trend toward deifying the monarch. Pharaoh was no longer a human being favored by fortune but was himself fortune—a god on earth to be worshiped in the flesh as a bringer of prosperity and stability to the Two Lands.

To understand what this means one has to see the perspective of civilization in the setting Egypt furnished. Civilization as mentioned above is by its very character out of balance with its immediate environment. Human cultures tend to establish a working equilibrium where social form, moral value, economic opportunity, and the like operate effectively for the whole of society. Cultures become suited to their environment and up to the limits of their individual technologies derive the maximum economic benefit from their local resources. The cultural forms used to derive this benefit may vary from one culture to the next but generally they operate efficiently for each, otherwise they would be changed. It is an anthropological axiom that no culture or cultural form can endure for long which is at variance with its environment or with adjacent cultures. Thus settling into a balance with the world about is a characteristic tendency of all cultures, even the most complex. A phenomenon of cultures seeking this balance is the continuity of experiment and change which marks the effort to adjust. A conservative in such a cultural phase finds himself hard put to maintain the older order of things. Cato, the paragon of republican Rome, did not protest against political change alone, his insistence was against the whole tendency to move from an ideal which had for centuries served Rome by its *gravitas*, welding a true nation out of the Latin tribes, to a Hellenistic materialism where men thought of personal wealth more than personal character. This tendency was expressed in a host of things ranging from style of dress to systems of teaching. What Cato was witnessing was the adjustment of Roman culture to a new environment, both cultural and geographical. Such an adjustment had to come about, for the stern ideals of republican Rome were completely out of balance with the large world Rome had created. Cato's demand for adherence to an older, unchanging order was impossible of fulfillment even should the desire be there. The cultural unbalance was a far stronger voice than even the patriotic virtues recalled by stern Cato. The tragedy is that the worldly Roman civilization that evolved in spite of noble effort was never quite able to bring about a lasting equilibrium and in a few centuries collapsed to revive only in other forms.

Anyone looking objectively at cultures in unbalance finds that its people make a fetish out of change. As long as there is change things are good. Tradition, conservatism, even ceremony, have little real voice in this context. Arts and crafts reveal a love of experimentation and exhibit endless variety in tastes. Such cultures tend to be aggressive and more often than not try to superimpose their way of life on others. The economic need for raw materials to give firmer foundation to the cultural structure is one cause of this aggressiveness. As indicated before, civilizations always seem to be short of what they need. Their very complexity ensures that there will always be needs exceeding the local supplies.

The remarkable achievement of Egyptian civilization is that once formulated, it lasted almost three thousand years, seemingly almost as impervious to foreign political controls as it was to cultural. Between the Egypt of the Pyramid Age and that of Cleopatra were many differences, but many of these seem superficial, for much of the hard core of Egyptian thought and institution was comparatively unchanged after some twenty-five centuries.*

Zoser's pyramid is an expression of the ascent of Egyptian civilization from a dynamic chaotic beginning to an active but harmonious adulthood. It would appear that the Egyptians had tamed their early civilization and brought it into balance with the world. This accomplishment was to need continual adjustment to keep it intact. That this was done is one of the real contributions of the ancient Egyptians to the textbook of experience which ought to enrich the modern world.

The Old Kingdom—Classical Egypt (2680–2258 B.C.)

The final conquest of the delta and the whole Nile Valley up to about the First Cataract at the gate of Nubia appears to have removed the need for further war. Nature had set bounds to Egypt. On the north the waters of the Mediterranean were probably too hazardous for more than an occasional venture by early boatmen; the Sinai desert in the same way allowed only a trickle of foreign contact to reach the delta across its arid wastes.† To the east the Red Sea and the barren hills made impossible any frequent intercourse with Arabia, which itself was largely a wasteland. To the west the Great Sand Sea spread its impassable miles between the Nile Valley and the next truly occupable region. The south, as we have

---

* John Wilson, a leading Egyptologist, qualifies this Egyptian seeming changelessness: ". . . the ancient Egyptian clung successfully to the main outlines of his cultural system by making constant adjustments within the system in order to resist the attacks of historical movement. It is a question, of course, how long one can continue to make changes in degree without effecting a change in kind, how long one can adjust and patch up the whole without having a system which is different in essence. The extraordinary phenomenon of ancient Egypt is her success in denying change by tacitly accepting change—in much the same way as she denied the flat fact of death by accepting death as renewed life." John A. Wilson. *The Culture of Ancient Egypt* (Chicago: University of Chicago Press, 1956), p. 91.

† Sinai, however, was early a good source of copper and turquoise, and was often visited by Egyptian expeditions sent to mine these materials.

seen, was also largely a desolate land with cataracts inter-
rupting the course of the river. The early warrior-chiefs
had created a kingdom up to the natural habitable limits of
the land. Beyond these limits were unknowns, hazards, and
inhospitable regions of little initial lure to a kingdom already
richly endowed.

Leading Egyptologists have noted the tendency toward
symmetry in ancient Egyptian culture, derived in part from
the natural duality caused by a river flowing between two desert banks. Only at the southern and northern ends of Egypt's
share of the Nile were foreign contacts usually made; between
were hundreds of miles of homogeneous country where
people lived in the same way and paid homage to the same
natural forces: the river, the sun, the moon, and the earth.
Annually the river rose and flooded the fields, annually it
subsided leaving the earth enriched with new soil. Two seasons, wet and dry, would be counted on forever and a day.
The sun rose and flooded the world with brilliant light; at
night the stars shone forth in countless array. Nothing impeded the celestial spectacle, no clouds veiled the skies of
what is in reality a desert land. No muttering monsoon, burst-
ing volcano, jangling earthquake, or all-erasing tidal wave
changed the face of the natural world from a beneficent
smile to a demon-creating frown. Not that hazards were
lacking. The demons that appear in the later Egyptian books
describing the terrors of the underworld are crocodiles and
snakes, and the deceased all too frequently cry out, "I hunger,
I thirst." But such terrors were small in comparison with the
good qualities of the land.

In such an environment Nature had an opportunity to bring
men into close harmony with herself. It is almost as if the
calmness of the natural setting finally gained dominance over
the turbulence of men. In any case the gradual crystallization
of the concept of Pharaoh as a god and the development of ceremony for, with, and by this god, is emblematic
of the tendency to "settle in." The warlike prowess of an individual in conquering human enemies seems replaced by the
idea that the presence of Pharaoh was the reason for
the fertility of the land. Accordingly, Pharaoh was to be
worshiped as the "bringer of good." This good was not the
Western concept of "bringer of new things," but rather the
continuance of the old—like the annual flood, and the repeated appearance of a flourishing crop. One becomes aware
that the Egyptians hated change because it usually meant in-

terruption of what was good. Low flood could mean drought, locusts could devour the year's harvest. Such disasters came about because of change. Fulfillment of one's daily task became a point of moral import. One followed in one's father's footsteps performing his tasks in the same way he did.

Artists and craftsmen lost the motivation for creating new forms. An absorption in already established traditions caused them to develop these to the utmost. It may come as a surprise to modern revolters against tradition to find mighty aesthetic power created within the bounds Egyptian culture was setting for its artists. The art of the Old Kingdom, that period which inherited the traditions of the Archaic Age, became a kind of classic standard awesome in its measure.

This was a time when Egypt was in full possession of its resources and just beginning to seek beyond its boundaries. The machinery of government was under the complete control of the monarch who delegated his authority to his officials, each of whom held a dread responsibility in the name of the king. The nobility was a landed one, but the local administration was, within the limits of human foibles, a moral one. The lord of the manor was the father of his serfs, servants, and family. A moral intent pervades the surviving literature of the time.

"If you are a leader, ruling a multitude of people, struggle to be worthwhile so that you may always act in the best way you can. Righteousness is of great value and infinitely worthy of preservation," was an oft-repeated precept accredited to the Vizier Ptahhotep.

Ptahhotep

The vigor of the Old Kingdom was due to the same reasons that created other great ages in human history. The stability of political and economic life led to an active inspection of the world around. Egyptian artists, already deeply involved with traditions, had their horizons stretched to include the whole of Egypt. With great intensity they observed the life around them. The famous painting of the geese at Medum, the graceful embossed hieroglyphs of Hetephere's canopy, the marvelous tomb reliefs and paintings depicting daily life of the Old Kingdom, were some of the results of this richly detailed observation of a living world.

Most wonderful of all perhaps are the sculptures. Here in wood, plaster, and hard stone, are a whole range of portraits depicting in ideal terms the calm, dignified, and earthly princes and officials of the time. Most apt to remain in one's memory are the royal statues. Here, in the best examples, the artists have created wondrous portraits. In particular a larger-than-life-size seated statue of King Chephren (Khafra), builder of the Second Pyramid at Giza, is one of the great treasures of the world. Carved in diorite, the massiveness of the stone block out of which the figure was created remains to impress one with an immutable power that does not belong to mortals. Nothing in the carving detracts from the life within the stone. The King and throne are one indivisible unit which welds the article to the monarch as if all things immobile and living were under the absolute sway of what the sculpture represents. There is a nonhuman geometry in the clean horizontal and vertical planes of the carving, the overwhelming frontality of the whole. The smooth, almost polished surface creates an impression of hardness that deepens the abyss between god and man. But the artist was a human and his subject in the form and in the midst of man. With chiseling that suggests rather than imitates, the swell of the chest, the form of limb, and the contours of face are revealed in specific units. They state totally, "This is a man." However, the humanness receives its final emphasis in the small hawk standing on the back of the throne whose stubby wings seek to enfold the head of the king as if to say, "This lord is mine." There is a tenderness in that single element of embrace which suddenly touches the whole with a pathos that imbues Chephren with a human heat that bridges the ages.

The deification of the monarch, the centralization of Egypt's political control at Memphis—strategically located at the apex of the delta fan, the increasingly elaborate mechanism of government and the waxing produce of the fields, together with a fully developed technology, gave opportunity for public works on a large scale. Certain it is that some of these works included irrigation-canal building as well as the construction of dams for water control. But most spectacular of all, it made possible the construction of the pyramid tombs of the pharaohs. Enough has been written of these to make the story familiar to all, yet one matter can still be disputed. In a world gone increasingly socialistic, the idea that the pyramids represent the tyrannical hold of the few over the many has popular support. Hollywood and the journalists, as well as the political philosophers and economic determinists of our time, represent these Old Kingdom monuments as the epitome of human futility—masses beaten to create a home for the corpse of a single man—slavery, vicious foremen, thousands toiling on ropes and levers, dying in agonies of thirst and exhaustion while Pharaoh smiled. The trouble is that while the pyramids undeniably took the muscle power of thousands, and that the great effort took the lives of many, I think it can be seriously doubted that villainous tyranny was involved. Every evidence we have points to the Old Kingdom as a going concern where prosperity was real and enjoyment of life consummate. We know that there were few slaves because foreign conquests were at a minimum. The labor for the pyramids came from the peasant farmers who, at times of high Nile, were comparatively idle and could be used for public projects. In such cases they were maintained at government expense, which in view of the job to be done could not have been meager. The number of pyramids, and the years it took to build each of them, indicates that a stable arrangement between government responsibility and peasant labor had been established. Abuses, no doubt, existed and the scope of the projects could not have made the job easy, but it is at variance with the facts to postulate mercilessness on the government's part and revolt in the mind of the people. Indeed one has only to recall the motivations behind the creation of the magnificent cathedrals of the medieval period to find the driving force that insured the construction of the pyramids. To the all-skeptical modern, the idea that a religious feeling would motivate such labor is incomprehensible. Yet it is to be doubted that the pharaohs could have stopped the construction of the tombs even if they had wished to. The idea of participation in an act of creating a tomb, a place of ascent for the god who brings good to all, must have motivated the humble people to acts beyond our conception.

The Old Kingdom brought about the first full appearance of Egyptian civilization on the world stage. We see it as a stable entity insured of longevity by its well-rooted traditions and well-balanced economy. The brilliance of its achievements in engineering, in the creation of a businesslike writing as an adjunct to hieroglyphic, the firm religious philosophy, the moral code, the technology which made efficient the use of raw materials, and above all the enormous agricultural productivity—made Egyptian culture increasingly dominant over all others in the vicinity and for a considerable distance beyond. Egyptian culture colors the form of Palestinian and Syrian cultures. Parts of Africa still reflect the ancient influences that drifted south from the northeast corner of the continent. It was not perhaps until the Arabs brought Islam beyond the Nile Valley that a cultural force of comparable impact to Africa was created.

The Old Kingdom and Africa

Nubia, for the next several millennia, is more often than not a reflection of Egypt, and this gives real reason for the emphasis of this and other chapters. For as Egypt went so did Nubia for many centuries, until a turnabout did occur in an unforeseen way. Later it was Nubia that maintained some of the more classic traits of Egyptian culture and was to help revive them in the land of their birth.

Nubia was frequently raided during the early days of the Old Kingdom—the raids carried out by Snefru being the most extensive. Ivory, ebony, cattle, and gold were the principal booty. By the Sixth Dynasty, toward the close of the Old Kingdom, Nubia had become the most important foreign field to command Egyptian attention. Mernera (ca. 2300 B.C.) had a channel made through the rocks of the First Cataract which opened up a considerable portion of Lower Nubia to Egyptian vessels. The ostensible purpose for making this passage was to create an easy waterway for carrying large granite blocks from the Aswan quarries to Egypt. This stone was admirably suited for the manufacture of various funerary monuments.

However, the caravan trade of the Sudan had a definite role in stimulating Egyptian interest in Nubia. Egyptian objects of this period have been found as far south as Kerma beyond the Third Cataract, and undeniably more will appear as investigations intensify. In return, the Egyptians acquired African exotica such as ostrich feathers, myrrh, leopard skins, and ebony. One noble boasted of acquiring a tusk ten feet long as a gift for Pepi II. There is a delightful account of the instructions sent by this pharaoh to Harkhuf of Elephantine who was bringing him a dancing dwarf out of the Sudan:

Royal seal, year 2, third month of the first season, day 15. Royal decree to the sole companion, the ritual priest and caravan conductor, Harkhuf.

I have noted the matter of this thy letter, which thou hast sent to the king, to the palace, in order that one might know that thou hast descended in safety from Yam with the army which was with thee. Thou hast said in this thy letter, that thou has brought all great and beautiful gifts, which Hathor, mistress of Imu, hath given to the ka of the king of Upper and Lower Egypt, Neferkere, who liveth for ever and ever. Thou hast said in this thy letter, that thou hast brought a dancing dwarf of the god from the land of spirits, like the dwarf which the treasurer of the god, Burded, brought from Punt in the time of Isesi. Thou hast said to my majesty: "Never before has one like him been brought by any other who has visited Yam."

Come northward to the court immediately; thou shalt bring this dwarf with thee, which thou bringest living, prosperous, and healthy from the land of spirits, for the dances of the god, to rejoice and gladden the heart of the king of Upper and Lower Egypt, Neferkere, who lives for ever. When he goes down with thee into the vessel, appoint excellent people, who shall be beside him on each side of the vessel; take care lest he fall into the water. When he sleeps at night appoint excellent people, who shall sleep beside him in his tent; inspect ten times a night. My majesty desires to see this dwarf more than the figs of Sinai and of Punt. If thou arrivest at court this dwarf being with thee alive, prosperous, and healthy, my majesty will do for thee a greater thing than that which was done for the treasurer of the god, Burded, in the time of Isesi, according to the heart's desire of my majesty to see this dwarf.

Commands have been sent to the chief of the New Towns, the companion, and superior prophet, to command that sustenance be taken from him in every store-city and in every temple, without stinting therein.[3]

Caravan routes in Nubia led to various areas of the Sudan. An ancient and much-traveled route led from Elephantine on the Nile, southwest via the oases of Selima and

Bir Natrum to El Fasher in Darfur. This point was a junction with routes leading westward to the Lake Chad area. Between the First and Second Cataracts there were several routes going south to Abu Hamed including the one from Korosko later described by Sir Samuel Baker. In addition, there were numerous roads going east into the Red Sea hills where gold could be mined. Obviously, control of the country from the First Cataract south gave the Egyptians marvelous mercantile opportunities.

This control was exercised in the name of the ruling pharaoh by a group of nobles whose native home was at Elephantine and whose tombs are a feature of the rock cliffs near there. These officials were probably all related, as they are all involved with the governorship or nomarchy of Elephantine. Elephantine was called the "Door of the South," and as the guardians of the marches the nobles of Elephantine were responsible for the protection of Egypt against raids from the south, and for the safety of caravans that moved far beyond the boundaries of Pharaoh's domains. To carry out these duties the Elephantine chiefs had soldiers at their disposal among whom were levies of Negro troops. These are said to have come largely from the Medjai who lived in the Second Cataract region. The Medjai appear to have been herders, some of whom may have carried on supplementary cultivation in the Nile flood plain. Perhaps they were cattle herders like the numerous warrior Bantu peoples of today. Perhaps the Medjai had a general contempt for cultivators, preferring to trade for agricultural produce rather than grow it. This would be in perfect keeping with an African habit encountered in modern East Africa—and the cause of considerable friction. We don't know, of course, but it is of no little significance that the Egyptians not only were able to use the Medjai as auxiliaries in their armies, but that the Medjai seemed perfectly willing to co-operate.

This use of Africans in the policing of Nubia gave the Egyptians considerable advantages. It provided them with a desert-wise, courageous people who made more impression on surrounding tribes by their presence perhaps than did the Egyptians themselves. In any case, we find these Elephantine nobles leading caravans far south—as far at least as the Fourth Cataract and maybe even to the Khartoum area, and beyond. Ivory, dwarfs (pygmies?), and ebony indicate more tropical settings and it may well be that some of these earliest of explorations penetrated to the Nuba hill country or to the flanks of the Ethiopian Highlands, though it is equally likely that the Africans themselves brought these things to the northern trade stations.

The caravans seem to have been made up of donkeys for carrying the loads and soldiers for guarding them. It is apparent that considerable negotiation with local Sudanese chiefs was carried on. As Egypt's power grew some of these negotiations were one-sided, however, for it is clear that the Lords of Elephantine were as capable of bringing a punitive force as they were of bringing peaceful trade. At the First Cataract a relief can still be seen showing Pharaoh Mernera receiving the homage of a group of Nubian chiefs whose combined realms extended as far south as Abu Hamed in the midst of the Land of Kush. This homage was not given as a mark of conquest, but rather as a token of Egypt's control of the Nubian, and in effect, the Sudanese trade. This control the Nubians had to support whether they liked to or not. Mernera's son Pepi II nevertheless had to send an army there under one of the "Keepers of the South" on several occasions. The Egyptian attacks broke the back of resistance by decimating the populace, seizing the leaders, taking hostages and immense booty. Revolts were frequent, and while boats enabled the Egyptians to control the Nile Valley, the caravan trade often must have suffered as warlike nomads could hit and run before they could be intercepted. However, in those days before the horse and the camel, the mobility of the nomad was restricted, and as long as the Egyptians could cow the reigning chiefs—just so long could the African trade be maintained.

In this crucible of war and under the stress of far-flung expeditions into the Sudan, the Elephantine nobles were shaped into powerful lords subject only to Pharaoh. They were probably the most influential among many important officials of the court at Memphis. They even directed the important Red Sea trade to Somaliland (Punt), and were often called upon to lead military forces in the service of the king. These nobles represent the rise to power of a powerful aristocracy that was to change the nation.

The Egypt of the last phase of the Old Kingdom was having difficulties handling civilization. The acceleration of contacts between north and south in Egypt, primarily because of the ease of travel on the Nile, bound the country into a whole. The court at Memphis became less and less a center where a god-king lived, to be worshiped and obeyed, and more and more a capital where a king supervised a large administrative body of officials. These officials were constantly growing more numerous with the increasing complexity of administration. Many of them were members of the old, landed aristocracy whose families ruled the various districts of the kingdom. The wealth of the land, while ostensibly the property of Pharaoh, was actually funneled into the hands of the nobles in return for services rendered. Titles acquired meant property acquired, much of which was tax free, as a gift of Pharaoh. Much wealth was frozen into the upkeep of the vast city of pyramids and temples which had arisen along the edge of the western desert. More and more of the tombs were for nobles who had no blood connection to Pharaoh but whose stake in an afterlife was assured by having burial in the holy burial grounds of the kings—a symptom of a kind of democratization of religious ideas by which more common folk were allowed entrance to Elysium.

It is obvious that the increased power of the nobles caused the weakening of the central authority. Pepi II, last king of the Sixth Dynasty, reigned for over ninety years, the longest reign in history. When he was placed on the throne he was but six years of age. As the son of the powerful Mernera, he inherited a well-knit administration and a rich kingdom. But it would appear that the whole organization depended upon the loyalty of the nobles, which could be kept only by the presence of a powerful monarch in their midst. What a familiar story this is in the history of man—whether speaking of courts or political parties! Pepi II appears to have been a vigorous administrator who kept things well in hand. But perhaps, like Emperor Franz Joseph, as his reign wore on and on, and those loyal to him from youth died off, his control weakened. The pharaonic house certainly did not possess the wealth of a Snefru in those last days. Much of it was held by the nobles or tied up in tombs and temples. Perhaps only the mystique of the old pharaoh prevented the final collapse. But at his death (2261 B.C.) the Old Kingdom ended. Weak monarchs in Memphis were unable to unite the quarreling provincial nobles and a period of chaos ensued. Nubia was lost and was itself subject to the influx of a new people, the so-called "C" group. For Egypt, civilization had brought harmony. Now the harmony was broken and the juggler disgraced—for a time.

Principal Kings of Egypt Before the Middle Kingdom

ARCHAIC PERIOD, Dynasties I-III (3200–2680 B.C.)
        Dynasty I (3200–2980 B.C.)
           Narmer (Menes)
        Dynasty II (2980–2780 B.C.)
           Khasekhemuwy
        Dynasty III (2780–2680 B.C.)
           Zoser

OLD KINGDOM, Dynasties IV-VI (2680–2258 B.C.)
        Dynasty IV (2680–2565 B.C.)
          Snefru
          Cheops
          Chephren
          Mycerinus
        Dynasty V (2565–2420 B.C.)
          Unas
        Dynasty VI (2420–2258 B.C.)
          Pepi I
          Mernera
          Pepi II

FIRST INTERMEDIATE PERIOD, Dynasties VII-X (2258–2052 B.C.)

4

Forts Along
the Belly of Stones

*Can we allow all these sites to be destroyed without their
having been at least partly explored, excavated and recorded?*—
J. VERCOUTTER, Director of the Antiquities Service, Republic of
the Sudan (*The UNESCO Courier*, February, 1960)

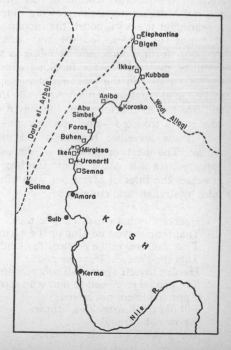

Among the more provocative accomplishments of the science of Egyptology is demonstrating to the modern world not only the material achievements of a people living some two thousand years before Christ but the emotional currents that swayed them as well. These wonderful reconstructions of the Egyptian past do not derive alone from the reading of texts. The art historian viewing the sticklike figures of the tomb paintings of the Middle Kingdom or the creased alert faces of the royal sculpture of that period is very much aware of distinct changes from the days of the Old Kingdom. He senses a shift-over from a prime acceptance of life as it is to an awareness that things are not as they might be. The student of religion finds that there is an increase in ritual paraphernalia. What was often accepted in the past on pure faith now requires the apparatus of magic to make one feel secure. The roots of the *Book of the Dead*, the famous compilation of rituals and charms needed by the deceased in the underworld, are found in the "Coffin texts" which cover great areas of the funerary coffins of the Middle Kingdom. The political historian notes the growing number of functionaries appearing at the royal court, the increase and the elaboration of tombs for nobles, and the war atmosphere revealed by weapons, fortifications, and standing armies. The economist examines the evidence for far-flung expeditions in search of raw materials and the great emphasis upon public works to make good land available. Add all these things together and one has to conclude that the Egypt of the Middle Kingdom was a troubled—albeit prosperous—world.

It is the literature that adds the ultimate piece to the mosaic. The detached pharaoh of the Old Kingdom has disappeared, in his place rules another pharaoh, one who possesses the titles of a god but who bitterly and realistically rules by strength and cunning.

> Hearken to that which I say to thee,
> That thou mayest be king of the earth,
> That thou mayest be ruler of the lands,
> That thou mayest increase good.
> Harden thyself against all subordinates.
> The people give heed to him who terrorizes them;
> Approach them not alone.
> Fill not thy heart with a brother,
> Know not a friend,
> Nor make for thyself intimates,

Wherein there is no end.
When thou sleepest, guard for thyself thine own heart;
For a man has no people,
In the day of evil.
I gave to the beggar,
I nourished the orphan;
I admitted the insignificant,
As well as him who was of great account.
But he who ate my food made insurrection;
He to whom I gave my hand, aroused fear therein.

Thus Amenemhet I warns his son, the Crown Prince Senwosret (Sesostris I). Some Egyptologists call these kings of the
Middle Kingdom the "Good Shepherds." Constant vigilance
and the ability to act effectively when necessary were prerequisites for the well-being of the kingdom. It is no wonder
that the royal portraits often have a frowning weary look.
The burden of monarchy was a heavy one.

Middle Kingdom Egypt rose out of the chaos of the so-
called First Intermediate Period (2258–2052 B.C.). That that
period was a chaotic time is underlined by the cryptic statement found in the writings of a contemporary, the sage Iper-
wer.

Great and humble say: "I wish I might die."
Little children cry out: "I never should have been born." [1]

Civil war between the rulers of the various most powerful
districts disrupted the harmony of the land. The rulers of
Memphis lost control completely. Various petty nobles quar-
reled much as later did the barons of the medieval world.
Certainly these conflicts must have upset the efficiency
with which the Egyptians controlled their agricultural activities, and as certainly prosperity with its motivation for
crafts and other industries became a thing of the past.
Foreign trade languished—in fact Asian peoples invaded the
delta area and effectively took that rich region out of civil
contention—at least for a time. Nubia on the south had a
respite from Egyptian raids but there is evidence that a new
pastoral nomadic people, the so-called "C" group, were oc-
cupying that region. These people are best distinguished
archaeologically by their pottery, a fine black incised ware.

The Mysterious "C" People

Initially the "C" group people buried their dead in shallow graves surrounded by stone rings, but later the graves were more elaborate stone-lined chambers in the midst of a round stone structure complete with chapel: the latter feature possibly due to Egyptian influence.*

They were extensive users of cattle which they milked. This milk was used for butter as well as for itself. The importance of milking is that it is evidence for an eastern origin of these people, according to Murdock.[2] The peoples of the Western Sudan are not milk users. Arkell believes, however, that the "C" people came more likely from the West because their pottery suggests Libya and points west.[3]

The "C" group people may be the Caucasoid ancestors to the modern Beja, who are still one of the dominant groups found in the Eastern Sudan. The modern Beja are pastoral nomads but their ancestors who settled in Nubia were also agriculturists and very likely were responsible for the reestablishment of a sedentary population decimated during the Old Kingdom. There was time for settlement in Nubia because the lords of Elephantine were probably too busy maintaining their home grounds for any expeditions into the south. Besides the motivation was lacking without the demand for dwarfs and ivory from a materially thankful pharaoh. Settlement was heaviest near the mouths of wadies. In this regard the Egyptologist, the late George A. Reisner's comments are worth noting:

> The Archaeological Survey of Lower Nubia found south of the First Cataract a series of centers of population each situated at the mouth of a wady, or ravine, in which the river had deposited a larger or smaller area of alluvial land. The material basis of life in these communities was obviously to a great extent agriculture, probably enriched by fishing, hunting, and trans-

* A. J. Arkell cites evidence to prove that the "C" people entered Nubia before the Middle Kingdom and were probably the ones with whom the Eleventh and Seventeenth Dynasty Egyptians had to deal when they invaded the area south of Kubanieh. Thus the Middle Kingdom forts were partly built to keep the "C" people subject. (*A History of the Sudan*, London, 1955, pp. 53-54.)

port service. Each community appeared to be continuous in time, as far as the continuity of its cultivable
land permitted. In some cases, new terraces were formed
by the river, or old ones left dry; but in most cases
the cemeteries of each community, in spite of plunder-
ing and denudation, ranged in time from the Predynastic Period to the present day. The size and the prosperity of the communities, however, varied greatly from
period to period. In some instances these variations
could be directly attributed to changes in the Nile level;
in other cases they depended on administrative and
commercial conditions.[4]

The dominant power in Egypt for a time was the nome
district of Herakleopolis located near the mouth of the Fayum. The rulers of this district extended their power north
into the delta; on the south the border was apparently near
Abydos, famous as the burial place of Osiris, Lord of the
Dead. South of this boundary was the nome whose activities
were increasingly centered about the minor town of Thebes.
Under a group of rulers known as the Inyotefs, Thebes
grew in power until it was the chief opponent of Herakleopolis
and its allies. Among the latter was the Assiut nome of Middle
Egypt—one of the richest in the land. To defeat such a
coalition Thebes must have been able to unite the southern
nomes whose proximity to Nubia made them well prepared
for conflict. These nomes were in a frontier area: their
survival doubtless depended on their increasing ability to
defend their lands against the raids of the Beja and other
nomadic peoples of the desert country. We can be sure that
long marches under the stress of heat, sandstorm, and
scanty food and water ending with savage hand-to-hand
fighting were customary. This hard soldiering must have
made a formidable fighting force out of the southerners.
Never great in number, they more than made up for this
lack by a military sagacity molded out of bitter experience.
Thus Nubia had a role in the creation of a new Egypt. It is
of interest that among the wives of the Theban king
Mentuhotep II there were several with Negro blood and some
with body tattooing, indicative of the closeness of Africa to
the southern nomes.[5] This king boasts also of his triumphs
in Nubia in his inscriptions, though it is hardly likely he
could have penetrated very far into that land.

Mentuhotep II eventually succeeded in crushing the

Herakleopolitan army and after a siege took their capital (*ca.* 2052 B.C.) and became indeed "Ruler of the Two Lands."

In the Shatt-er-Rigal, a small valley running west from the Nile Valley a few miles north of Gebel Silsileh, a narrow canyonlike stretch in the Nile Valley where there are dangerous rapids, the late Herbert Winlock of the Metropolitan Museum of Art was able to trace a number of graffiti made by courtiers of Mentuhotep II. It would appear from these that it was frequently necessary to go overland into Nubia leaving one's vessel below the rapids. Apparently the rulers of the Eleventh Dynasty were able to send expeditions into Nubia from the Shatt-er-Rigal. These expeditions were like those of the Old Kingdom in which soldiers were a prerequisite for the success of the trip. The fact that it was not Elephantine that was the jumping-off point for these expeditions and that their return was of such moment as to bring Pharaoh and court to this rather remote post is surely indicative of the uneasy status of Egyptian strength in Nubia. This was to change with the powerful kings of the Twelfth Dynasty.

The throne was a troubled place for these Theban kings of the Eleventh Dynasty, and their tombs and those of their courtiers, when anything is found in them, have quantities of bows and arrows, axes and spears lying about—a reflection of the time. As so often happens in history during wartime the commander of the armies possesses a power useful to himself if he so wishes. One of these commanders, Amenemhet, apparently took over the throne and ended the Eleventh Dynasty, opening at the same time the prosperous days of the Twelfth, a dynasty that had a profound effect on Nubia and eventually on much of Africa.

Early Imperial Egypt (2000–1785 B.C.)

Traditionally and strategically, Memphis was the real capital of Egypt, and in the Twelfth Dynasty the founding monarch, Amenemhet I, moved his capital from Thebes to Lisht just south of the old city and close to the Fayum. Here was the nerve center of the kingdom. It was like a watchtower supervising a vast flat land. In fact, as Breasted has pointed out, "The name given to the residence city was significant of its purpose; Amenemhet named it Ithtowe, which means 'Captor of the Two Lands.' In hieroglyphic the name is always written enclosed within a square fortress with battlemented walls. . . ." [6]

The vigilant Middle Kingdom monarchs brought recalcitrant nobles to heel even though it is obvious from such speeches as that of Amenemhet to his son quoted at the beginning of this chapter that there were conspiracies, revolts, and the like at every hand. However, these rulers were men of great natural gifts and were able to gather loyal followers and thus bring peace to the land. Part of their control came about because of a small standing army, a bodyguard, which was at the heart of larger forces commandeered from all Egypt in time of need. A military establishment was from now on a regular part of the Egyptian court. In fact, military art took a giant step forward and it was Nubia again that furnished the impetus.

With strong central government re-established, prosperity rapidly returned to Egypt. Egyptian civilization was bound to a monarch who, though still regarded as a god-king, ruled less through his godliness and more through his personal talent than did most of the pharaohs of the Old Kingdom.

The leading god was Amun—a rather amorphous divinity among whose abilities was that of holding the ultimate power which lay behind all the gods. Amun was now the patron god of Thebes, and while Pharaoh was the son of Amun and capable of calling upon him for whatever purpose, he was not technically Amun himself, a distinction which Pharaoh acknowledged by ritual. The more worldly monarchs of the Middle Kingdom were thus more accessible to their followers and in this sense at least more vulnerable to human foibles than hitherto. The critical point is that far more individuals were sharing in the advantages given by improved technology, balanced administration, and benefits brought by public works because of this descent of Pharaoh to more earthly levels. Accordingly civilization intensified its demands, that is, more of everything. In the Old Kingdom a few dozen ivory tusks were sufficient for royalty; now they were required by the hundred. Fine stone for sarcophagi, always in demand for Egypt, was now required in extraordinary amount as the nobles down to the very least built tombs to preserve themselves for immortality. Gold, ebony, ostrich feathers, slaves, sweet-smelling wood, et al., were demanded in quantity. For an Egypt at peace the status quo, no matter how harmonious, was simply not possible. Raw materials were sought far beyond the borders. Trading expeditions to Lebanon and Palestine moved successfully overland and along the coasts. The mines in Sinai were reopened, and the old Red Sea trade to Punt via the Wadi Hammamat was revived. These were generally peaceful mercantile journeys giving the impression that Egypt was loath to give trouble in Asia. It was very probable that Asians in turn were impressed with Egyptian wares and welcomed the trade.

The Middle Kingdom and Africa

Nubia, however, was another matter. Egyptians regarded Nubia and the lands beyond as their own. The ascendancy of Theban power was probably a factor in this. For Egyptians living near the "Door of the South," Africa was the land of promise, and it was only natural that their interests lay in controlling the Nile Valley as far south as they possibly could. In short order Nubia became an integral part of Egypt. The frontier was no longer at Elephantine but at the Second Cataract above modern Wadi Halfa. Beyond that point there were garrisoned trading posts of which the most famous was Kerma, called then "The Walls of Amenemhet, the Justified." Technically, Kerma, situated as it was beyond the Third Cataract, was in Kush, the vast land inhabited by Negro peoples above Nubia.

Control of Nubia was sustained by a line of fortresses placed at strategic points along the Nile Valley. Each of these fortresses contained a garrison of Egyptians and probably a few mercenary African troops, among these being the Medjai, the celebrated desert warriors used in the Old Kingdom. Now Egyptian conquest was a reality and there was an imperial side to civilization.

Actually the Second Cataract extends over one hundred miles along the Nubian Nile. One stretch is so studded with rock outcrops and islands that it is known locally as the Belly of Stones (Batn-el-Hagar). This region is excellent for those who wish to supervise the Nile traffic as did the Egyptians of the New and Middle Kingdoms. During the latter period there were several forts built between Elephantine and the Second Cataract, but the greater emphasis was placed on the "Belly of Stones." Somers Clarke, who early made a study of these forts, records nine located there, at least five of which were built originally during the Middle Kingdom (Buhen, Mirgissa, Semna East, Semna West, Uronarti). [7] Alan H. Gardiner, on the basis of a find of papyrus at Thebes which recorded the names of fortresses, believes that there were at least eight along the Second Cataract.[8]

But a papyrus found by Flinders Petrie mentions fourteen Middle Kingdom forts: eight in the stretch between Elephantine and the Second Cataract and six in the "Belly of Stones" stretch.[9]

Egyptian Reference

BELOW SECOND CATARACT	Modern Location
Senmet	Bigeh
Yebu	Elephantine
Baki	Kubban
	Ikkur
Ma'am	Aniba
Hesef-Medju	Serra East?
Ink-tawi	Faras?
Buhen	Wadi Halfa
Iken	Kor

SECOND CATARACT REGION	
	Mirgissa
	Shelfak
	Uronarti
	Semna (3 forts)

The fortresses of the Middle Kingdom were largely traced by the archaeologists of the Archaeological Survey of Nubia in the days when the Aswan Dam was being built and there was some threat to their situation. Now the fortresses will be inundated completely. Their structure is of brick and inundation will destroy them. However, some are being studied with considerable intensity at the moment.

To understand the character of these ancient military posts one has to recall that not only the river routes were involved but the overland roads as well. It is as much a matter for observation as for defense that these fortresses were usually erected on natural elevations. At the head of the long stretch of the Second Cataract above Wadi Halfa at Semna the river is forced into a narrow channel. A rock barrier crosses the Nile at this point. This is overflooded at high Nile but divides into three distinct channels when the flow is more moderate. At low Nile, however, only one channel some hundred feet wide carries the water. There are rocky heights on the banks on either side of the river barrier, and these were the sites of two fortresses located only some fifteen hundred feet apart. Obviously the command of the river passage depended on who held these fortresses. Some three miles to the north another fortification (Uronarti) was situated on the ridge of a rock-bound island in the midst of the stream. This fortress is within easy signaling distance of the two fortresses at Semna (Semna East and Semna West). The three thus form a strategic complex of enormous military strength.

There were two roads running north and south along either river bank which were bound to converge on the Semna-Uronarti fortifications. The most used road, that of the west, led right through the Semna West fortress. Gateways on the north and south of this fortification provided a "thruway," but it is certain that inspection of baggage and possibly the payment of a tariff were required before the second gate

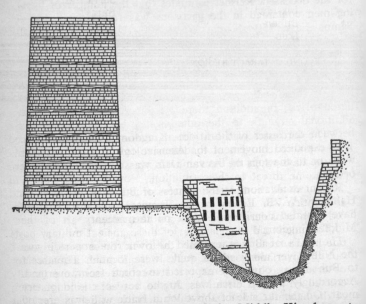

SECTIONS OF FORTIFICATION of the Middle Kingdom at Buhen (*after Emery*).

was passed. The large number of seals and sealings both official and private indicate that a considerable commerce was carried on and undeniably a quantity of red tape had to be cut even in those remote days of about 2000 B.C.

Access to the river was obtained at Semna West by a covered stairway which ensured the water supply in time of siege. The great rock barrier across the river caused the formation of pools above and below the cataract channel. Here ships could await their turn to be hauled against the current or guided downstream. This forced delay gave further advantage to the location of the fortifications which commanded the pools as well as the channels. Needless to say, small craft were available to the Egyptian soldiery for the inspection of cargoes moving in either direction.

The interior of these forts was geometrically divided up by a main street from which cross streets radiated, the whole forming blocks where the administrative and garrison offices and habitations were located. Outside the walls there were quarters for non-Egyptian habitation and cemeteries for the deceased. Reisner estimates that the number of fighting men contained in the garrisons was rather small (50—Semna East; 150—Semna West; 100—Uronarti),[10] but if one adds the families of the soldiery to the population there were a sizable number of people resident.

The forts were constructed of mud brick. The outer walls were thick (16–20 feet) and rested on a rock-and-rubble base. In these walls were stout beams as reinforcement to the tiered brick. In addition there were buttresses which gave additional strength to the outer walls. Inside, a road ran between the outer wall and the habitations of the garrison. This expedited movement to defensive towers built into the walls or to the tops of the ramparts via stairways or ladders or both.

Recent excavations at the fortress of Buhen opposite Wadi Halfa by W. B. Emery of the Egypt Exploration Society have revealed considerable data on the military art of the Middle Kingdom.[11]

The walls of Buhen enclosed a town: on one side was the Nile River along which quays were located. The threat to Buhen was obviously expected to come from overland. Accordingly a deep ditch was dug to act as a kind of dry moat. On the far side of this ditch a brick wall was erected on which a covered way provided protection for a first group of defenders.

On the town side of the defensive ditch was a brick rampart broken at intervals by circular towers. These towers and the rampart walls that connected them commanded the ditch below, loopholes being arranged so that arrows could be fired at anything appearing in the ditch. Beyond this bastion tower wall was a narrow way at the foot of

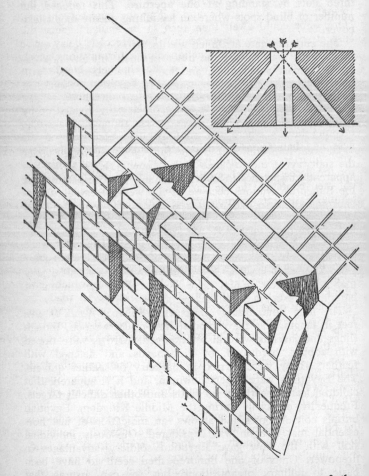

CONSTRUCTIONAL DETAILS of the loophole system of the Buhen Middle Kingdom fort *(after Emery).*

massive main walls which were a full five meters thick and rose some thirty feet in the air. An assault on these overlapping defenses, if they were resolutely held, would have been highly impractical, if not impossible.

The loopholes in the bastion rampart were ingeniously arranged so that a single archer or slinger had a choice of three slots by standing at one aperture. This reduced the number of blind spots where an assaulting enemy might take cover.

The entrance gate at Buhen was located between two enormous walls that crossed the outer parapet, "moat," first defense rampart, inner alley, and joined the mighty city wall at right angles. The narrow way between was distinguished by a wooden drawbridge over the dry ditch which moved on rollers. The gateway was closed by double doors. The main wall was broken by square bastions and there were high towers at the corners.[12]

Of great future interest are the torn-up papyri found under the stairway of the so-called Commander's House which are apparently dispatches to Buhen from Egypt. The potential of the Buhen excavations because of the well-preserved ruins is enormous if these finds of papyri are in any way indicative of what is to come. One shudders to think what will be lost if these fortress towns are not thoroughly excavated before the final floods which extinguish them.

The weapons available to the Middle Kingdom soldier were somewhat limited. The desert conditions and the long marches required of him helped in dictating the amount of equipment he could carry.

The long bow, usually measuring between four or five feet in length, was the principal long-range weapon, though slings and javelins were also employed. Arrows were tipped with copper, hardwood, or flint heads and fletched with feathers. They were carried in basketry or leather quivers. The Egyptians were expert bowmen, and it is apparent that children learned early to hit birds and other difficult targets. Frequently, especially during the Middle Kingdom, Egyptian burials contain bows and arrows, an indication of just how essential that weapon was considered. Obviously individual skill with the bow gave Egyptian soldiery advantages in firepower. Units of one hundred men seem to have been basic to military organizations, but we can assume that smaller units were frequently employed. Several fine bowmen could punish raiding enemies at considerable range, and if one coupled these with Medjai scouts or Sudanese spearmen, an Egyptian patrol was something to command respect. We don't know how well Egyptian commanders knew their military arts, but the evidence available to us indicates that they were quite aware of the advantages gained by mass and perhaps unison fire. A hundred archers firing at an advancing enemy would have been no mean deterent to an attacker. There is a wooden model found at Assiut which depicts a body of soldiers marching in ranks in perfect order, and the placement of loopholes at Buhen, the apparent standardization of equipment illustrated by numerous finds, all bear witness to a military organization of considerable scope. This may have taken place because of the recognition of the effectiveness of archery when it can be regulated.

Shields were the only body defenses. These were made of cattle hide, sometimes backed with wood. They were either small like a buckler or full and capable of guarding most of the body. Soldiers had thrusting spears, daggers, clubs, and battle-axes for hand-to-hand combat. The business end of the spears, daggers, and axes was usually of copper, bronze being still a rare metal.

The soldiers were probably not too unlike the Roman soldiers of republican and early Empire days in their ability to perform a variety of tasks. Every peasant knew how to dig, cultivate, make bricks or adobe, build reed huts, perform repairs on equipment, and use the boomerangs and nets which caught birds and fish on the banks of the Nile. In the Nile and desert environments Egyptian soldiers were remarkably self-sufficient and, aside from certain homesickness, perfectly capable of holding these African outposts efficiently and well.

After battle the wounded, according to the formula for doctors set forth in the Edwin Smith surgical papyrus, were examined and the doctor decided one of three ways: (1) to proceed with treatment; (2) to observe and wait; (3) not to do anything. A number of Egyptologists have pointed out that much of this early Egyptian medicine was scientific and that the god and demon-ascribing cause of illness and injury which was prevalent in later times had little role. These early physicians looked to the wound for the cause of the ailment and insofar as they were able tried to effect a cure.[13] That there was a practical aspect to military medicine does not seem unlikely in view of the intense practicality of all the other aspects of the Egyptian control of the far frontiers. The setting of broken bones, the sewing up of wounds, and the alleviation of some fevers by means of herbs, some of which they obtained from local practitioners, were all within Egyptian capability, and their medical accomplishments were certainly far superior to the primitiveness with which they are often accused of acting.

Obviously the control of the Second Cataract region provided a secure limb upon which a large body of commercial enterprise might lean. Gold and fine stone might be obtained in the areas east and west of the fortifications, but it was the ivory, resins, fine wood, ostrich feathers—and by this time, the black slaves of the south—that were in increasing demand. This southern region was beyond Nubia and was given the general name Kush, with local areas designated within the main region. In order to tap the trade of Kush, which itself was only intermediate for the rich merchandise of inner Africa, trading colonies were established far up the Nile. The most important of these was located at Kerma, some six days' land journey south of the last fortresses of the Second Cataract at Semna. This was a town of considerable size with a citadel in its midst known as the "Walls of Amenemhet" (Inebuw-Amenemhet). Here an almost completely self-sufficient group of Egyptian officials, scribes, soldiers, etc., lived, peaceably it would appear, amid the local African populace. They were governed by a high official from Egypt, and their daily job was apparently to trade for and expedite the shipment of goods to Egypt. It is more than likely that the profits from this trade were reciprocal, since the Egyptians were certainly in a vulnerable position so far to the south. Much was gained by both parties in maintaining this post.

The remarkable excavations of the late G. A. Reisner of the Harvard-Boston Museum of Fine Arts Expedition which excavated at Kerma beginning in 1913 have given us a truly extraordinary insight into the life of an Egyptian colony so far from home. It must be remembered that like the Chinese the Egyptians were very much aware of being Egyptians. They regarded themselves as a superior people and, not unnaturally, their culture as the best. It is not so unusual then for the archaeologist to find many Egyptian articles when excavating the buildings and tombs at Kerma. One of the most poignant aspects of the finds at Kerma is the graves in which the bodies have been interred with face to the north toward the land of the deceased's birth, head placed on its pillow, sandals for the journey, and funerary furniture placed in position similar to the arrangement in the tombs in Egypt. Obviously a spiritual return was expected even if the body was interred far in the Sudan.

But if Egyptian culture was sustained so far south of its homeland the ways of Africa were still not to be ignored. Kerma was located above the Third Cataract at the head of what is now known as the Dongola Reach of the Nile. In more recent times Dongola, birthplace of the Mahdi, has been the Nile terminus for numerous caravan routes coming from the west. These routes intersect the Darb-el-Arbain, the main caravan road connecting Egypt (Elephantine, Abydos, Assiut) with the El Fasher area in Darfur via numerous oases of the Libyan Desert. Kerma is only a few miles north of Dongola and must certainly have played the same commercial role. The Nile stretch below Kerma as far as the Fourth Cataract is thoroughly navigable. Between Kerma and the Fourth Cataract are Old Dongola, Debba, Korti, and Kereima, from all of which points caravan routes go overland to the Khartoum area and beyond.

Kerma was wisely chosen as a base for Egyptian trade. One trouble is that we know so little of the people with whom they were trading. Ostensibly the Caucasoid Libyan pastoral nomads, as well as an older agricultural populace of the same general physical type, were indigenous to the immediate Kerma region. But it is not unlikely that these people gradually were replaced by Negro groups as one went farther south, whether in the more fertile stretches of the Nile Valley beyond the Dongola Reach or at the termini of the caravan routes previously described.

It was these Negro groups, whose origin was Central and West Africa, who carried the cultural patterns most apt to influence outsiders coming into their midst. Just what these Negro cultures were like awaits further work by the archaeologist and perhaps a bit more awareness of history by the ethnologist working with primitive African cultures south of Khartoum. Certainly agriculture and cattle domestication were given varying emphasis even in those times. It seems likely that among the cattle users at least, especially in the grassland areas of the sudd where cattle seem to have been more successful than crop growing, that there was a social hierarchy in which a chief governed both secular and sacred affairs. Belief in an afterlife where the sacred ruler required his wives, retainers, and domestic servants much as in the days of his living existence may have been derived

14. THE RUINS OF THE FORTRESSES at Semna as seen by the traveler G. A. Hoskins in 1833.
(The American Museum of Natural History)

15. LIMESTONE RELIEF FROM MASTABA TOMB from the North Pyramid, Lisht. Dynasty III-VI.
(Courtesy of The Metropolitan Museum of Art, Museum Excavations, 1920-1922; Rogers Fund, 1922)

16. BAS-RELIEF DATING FROM THE OLD KINGDOM. Dynasty V, re-used in Dynasty XII. From Lisht.
(Courtesy of The Metropolitan Museum of Art, Museum Excavations, 1913-1914; Rogers Fund, 1915)

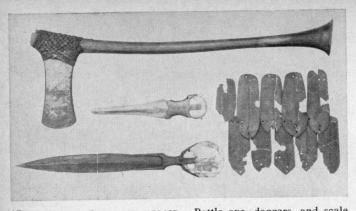

17. EGYPTIAN ARMS AND ARMOR. Battle axe, daggers, and scale armor.
(Courtesy of The Metropolitan Museum of Art, Museum Excavations and Rogers Fund)

18. WOODEN FUNERARY MODEL OF A GIRL BEARING offering of meats and a live duck from the tomb of Meketre, Thebes. Dynasty XI.
(Courtesy of The Metropolitan Museum of Art, Museum Excavations, 1919-1920)

19. PAINTED LIME-STONE FIGURE OF A BREWER straining the mash, a servant to accompany his dead master to the other world.
(Courtesy of The Metropolitan Museum of Art, Rogers Fund, 1920)

20. A MODERN EGYP-TIAN BOATMAN who, in the tradition of his ancestors, ferries people across the Nile at Thebes.
(W. Fairservis)

21. TEMPERA REPRODUCTION OF A WALL PAINTING of a Nile ship from tomb of Menana, Scribe of the fields of the Lord of Two Lands, Thebes. Dynasty XVIII, *ca.* 1415 B.C. *(Courtesy of The Metropolitan Museum of Art)*

22. THE KING AND QUEEN OF PUNT as represented by Egyptian artists on the walls of Queen Hatshepsut's Deir-el-Bahri temple at Thebes.
(The American Museum of Natural History)

23. FRAGMENT OF LIMESTONE BAS-RELIEF bearing the head of King Thutmose III. Dynasty XVIII.
(Courtesy of The Metropolitan Museum of Art, Carnarvon Collection, gift of Edward S. Harkness, 1926)

24. TEMPERA REPRODUCTION OF A WALL PAINTING of a man hunting in a chariot from the tomb of User-het, royal scribe, Thebes. Dynasty XVIII, *ca.* 1430 B.C.
(Courtesy of The Metropolitan Museum of Art)

25. ALABASTER SCULPTURE OF A DWARF. Dynasty XVIII.
(Courtesy of The Metropolitan Museum of Art, gift of J. Pierpont Morgan, 1917)

26. AVENUE OF SPHINXES AND THE NILE VALLEY from top of a
pylon, Karnak. One of the grand approaches built by Amenhotep
III. The stone platform is the ancient landing for Nile boats. Note
how far in the distance is the modern Nile.
(The American Museum of Natural History)

27. TEMPLE OF LUXOR across the Nile from west bank, Egypt. The Luxor temple was probably designed by the architect Amenhotep in the reign of Amenhotep III, father of Akhenaton. It is one of the finest building groups of the New Kingdom.

(The American Museum of Natural History)

28. G. A. HOSKINS' DRAWING of the ruins of the Amenhotep III temple of Soleb (Sulb) in 1833.
(The American Museum of Natural History)

29. RED QUARTZITE
SCULPTURE OF KING
AKHENATON. Dynas-
ty XVIII.
*(Courtesy of
The Metropolitan
Museum of Art,
Rogers Fund, 1911)*

30. NUBIAN TRIBUTE-BEARERS from
tomb of the Viceroy Huy.

31. TEMPERA REPRODUCTION OF A WALL PAINT-
ING of freight boats from the tomb of Huy,
Viceroy of Nubia, Thebes. Dynasty XVIII.
(Courtesy of The Metropolitan Museum of Art)

32. REPRODUCTIONS OF WALL PAINTINGS of the viceregal *Dahabiyeh*
sailing up the Nile in one picture and tied to the dock in the other.
From the tomb of Huy, Viceroy of Nubia, Thebes. Dynasty XVIII,
ca. 1355 B. C.
(Courtesy of The Metropolitan Museum of Art)

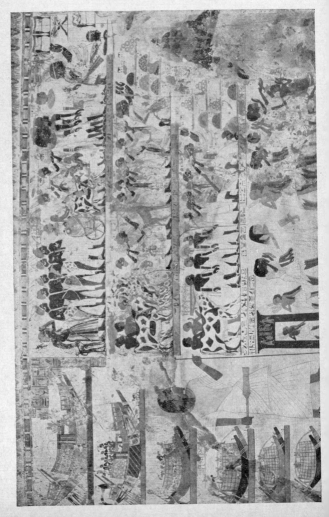

33. PRESENTATION OF NUBIAN TRIBUTE TO THE KING. Tempera reproduction of wall painting from the tomb of Huy, Thebes. Dynasty XVIII, *ca.* 1355 B.C.
(Courtesy of The Metropolitan Museum of Art)

from an ancient tradition widespread during late predynastic and Archaic Period times. But whereas the Egyptians rarely used human sacrifice as a means of providing these companions for the afterlife, the custom was far more common to the south of Nubia. In fact, until very recent times, the custom, like suttee in India, was a very real thing even in the Sudan. H. C. Jackson, formerly governor of Berber and Halfa, recorded an incident among the Azande of the Southern Sudan which happened during his travels there in 1926.

One day an Inspector of the Woods and Forests department (whose name, I think, began with R) was looking for rubber vines in the Tembura district when he heard shrieks coming from the jungle. He walked along a narrow track towards the sound of the shrieks until he suddenly came upon a clearing where scores of men and women were gathered beside a group of young girls. The men, some with their heads completely shaved, or with a parting carefully cut down the middle, others with plaits adorned with a feather, wore the usual skirt of bark; they were drunk with banana beer and mad with excitement. The women were naked except for a bunch of leaves in front and behind, suspended from a fibre string around their waists; they, like the men, were infected by some deep emotion. But it was fear and horror that were depicted upon their faces, not the ferocious blood-lust that transfigured the men into creatures frenzied and obscene. Alone, but for a few terrified carriers, the Inspector made straight for the middle of the throng, despite the angry protests of the crowd, and saw a large open pit some four feet across. At the bottom was the trussed body of the dead Sultan surrounded by calabashes of food and drink, and beside the pit R. saw some young girls whose screams had first attracted his notice. R. asked the Sultan's son—a brutal, truculent young man—what had caused these screams and shrieks. The youth explained that when a great chief died young girls had to accompany him into the world beyond the grave to minister to his wants. "This," said the Sultan's son, "is the custom of my people and I will carry it out whatever you or the government says or threatens; the legs of these girls will now be broken and the girls will be thrown into the grave and buried alive with my dead father." R., alone though he was, and faced with a mob half mad with fanatic exaltation, ordered the ceremony to stop. The Sultan's son raved and fumed; R. stood calm and resolute; and such was the respect in which the white man was held, and such the indomitable courage with which R. faced the frenzied crowd that, gradually, with many curses and threats of what they would do to him later, the cruel mob dispersed to their homesteads and the girls were spared.[14]

One of the most wonderful discoveries in modern archaeology was made by the Egyptian Expedition of the Metropolitan Museum of Art at Thebes, in 1920, of an intact cache in the looted tomb of an Eleventh Dynasty noble. In one of the corridors of this tomb a little secret chamber was revealed in which were stuffed a great many wooden models and small painted statues. In a striking and charming way the collection was succinct evidence for the manner of daily life during the Middle Kingdom. There were homes with gardens, a butcher shop, carpenter's shop, brewery, granary, weaving room, stable, a whole fleet of boats, and even a scene of the nobleman, one Meketre, reviewing his cattle holdings. Two exquisite statuettes of young girls carrying baskets of food on their heads rank among the great treasures of the past. These models serve to emphasize the Egyptian's desire to carry the good life of the present over into the next world. The spirit of the deceased was served in the afterlife by the spirits of his servants as they were represented at their tasks in the models. Sometimes magic formulas were appended to these statues which accompanied the dead as a means of ensuring their revival after death. But in any case their association with the tomb of itself had a magical quality. It was a prerequisite for proper burial in the Middle Kingdom then to have at least some modeled image of a servant, of food, etc., interred in the tomb.

At Kerma the Egyptian officials were buried under earthen tumuli surrounded by a brick wall. A number of the larger tumuli in the necropolis there represent the tombs of the governor or "Chief Headman of the South," who acted as Pharaoh's agent.* Reisner's excavations in these tumuli re-

* Arkell, Junker, and Steindorff and Seele have considered Kerma as an Egyptian trading post ruled by native chieftains, even calling the culture there the Kerma culture. W. Smith and J. Wilson on the other hand uphold Reisner's original theory that the rulers of Kerma were Egyptian governors-general whose tombs were in the tumuli. (Arkell, *History of the Sudan*, pp. 69 ff.; G. Steindorff and K. C.

vealed an extraordinary blend of native Africa and Egypt. Hundreds of bodies were found in the tumuli representing human sacrifice on a very large scale. Almost all the individuals found had objects that showed their role in the life of the time: soldiers had their daggers, servants their carrying jars, hareem women their finery. There seems no doubt that these people were meant to serve the dead in another world. However, unlike the charm of the Meketre models, the ranks of sacrificed victims found at Kerma cannot but horrify. What is perhaps most bizarre is that there is every indication that the victims were buried alive!

Prince Hepzefa (Djefa-Hapi) was one of the earlier governor-agents at Kerma. His home was at Assiut in Middle Egypt where he had a fine rock tomb built for himself and where at his death full funeral services were carried out—without the body of the deceased. Hepzefa died at Kerma surrounded by his family, which seems to have included a rather large hareem. One gets the impression that once established in these far places some Egyptians at least resembled the old officials of British India who had put down their roots in alien soil and stayed so long that their life and language became one with their surroundings. The step from the Egyptian mortuary custom of using models for servant and familial representation and the African method of human sacrifice for one and the same purpose was certainly not a very great one in a world where magic and the supernatural had a dominant role. Reisner has pointed out that the conservative elements in some societies are usually women. The number of Africans in these princely hareems was very large and their normal way of life may have included a total acceptance of the idea that their role in daily life involved an eventual journey with their lord to the "other world." The manner of undertaking that journey was of small import. Reisner in a classic interpretation of archaeological evidence describes some of the feelings involved with the participants as well as describing the assumed funeral of Hepzefa.

. . . But whether the spirit of Prince Hepzefa, (who

Seele, *When Egypt Ruled the East* [Chicago: University of Chicago Press, 1942], p. 96; W. S. Smith, *The Art and Architecture of Ancient Egypt* [Baltimore: Pelican History of Art, 1958], pp. 121-122; John A. Wilson, *The Culture of Ancient Egypt* [Chicago: University of Chicago Press, 1956], p. 139.)

was buried in tomb K III) for example, was setting out on the long journey to Egypt or was remaining to face the unknown spirit-world of the Sudan, his need for the company of his family was more urgent than in Egypt. The family itself was in a still more difficult situation. If they lived on and died singly, whatever perils the afterlife might bring, whether those of the journey to Egypt or those of a shadow-world filled with the spirits of the wild tribes and the raging gods of the south, all must face it alone without the aid and protection of their master. Only a few moments of present pain separated them from his familiar presence. Existence was not to cease. The fact of continued existence under the accustomed habits of life on earth was not a matter of doubt. From their point of view manifestly the safest and the most desirable act was to pay the small price and to enter the future life in their familiar family environment. . . . Thus self-sacrifice as practiced in the sati-burials at Kerma was not a cruel inhuman thing, but rather a kindly custom, an act of loyalty which provided both him who had died and those who offered themselves to a living death, with the assurance of the continuation of the long-accustomed family life in the other world.

Under such circumstances, the mind attempts to reconstruct the funeral of Prince Hepzefa, probably the first of the Egyptian governors to be buried in Ethiopia. Many of the preliminaries are quite beyond our ken—whether the chapel, K II, and the skeleton of the tumulus had been built before the actual death; to what extent the body was mummified or prepared for burial, whether it lay in state in the thick-walled chapel for some days with the funeral equipment gathered about it; and many similar details. It was entirely in accordance with Egyptian custom to slaughter cattle for a great funeral feast, and the skulls of over a hundred oxen laid on the surface and buried by drift sand around the southern circumference of the tumulus form ocular evidence of such a feast at the funeral of Hepzefa. The disposal of these skulls without rather than within the tumulus seems to indicate that the actual eating took place after the burial. A meat-feast was and remains among primitive people a rare occasion of which advantage was taken by every person within reach and such a ceremonial feast as was provided at the funeral of Hepzefa must have called together almost the whole population of the district for more than fifty miles around, if the delay between death and burial was greater than a few days. I imagine the procession filing out of the chapel, K II, and taking the short path to the western entrance of the long corridor of the tumulus, K III; the blue-glazed quartzite bed, on which the dead Hepzefa probably already lay covered with linen garments, his sword between his thighs, his pillow, his fan, his sandals in their places; the servants bearing alabaster jars of ointments, boxes of toilet articles and games, the great blue faience sailing boats with all their crews in place, the beautifully decorated faience vessels and the fine pottery of the prince's daily life; perhaps the porters straining at the ropes which drew the two great statues set on sledges, although these may have been taken to the tomb before this day; the bearers who had the easier burden of the statuettes; the crowd of women and attendants of the hareem decked in their most cherished finery, many carrying some necessary utensil or vessel. They proceed, not in the ceremonial silence of our funerals, but with all the "ululations" and wailings of the people of the Nile. The bed with the body is placed in Chamber C, the finer objects in that chamber and in the anteroom, the pottery among the statues and statuettes set in the corridor. The doors of the chambers are closed and sealed. The priests and officials withdraw. The women and attendants take their place jostling in the narrow corridor, perhaps still with shrill cries or speaking only such words as the selection of their places required. The cries and all movements cease. The signal is given. The crowd of people assembled for the feast, now waiting ready, cast the earth from their baskets upon the still, but living victims on the floor and rush away for more. The frantic confusion and haste of the assisting multitude is easy to imagine. The emotions of the victims may perhaps be exaggerated by ourselves; they were fortified and sustained by their religious beliefs, and had taken their places willingly, without doubt, but at that last moment, we know from their attitudes in death that a rustle of fear passed through them and that in some cases there was a spasm of physical agony.

The corridor was quickly filled. With earth conveniently placed, a few hundred men could do that work in a quarter of an hour; a few thousands with filled baskets could have accomplished the task in a few minutes. The assembled crowd turned then probably to the great feast. The oxen had been slaughtered ceremonially to send their spirits with the spirit of the prince. The meat must be eaten, as was ever the case. If I am right in my interpretation of the hearths, consisting of ashes and red-burned earth, which dot the plain to the west and south of the tumulus, the crowd received the meat in portions and dispersed over the adjacent ground in family or village groups to cook and eat it. No doubt the wailing and the feasting lasted for days, accompanied by games and dances.[15]

The Twelfth Dynasty marked the climax of the Middle Kingdom. Even though the capital was near Memphis, the pharaohs were of Upper Egyptian derivation. The advantage of Nubia and the wealth of Kush were well known to those monarchs. The seven chief monarchs of the dynasty (four Amenemhets and three Senwosrets (Sesotris) depended on their African holdings for much of the stability of their regimes. The gold of Nubia and the slaves, cattle, and luxury items of Kush were wealth that not only enriched the court but had a very practical application in keeping the nobles happy. In addition the large body of administrative clerks, overseers, stewards, and military officials required upkeep that the surplus wealth of Egypt itself was apparently not sufficient to uphold. Undeniably a certain covetousness among the great majority of officials made the cost of administration higher than during the Old Kingdom. The morality that was praised in the Pyramid Age seems to have been modified at least by a materialism which can be but summarized as "Live today, you are gone tomorrow." In the famous Song of the Harper, written during the period, the repeated refrain is heard:

> Increase still more the good things which you possess, and stop worrying. Do what you feel inclined to do and will give you pleasure. Enjoy yourself while you are here, and don't worry until the end comes.
>
> Enjoy each day to the fullest. For be sure no one can take what he possesses with him, and no one who has passed on can return.

The power of the officials was a continual headache to the pharaohs. Breasted found evidence, for example, of an officer of the army of Amenemhet I, in command of a garrison in Nubia, who made so much of himself that he apparently began to rival the King. Needless to say, he was removed from his post.[16] Even an attempt on Amenemhet's life was carried out which may have succeeded but about which we are uncertain.

The powerful Twelfth Dynasty monarchs gradually welded together a body of loyal followers whose duties included both civil and military functions. So long as this group could be maintained and their loyalty kept, so long would the monarchy last. For almost two hundred years the monarchy did function effectively, and the nobles, rather than being recalcitrant, took an effective and loyal part in the administration. Undeniably Pharaoh's possession of a standing army, as well as control of the Nubian sources of wealth, had a lot to do with this harmony which restored Egypt to its former prosperity.

The vigorous successor to Amenemhet I, founder of the Twelfth Dynasty, was Senwosret I who as Crown Prince had led an expedition to Korosko where the desert route to Abu Hamed began. Probably a garrison was maintained there as much to control the Egyptians on the frontier as to keep the door to Nubia open. Almost as soon as Senwosret I ascended the throne he was again in Nubia, only at this time he pushed beyond into Kush. This seems to have been partly an exploring expedition and partly a mercantile one which did not set up permanent posts so far afield. Initial interest was very likely centered on the gold resources to be found in the Red Sea hill country to the east of the Nubian Nile.

The two succeeding pharaohs (Amenemhet II and Senwosret II) were content with reinforcing their position in Nubia itself, and it is to them that the fortresses previously described owe at least a portion of their origin. As an adjunct to the Nubian interests there was a considerable revival of the Red Sea trade to Punt. This trade as in the Old Kingdom was sustained via the Wadi Hammamat route from the Theban region. Nevertheless the Red Sea ships must have touched at various points along the Sudanese coasts en route to Somaliland. The location of the Red Sea landing ports is one of the problems to be solved by future archaeology.

It was Senwosret III (Sesostris III) who had the greatest impact on Nubia and Kush. So much so, in fact, that he became a kind of patron deity there and was actually worshiped in the Sudan for centuries after his death. In order to expedite river travel across the First Cataract at Elephantine he had a channel cut into the granite which was some twenty-six feet deep and wide enough to easily accommodate the river craft of the time. This was a larger canal than that cut during the Old Kingdom, which by now at any rate had fallen into disrepair. Senwosret III strengthened existing fortifications in Nubia and constructed the fortress system at Semna. The Semna area was the southern boundary of Egypt, Nubia being regarded as an integral part of Egyptian territory. To mark this boundary stelae were set up with the following inscription:

> Southern boundary made in the year eight, under the majesty of the king of Upper and Lower Egypt, Senwosret III, who is given life for ever and ever—in order to prevent any Nehsi [Negro?] should pass it either by water or by land, with a ship, or with Nehsi herds; except Nehsi who cross for purposes of trade . . . or by proper authority . . .

From the Nubian fort bases Senwosret III was able to campaign into the eastern hills, west to the Sahara oases, and south into Kush. Some of these campaigns he led himself, others were headed by his officers. The punitive expeditions obtained cattle as the prime loot and subdued the recalcitrant populace by a program of devastation. In these desert regions the loss of cattle and the destruction of crops was a very serious matter, and certainly the inhabitants of the more settled and therefore more vulnerable regions of Nubia and Kush were more apt to remain quiescent after one of these raids than the less vulnerable nomad of the desert. One has the feeling that the obvious natural riches of the only dimly known Africa that lay beyond Kush must have intrigued the Egyptians of those days just as it did the nobles of Elephantine in the days of Pepi II. Senwosret III himself appears to have been attracted to far places. He led the first major Egyptian campaigns into Syria and seems to have headed several comparatively nonmilitary expeditions into Kush. It seems more than likely that individuals were sent far into Africa to find out more about the sources of the rich trade which made the control of Nubia so vital. The pity is that at the moment anyway we have no records that tell of some of these journeys. Perhaps in the ruins of one of the doomed buildings of Nubia such records will be found as archaeologists intensify their researches with one eye on the calendar.

We have very little idea what Africa was like in those far days. The archaeology of that period is still in its infancy. There were shellfish eaters living on the shores of the great lakes of East Africa. These people wore beads and made a very coarse pottery. They were small in stature, though they had large heads suggesting the bushman types known in South Africa today. The plateau country of Ethiopia and the coasts of Somaliland were apparently inhabited by hunters who made fine diminutive flint tools and knew pottery-making. They seem to have lived in rock and cave shelters, though brush and wattle and daub structures were probably used as well. More settled people lived in Kenya, some made pithouses and others buildings with stone walls. These settlements were small and much as in prehistoric Egypt the dead were buried in a contracted position frequently in the floor of the houses.

Hunting was the principal means of livelihood in the Congo forests, especially among the Pygmies. However, if the Murdock thesis for early agriculture in Western Africa is correct, it is not unlikely that Negro agriculturists were penetrating to the fertile lands of the Congo region, forcing the Pygmy toward the Ituri area where he survives today. In the Sahara region pastoral nomadism supplemented with hunting and some limited agriculture was the pursuit of most of the inhabitants. The bulk of these people were Negroes, but there was a considerable Caucasoid element in Libya extending to the Mediterranean coast.*

These paltry facts do not hint of the lure that Africa must have had in the days of Senwosret III. The myriad animal life, the rich flora, the immensity of the geographic prospects which met one on all sides, and, of course, the stories of rich treasure and magical wonders that must have been repeated by travelers foreign and native were sufficient to create a wanderlust that seems to have affected even the Pharaoh. There is a wonderful story of a shipwrecked sailor that has come down to us on a papyrus of the Middle Kingdom now in Leningrad. Though the adventure took place on the Red Sea route to Punt, it serves to illustrate the aura which surrounded distant lands.

* Dating of the various phases of prehistoric art found by Henri Lhote in the Tassili region for example should tell more of the life at the time of the Middle Kingdom.

The sailor was the captain of an Egyptian ship on the Red Sea. During one voyage a storm wrecked the vessel and all perished except for the captain, who managed to crawl onto an island. The island fortunately was richly endowed with grapes, fish, figs, game, and other good edible things. In gratitude he made an offering to the gods. While doing this there was a violent earthquake and suddenly there, crawling toward him, was a gigantic serpent. This monster was marvelous to look upon. His body was entirely gilded, he had an immense beard, and his eyebrows were of pure lapis lazuli.

The serpent threatened the sailor, but when he heard his sad story he prophesied that after four months an Egyptian ship would come and bring him home. The snake's story was also a sad one. He had been one of a very large serpent family, but one day a star fell on the island and burned them all up, leaving him the only survivor in a place of death.

The sailor was overjoyed at the prospect of a safe return home and promised that once back in Egypt he would send to the serpent on his island a great number of gifts, including incense. But the snake laughed, for he was also King of Punt, as it turned out, and had more than enough myrrh and other good things. Besides, once the sailor left the island, it would disappear and he would never find it again.

After the four months were up a ship did come, and the Serpent King of Punt loaded it with "myrrh, hekenu-oil, yawdanub, khesait, tishepes wood, shaas, eye-paint, giraffe-tails . . . incense, elephant tusks, greyhounds, baboons, monkeys, and many beautiful and precious things." [17]

Senwosret's son, Amenemhet III, was a worthy successor to the throne. His father's aggressive enterprise seems to have pacified most of the surrounding peoples; thus the son was enabled to develop Egypt's resources in peace. The Fayum dam was completed and the mines in Sinai and Nubia more fully exploited. At Semna a nilometer was kept which recorded high Nile each year. It is of interest that these records still existing on the rocks of the gorge evidence a fall of nearly thirty feet for the river there in almost three thousand years.

Amenemhet III's rule marked a climax of a revived Egypt. It was a time of great enterprise in which temples, tombs, forts, dams, canals, mines, and certainly city and town were built, renewed, and enlarged. A considerable literature developed and both fine arts and handicrafts attained high degrees of aesthetic accomplishment. The rich revenues of

Africa and the trade of Asia, plus a full prosperity in the Two Lands, made the reign a memorable one. Yet its extent of about fifty years was similar to that of Pepi II in that it was probably too long. The shepherd-king was unable to maintain his vigilance. The Egyptian civilization may have become too prosperous, too demanding, as it sought to augment its luxuries at the cost of its resources. The last Amenemhet, the fourth of the line, ruled about nine years, but dissolution had already set in. The weakness of the monarch and his successors of the Thirteenth Dynasty was all too evident as the nobility took hold and squabbled authority away. Central rule was lost and the divided states fought one another for the now almost meaningless title of Pharaoh. Even a Nubian or at least one who resided in Nubia seized the title at one time. A certain Sebekhotep, descendant of a commoner, may have held part of Egypt, Nubia, and much of Kush for a time, since a statue of his has been found near the Third Cataract. But it was a short-lived control, and the Egypt of the next two hundred or so years was a sadly divided shadow of itself. Nubia, Kush, and the Red Sea trade were mostly gone. The fortresses were attacked and the "Walls of Amenemhet" at Kerma were destroyed.*

Principal Monarchs of the Middle Kingdom

FIRST INTERMEDIATE PERIOD, Dynasties VII-X (2258–2052 B.C.)

MIDDLE KINGDOM, Dynasties XI-XII

Dynasty XI (2150–2000 B.C.)

Intef II	2150–2090 B.C.
Intef III	2090–2085 B.C.
Mentuhotep I	2085–2065 B.C.
Mentuhotep II	2065–2060 B.C.
Mentuhotep III	2060–2015 B.C.

* It is worth repeating here that there exists a disagreement among scholars about Kerma. Some in more recent years consider that place as the center for an African culture with Egyptian affinities. The people buried in the tumuli would not have been Egyptians but Sudanese. A cemetery similar to that of Kerma has been found on Sai Island located about halfway between Kerma and Semna. The Reisner theory still seems more logical in view of the undisputed Egyptian penetration into Kush during the Middle Kingdom. See J. Vercoutter, "Excavations at Sai 1955-7," *Kush*, VI (1958), 144 ff.

Mentuhotep IV   2015–2005 B.C.
Mentuhotep V   2005–2000 B.C.

Dynasty XII (2000–1785 B.C.)
Amenemhet I   2000–1979 B.C.
Senwosret I   1970–1936 B.C.
Amenemhet II   1938–1904 B.C.
Senwosret II   1906–1888 B.C.
Senwosret III   1887–1850 B.C.
Amenemhet III   1850–1800 B.C.
Amenemhet IV   1800–1792 B.C.

SECOND INTERMEDIATE PERIOD, Dynasties XIII-XVII
(1785–1580 B.C.)
Hyksos Rule   1730–1580 B.C.
King Kamose   1583 B.C.

5

Imperial
Civilization

Had it not been unknown and buried in the sand for so many centuries it might well have ranked among the Seven Wonders of the World. From Burckhardt to Barsanti, travellers, explorers and scientists of all nationalities followed each other during the 19th century in order to free one of the finest masterpieces of Pharaonic art from its tomb of sand. Their example justifies the hope that a second wave of international solidarity will save the great temple of Abu Simbel from the watery grave that now awaits it.—LOUIS A. CHRISTOPHE, Member of the Egyptian Institute, Cairo (*The UNESCO Courier*, February, 1960)

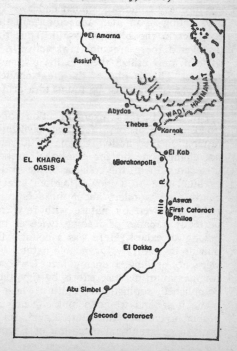

A common question asked of historians is "Does history repeat itself?" I seriously doubt that any historian could reply other than in the affirmative in view of the evidence. The history of man is full of accounts where a vigorous people seize the advantages that evolving civilization has given them for one reason or another and created posperous, expansive cultures which for a time achieve a golden age of accomplishment in many fields of endeavor. Successful and enduring in appearance, closer scrutiny reveals signs of decay even at the supreme limit of achievement. At last decay spreads in spite of desperate measures and collapse ensues. The measurement of this phenomenon is a matter of controversy, of course. But one may use any aspect of a civilization as a standard of measure whatever it be: the course of empire, the status of the individual, economics, religion, or art; and still find a general coincidence of evolution from youth to maturity to collapse. Of course, all that meets the eye may not upon investigation be really valid, yet one of the exciting aspects of the study of history is the tracing of the evolutionary trends of human endeavor. It is as if there were laws acting upon man and culture in the same way natural laws act in the physical world. Thus the historian seeks to discover if there are such laws active in human events and if so, can man utilize them to his own advantage and in fact survival. This is one of the great challenges facing research today—answers must be found to a profound problem of the modern world.

Ancient Egypt's exemplification of these evolutionary trends in the history of human civilization has a laboratory fascination for one living some 3,500 years later but this does not change one bit the emotional stress that was undergone for example with the collapse of the Middle Kingdom and the eventual rise of a New Kingdom after several centuries of chaos. One wonders about those times. Here was Egypt so richly endowed by nature with food resources that it was perfectly capable of feeding twice as many people and still having an excess. Here was a country firmly protected from outside invasion by formidable natural borders. Initially there were no organized enemy forces whose harassments called for maximum defense efforts by Egyptians. Egypt had an accomplished, sophisticated culture whose ethical achievements made it second to none in the Near East. Then there was Nubia, a kind of miniature Egypt, for all intents and purposes a geographical extension of Egypt itself. An extension that probed toward the rich heart of Africa, source of valuable raw materials that made for some of the splendors found in the Two Lands. With almost a minimum of effort Nubia could be kept in the Egyptian sphere a strong prop to the structure of that civilization.

With so rich and secure an endowment we have reason to wonder at the collapse of the Middle Kingdom. We know very little indeed about the causes of this catastrophe but it is obvious that the struggle for power, personal ambition, jealousy, quarrels over possessions, and certainly greed were contributory causes. In the weakening of central control and the re-establishment of district control by local governors we find an early example of an event which has occurred with almost cyclic frequency throughout history. In the West we have been so educated to the benefits of strong central government that we almost regard the establishment of petty states as an evil. Obviously, large public works, elaborate foreign trade, and imperial splendors are beyond the reach of the little principality. On the other hand the rule of the petty state is more apt to be influenced by the common man than is possible in a great nation. The Greeks knew that democracy operated best in a small city-state, and that the oppression of the absolute monarch or the control of the mob increased as the state grew larger. For Egypt one wonders whether this repeated demonstration of distinct loyalties, which occur from the Archaic Period on, were not a part of a struggle for a kind of local independence. The old totemic traditions survived in local religious beliefs and there may even have been folk heroes derived out of old wars among Thebes, Memphis, Herakleopolis, etc. There is a vast propaganda associated with the rise of Theban control in which Amun, the chief god of that city, supersedes all the gods and appears to be the true God of Egypt. The great emphasis upon him may have been motivated by a desire to lower the predominance of local deities in favor of the Theban patron god. In this way one of the props for insurrection was removed. This is, of course, the most rank speculation, and it would not have been introduced here except that it is a historical fact that once the central control weakened, Egypt fragmented into traditional units.

The Middle Kingdom collapsed from within. The small fragments of comparatively autonomous states resulting survived. For the annalists and poets these were dark days, but one doubts that the Nile ceased to flow or the sun to shine, so that it is just possible that the relief from high taxes and the demands for labor in enormous public works brought a modicum of happiness to many people that they had not had before—at least in those places where local rule owed something to the immediate inhabitants. One wonders if little states allowed to work out their differences and free from outside interference might not have developed a kind of utopia in a land so naturally gifted—but that is speculation for philosophers.

The stark reality of the course of events intervenes. Nubia was gradually lost as both the nomadic peoples of the desert and various Negro princes of Kush raided and conquered. This Nubian loss was gradual and the Egyptians were able to sustain their rule there for a long time after the last of the house of Amenemhet had gone to his pyramid tomb. But the African trade must have suffered quite early in this, the so-called Second Intermediate Period, and the loss of this revenue must have played a part in the deterioration of Theban rule.

The Pan-Grave People

Interestingly, a number of graves located in Upper Egypt south of Assiut, belonging to a Nubian people of mixed Negro-Caucasoid type, can be dated to this period. These people are called the Pan-Grave people after their shallow panlike graves found at Abydos where they were first identified. These Nubians appeared to have been soldiers, and excavators feel that they were professionals, possibly Medjai who were used by the Theban rulers in the long wars in the north. Of great interest are the decorated ungulate skulls with fine horns found in the graves. These are painted with simple designs and were very likely meant to hang in front of the doorway as "good luck" amulets.

The Pan-Grave people were buried in the old predynastic contracted position with heads to the north and faces east or west. Grave furniture included the usual pottery and jewelry, and of course, the weapons that mark their profession.

The Hyksos Conquest

But it was from Western Asia that the fatal blow came. A heterogeneous body of nomadic people known to history as the Hyksos suddenly entered the delta bent on conquest. In no time they possessed all Lower and Middle Egypt and were in position to demand and receive tribute from the local rulers from Thebes to Nubia. The Hyksos were a part of a general movement of people that took place in Asia toward the middle of the second millennium B.C. This movement had its origin in the migration of Indo-European-speaking peoples out of Central Eurasia into the more settled regions of the South from India to the Near East. In Western Asia the movement was enhanced by additions of various nomadic and seminomadic peoples who inhabited the Syrian and Palestinian regions. The Hyksos were of that tough, wonderfully adapted culture of Central Asia which had domesticated the horse, perfected the composite bow, developed scale armor and a repertoire of efficient weapons dominated by the sword, the latter to be used as a slashing weapon. Bronze was the material from which these weapons were made and its toughness was so much greater than copper that initially the Egyptians must have been at great disadvantage with their weapons of that softer metal.

The Hyksos were adaptable, and like many of these Central Asian peoples, readily grasped new ideas. One of these ideas was the horse-drawn vehicle. The Sumerians in the third millennium B.C. had a four-wheeled chariot drawn by onagers, which they used in battle. The idea of the wheeled vehicle probably spread to Central Asian peoples from the Tigris-Euphrates region. Carrying a man may have been the first domesticated task of the horse if his domestication took place as a result of contact with man in the steppes of Asia before men knew of the wheeled vehicles of Sumer. We don't know for sure which came first but in any case the horse-drawn, two-wheeled chariot is the principal war arm of these people when they first appear to history.*

* At Buhen, W. B. Emery has found the skeleton of a horse in Middle Kingdom context. This is about two hundred years before horses were supposed to have been used in Egypt. It is possible that nomadic peoples of Nubia acquired the horse before the Egyp-

The Hyksos were efficient in fortress making. Ignoring the laborious brick construction typical of the Near East, they simply threw up high thick walls of pounded earth. These walls were formed into great rectangles—one in Palestine being one thousand yards on the long side.

The Hyksos sacked Egypt and remained as conquerors. Generally they were content to leave Egyptian culture alone. Not so the Egyptians. It took about one hundred years, but after a succession of humiliations which we can only guess at, the conquered learned how to make and use the weapons of their masters.

The War for Independence

The war of liberation was spearheaded by Thebes and one can be certain that alliances in Middle and Upper Egypt were not too difficult to come by. However, the Theban rulers of the Seventeenth Dynasty (ca. 1660–1580 B.C.) do not seem to have been very successful in their struggle. The mummy of King Sequen-re of that period is marked by severe wounds on the head as if he had been killed in fighting the Hyksos. Kamose, the last king of the dynasty, left a record of his efforts which is of interest because of the view of Nubia which is given. One evidence for this record was a schoolboy's copy of part of a stele of Kamose which had been set up in Karnak and eventually lost. This wooden tablet was found in 1908 by Howard Carter and Lord Carnarvon, later the discoverers of Tutankhamun's tomb. Kamose had called his nobles together and in evident disgust pointed out that he, a powerful king, had to share Egypt with the Hyksos King and the King of Nubia. In order to remedy this situation Kamose overcame the doubts of his nobles and at the head of an army moved against Apophis, the Hyksos King. A recent find of the actual stele which the schoolboy had only partly copied continued the story where he left off: Kamose's raid was crowned with such success that the Hyksos ruler sent a messenger to the Nubian prince advocating a united attack on Kamose from two directions. Fortunately, Kamose's forces captured the messenger as he was going around the Theban

tians, possibly from Arabia. In this case the horse was probably used for riding. For the discovery see *Illustrated London News*, September 12, 1959, pp. 250-251.

forces and foiled the plot. This effort by Apophis would indicate that there was some unity among the rulers of Nubia, perhaps a kind of confederation.

For the Egyptians the Hyksos were the people to be beaten. Ahmose I, founder of the Eighteenth Dynasty and thus of the New Kingdom (1580–1085 B.C.) was a vigorous monarch who lost no time in assaulting Avaris, center of Hyksos control of Lower Egypt. It is of interest that much of the Egyptian fighting was on the river and the canals where ship battles took place. The Hyksos were out of their element on the water and her river-wise men gave Egypt advantage. The light chariot, the slashing sword, the hard bronze, and the composite bow now were in Egyptian hands as well as Hyksos. A patriotic fervor, reinforced by a unity induced by a common foe, roused the Egyptians as never before. Avaris fell and the Hyksos were driven out of Egypt. Ahmose I moved down into Nubia and apparently broke the back of Nubian control by a deep raid as far, possibly, as the Second Cataract. A group of cave-dwelling seminomads were apparently the main resisters to the new Egyptian invasion of Nubia, but both Ahmose and his successor-son Amenhotep I flattened this resistance with little trouble. These were really no more than raids into Nubia but sufficient to indicate Egypt's new strength. Presumably, fortified posts were reconstituted along the "Belly of Stones" and a watchful eye kept for nomadic raids. The canal at the First Cataract was cleared so that ships could pass to reinforce these posts. The horse and chariot gave the Egyptians a mobility that so greatly enhanced their striking power that nomadic raiders were wary about attacking the posts along the Nile. Control of Nubia was made much easier.

The real goal in Africa was not Nubia but Kush. The Dongola Reach above the Third Cataract is one of the most fertile stretches in the Northern Sudan. The valley is wider and there is more good soil available. Presumably, a considerable population lived here under the rule of numerous petty princes of Kush. Much of their revenue probably derived from tariffs each could impose upon the trading caravans coming up from the south en route to Egypt. Their control in some cases may have extended to the Western oases. This restriction on the African trade, plus the threat to Nubia which their alliances constituted, was sufficient to bring Egyptian armies south of the Second Cataract.

Thutmose I, successor to Amenhotep I, was already the

possessor of an army of veterans when he ascended the throne. Among these experienced men were officers who had served his father well, men like Ahmose-Pen-nehkbet, and a fighting Admiral, also another Ahmose. Significantly, both these warriors were from El Kab above Thebes. On the walls of their tombs they had inscribed the records of the campaigns they had fought under the various pharaohs they had served. Ahmose the Admiral (sometimes called Ahmose Ebana) was encharged with transporting the troops beyond the cataracts. In less than two months this river-wise sailor had the Egyptian army above the Second Cataract, where a battle was fought. The Nubians were drubbed severely, and the Egyptian forces, losing no time, swept by land and river south to the Third Cataract. At Tombos Island a fortress was constructed which was apparently the base for a series of successful conquering expeditions in various directions. Here in the Third Cataract area Thutmose set up a number of steles commemorating his victories in which it is obvious that he recognized how much he had exceeded the conquests of the Middle Kingdom pharaohs. "He pressed on into valleys which the ancestors had not known and which the wearers of the vulture and the serpent Diadems had never seen."

The swiftness of this Sudanese campaign must certainly have awed some of the chieftains. The Egyptians were capable of sudden retaliation either by land or by the river. The very fact that Pharaoh himself had come south at the head of an indomitable military machine was proof that the old days of profitable interference with the trade caravans was at an end. However, Thutmose had to return rapidly north for a campaign in Syria where Egyptian control was hardly established. Very likely this meant the almost complete withdrawal of the veteran troops he had brought with him. Thutmose had appointed a viceroy, one Thure, who had the titles "Governor of the South Countries, King's-son of Kush." Apparently his jurisdiction extended from Wadi Halfa (Buhen) to Napata (Kereima) at the Fourth Cataract, even though the Egyptian army itself had not yet gone that far.* Very likely the Kushite princes of the southernmost region had

---

* A. J. Arkell, eminent archaeologist and historian of the Sudan, suggests that Egyptian penetration of the Sudan after the conquest of Kush by Thutmose I may have gone at least as far as Merowe. There is a boundary inscription of Thutmose I recently identified at Kurgus which is located well south of Abu Hamed and there is evidence for a fort at this far-distant point. (*A History of the Sudan*, London, 1955, pp. 84-88.)

participated in the battles near Tombos and after their defeat had offered token tribute at least.

Thure, unable to hold down the hardly subdued tribes of Kush, soon found himself calling for aid. Thutmose, with that extraordinary energy which so marks the early monarchs of the Eighteenth Dynasty, came all the way back from the shores of the Euphrates in the land then called Naharin, back to Tombos. Somewhere in Kush another battle was fought and the leader of the rebellious Sudanese was killed. With the body of this chief hanging by its heels from the bow of the ship, the King returned through Nubia with the tangible evidence of his terrible power dangling before the awed eyes of the populace.

It is a characteristic of the East that when the old ruler dies his successor has to deal almost immediately with revolts aimed at testing his strength and weakness. Thutmose I died, aged and worn out after a vigorous reign of about fifteen years. He was succeeded by the physically weak Thutmose II, whose weakness made him unable to accompany the forces sent to Kush when there was a major revolt in that still unpacified province. Apparently there were many Egyptians or Egyptianized Nubians resident in Upper Nubia and Northern Kush whose possessions were imperiled by the revolt. They took refuge in the fortifications set up by Thutmose I. The field forces acted with relentless efficiency:

> This Army reached the wretched land of Kush; the might of his majesty guided it and the terror of him cleared its course. Then the army of his majesty cast down these barbarians, and not one of their males was permitted to live, even as his majesty had commanded, with the exception of one of the sons of the prince of Kush who was brought as a prisoner along with . . . their subjects to the place where his majesty was. . . .

This savage response to revolt seems to have broken the back of resistance. Nubia and Kush settled down under viceregal rule. The African trade flowed north by caravan and boat and the Theban capital was colored by the ostrich feathers, giraffe tails, leopard skins, golden rings, ivory tusks, baboons, exotic woods and perfumes, wrinkled dwarfs, and black slaves familiar during the proud days of the Middle Kingdom.

The reign of Queen Hatshepsut (1515–1484) was one of

peace. It was a period of great building enterprises and of mercantile expansion. On the walls of her fine temple at Deir-el-Bahri opposite Thebes, her architect depicted a celebrated voyage to Punt. Five ships sailed down the Nile, through a canal in the delta, to the Red Sea and so to Somaliland. Here was the myrrh the Egyptians so desired. Not only was this brought back to Egypt as a resin in baskets, but living trees were carefully boxed and transplated in the garden of her temple. It is of interest that Punt and Nubia were classified together when an offering was made to Amun, patron god of Egypt, at the successful termination of the expedition.[1] Cattle seem to have been one of the major contributions made by Nubia itself, suggesting that grasslands were perhaps more extensive in those days than they are today.

Hatshepsut also had a number of temples built in Nubia including a small but lovely one at Buhen.

Thutmose III, the so-called Napoleon of Egypt succeeded Hatshepsut, in fact it is not unlikely that he murdered her and all her leading supporters. The struggle for the succession is another story, but if ever one wanted a symbol for the times it would be that tragic event. Thutmose spelled an end for the old traditional Egypt. He was no one's fool. He brushed aside all internal opposition ruthlessly. The Hyksos had brought the outside world forcibly to Egypt; now Egypt was to bring Egypt to those foreign fields. In no less than seventeen campaigns into Asia, which even took him twice across the Euphrates, Thutmose III annihilated resistance. His army was organized into divisions complete with units of bowmen, axmen, and spearmen, and of course the crushing power of clouds of chariots. Ships carried supplies to bases in Palestine and Phoenicia, while communication was sustained by a system of interlocking garrisons. This was an Asian empire which made the surrounding peoples very much aware of Egyptian accomplishment and eager to acknowledge her power.

Thutmose did not neglect Egypt within, and as quickly as he returned from Asia, he was off on trips of inspection up and down the Nile, watching for corruption and encouraging by his presence the enterprise of his officials. So well had his grandfather Thutmose I done his work in Nubia and Kush that Thutmose III had only to go there once on a punitive expedition against some desert tribes—probably the incorrigible Beja. Napata, at the Fourth Cataract, was a thoroughly Egyptian town, and like revived Kerma, was a focus for the southern trade. Nubia, once a frontier area, was so Egyptianized that one would have been hard put to indicate where Egypt began and Nubia ended. Temples rose on the sites of new generally disused forts. Towns, like Buhen, were twice the size they had been in the days of Senwosret III. But that famed king was not forgotten, for at Semna his temple was restored and his worship continued. Fine temples were raised at Kalabsha and Amada in Lower Nubia where the Nile flows along one of its narrowest passages. Even at Sulb (Soleb) above Sai Island, Thutmose had a temple erected.

It is of interest that in addition to the worship of Senwosret III in Nubia, the Egyptians included Dedun, a local god, in some of their temples there. This is yet another indication of the elastic quality of the Egyptian pantheon, which found little difficulty in including other deities when it was expedient to do so. Dedun was a hawk-god and his similarity to Horus of Egypt probably expedited his recognition—possibly as a manifestation of the Egyptian diety.

At Karnak, among the numerous inscriptions recording the military campaigns, there is a list of the localities in both Africa and Asia which were ruled by Thutmose III. The evidence indicates that once and for all the Fourth Cataract (the Napata area) was the boundary of Egypt's empire to the south.

South of this boundary were a number of kingdoms or territories ruled by local chiefs. Apparently with Napata as a base the Egyptians were nothing loath to venture into these lands, even though they had no real sovereignty over them. The Viceroy of Kush was responsible for a great many things, including the annual shipment of gold and other precious things to the court at Thebes. Raids into areas beyond Egyptian control would have had the dual advantage of cowing possible raiders and obtaining loot to augment the annual tribute. As a result of these excursions the claim of lands up to the Sixth Cataract and beyond by land as far as Eritrea was made at Karnak, though it is highly unlikely that garrisons were maintained so far south.[2]

Amenhotep II, the celebrated archer and horseman, was no less vigorous than his father. In the second year of his reign he put down a major revolt in Northern Syria and crossed the Euphrates. In the fashion of the time he killed seven Asian princes and took their bodies back to Egypt. Before the walls of Thebes he had six of them hung head down from his boat. The seventh was sent far south to Napata where the body was hung on the walls. The fact that he took the trouble to impress the people of Kush with his power is an indication that there were still seeds of rebellion sown in the African territories. However, his viceroy had what he needed to keep things running smoothly. Boundary steles were set up in the Fourth Cataract area as a further demonstration of the far-reaching realm of Pharaoh.

Thutmose IV had to put down a revolt in Nubia, probably a raid by some powerful chiefs of the Beja nomadic groups who by now had adopted the horse. Amenhotep III, called the "Magnificent," the last of the really powerful pharaohs of the Eighteenth Dynasty, was not compelled to fight in Asia, perhaps because the lesson of retaliation had been finally learned in that hapless land. However, Kush was again a source of trouble. The Pharaoh brought an army up the Nile and joined the Nubian forces of his viceroy to attack the enemy, who had advanced probably overland to a point somewhere above Semna. The Egyptians won easily, probably because of better organization. The revolting forces may have been made up of a combination of desert people and of more settled groups from regions south of Napata. Amenhotep may have left the punishment of the desert people to his viceroy. These people had camps in the oases and by the watering places of the desert. The Egyptian troops probably enslaved the women and children and took away the livestock which was the basis of desert pastoralism. Meanwhile, Amenhotep pushed south as far as the "height of Hera," an unknown area perhaps as far as the Atbara River or somewhat beyond.[3] The expedition finally turned back, but it had done its work well, and the name of Amenhotep was properly worshiped for generations to come.

Among the reasons for Amenhotep's "magnificence" was the interest he took in building fine temples. Among the marvelous buildings he erected was the temple at Luxor, so readily accessible to the tourist from the two hotels just to its south. He built the great mortuary temple across the Nile, of which only the two colossi, accredited by tradition to "Memnon," remain. At Soleb (Sulb) near the Third Cataract, the ruins of one of the finest of all his temples can be seen. At Sadenga in Kush just below Soleb, Amenhotep III also erected a now badly ruined temple for his wife Queen Tiy. These are being excavated at the present time by an Italian expedition and from their work more should be learned of Egyptian life in the African provinces.[4]

As an example of the disasters so frequently suffered by archaeologists, the late Sir E. A. Wallis Budge, Keeper of the Egyptian and Assyrian Antiquities in the British Museum, described an incident at the Soleb temple:

When I first saw these ruins seven or eight years ago there were in the second large court a number of inscribed and sculptured slabs which I hoped would one day come to the British Museum. They appeared to have formed a sort of screen wall between the pillars, and being of hard sandstone, they had suffered less than the other stones in the building. The Inspector and I went at once to look for these, but when we came to the place they were nowhere to be seen. Looking round we saw that several large blocks and slabs of stone showed signs of having been recently broken, and the fractures were so clean and fresh-looking that they might have been made only the day before. The Inspector began to ask questions of the natives who were with us, and little by little he learned that during the last two years parties of men had come in boats, and had carried away many loads of stone to be used in erecting Government buildings. These men had naturally rejected the blocks which were weathered badly or soft, and they selected the hardest and firmest for removal; when the blocks were too large to haul away they broke them into pieces of a size convenient for transport and stowage in the boats. The sculptured slabs which I had seen there were about 4 feet long and 3 feet wide, and as they were made of good, hard sandstone, they were undoubtedly chosen by the men who came with the boats, and were broken and carried away first of all. The natives of Sulb were powerless to prevent this work of destruction, even if they had wished to do so, because there were officials of the Government with the boats, and they had the "order of the Government" to get stone. In spite of this, however, it is impossible to blame the Sudan Government for such an act of vandalism, for it was committed without the knowledge of any responsible official. The overseer of works told his men to get stone, meaning of course that they were to go to the quarries in the hills, but it was far easier for them to go to the ruins of the temple and break up the blocks there, especially as the stones lay near the river, and this they did with the result already described. One could not help feeling sorry that such a thing should be done under British rule in the Sudan, and done too at the very time when Sir Reginald Wingate and his officials were making every effort possible to preserve ancient monuments and buildings all over the country! [5]

The buildings of Amenhotep III at Soleb are of great interest because they seem to have been created by the second known architect of Egypt, Amenhotep son of Hapu, builder of the Luxor Temple. The scheme involved a columned entrance hall which led up to a pylon gate through which one had access to a succession of magnificent colonnaded courts terminating in a now vanished "holy of holies" complex of inner rooms. Part of the splendor of this building was the sculptures of lions and sphinxes which lined the way to the temple entrance. These were so fine that they were taken to the Napata area by later monarchs. Some of the lions are now among the treasures of the British Museum.

Amenhotep III ruled some thirty-five years. In his time the wealth of empire was enormous. The priesthood of Amun, the patron deity of imperial Egypt, held such treasure that we cannot even guess at its worth. With both Asia and Africa paying material homage and with the natural wealth of a superbly endowed homeland as the solid basis of the empire, it appeared that Egypt's prosperity would endure for centuries. Of course this was not to be and could not be. Crown princes of the past had been vigorous, dashing fellows with a good deal of physical strength and a willingness to face the reality of empire. The necessity of personally leading the varied forces which made up the empire required men of dynamic leadership qualities. Again the fatal repetition of the historical cycle which was to recur time and again in the history of the world, took place. The Egyptians who with patriotic zeal had hurled the Hyksos out of the delta and chased them across Syria were gone. Empire was now the glory and the defeat of Egypt. In order to hold the frontiers, mercenary troops were gathered. In particular the Sudanese of the south were called upon to act as a kind of civil police as well as acting as one of the striking units of the regular army. A vast officialdom became fixed into positions of wealth while hordes of slaves and servants did the physical labors and irksome tasks of each day. The enormous wealth of the temple communities gave them an independence of operation which made them a political entity in competition with other interests. A trade that reached into Ethiopia and Central Africa and up to the Aegean, including Cyprus and Crete, and to Babylonia, brought an enormous number and variety of articles to Thebes. All this was listed meticulously by an army of scribes and treasurers. Corruption most certainly had a place in the bureaucracy of the time. In this incredible complexity of administration resulting from the imperial successes, petty thefts, altered records, graft, and the like began the rot that would bring Egypt to her knees.

A crown prince brought up in a world where everything has been done for him, but who is expected to be as vigorous as his ancestors, has a struggle to find himself. The sickly boy Amenhotep IV, known to history as Akhenaton, seems to have retreated from the reality of empire. He resisted, apparently, the pharaonic duties increasingly imposed upon him, especially those that dealt with the enterprises of the warlike tribute-conscious priests of Amun. His religious convictions were those of the cult of Aton, in which love of nature and the creative power of the sun were combined into a faith of considerable power. There was a kind of mystique in Akhenaton's adherence to this growing faith. Perhaps as a dispirited young man he had sought some goals to follow and found them in Atonism. In any case, he became more and more fanatic, not only in his religious feeling but in his resistance to the priesthood of Amun. As coregent with the aging Amenhotep III he moved the capital from Thebes to a new site at Tell-el-Amarna where, with his wife the celebrated Nefertiti, he tried to rule Egypt in terms of the values of his Aton faith.*

Chaos resulted, the princes of Asia rebelled, the wealth-streams of Empire slowed to a trickle, dissatisfactions popped up on every side, and at the death of the disillusioned king his feeble successors Smenkhare, Tutankhamun, and Ay had to acknowledge Amun, repudiate Aton, and move back to Thebes. Their combined reigns only totaled some twelve

---

* At Sesibi near Sulb, Akhenaton built a temple which is of interest principally because the presence of drains in connection with the temple structures indicate that rainfall was somewhat more abundant than in later times: a consideration apparently supported by the constant inclusion of cattle in the New Kingdom accounts of the tribute from Nubia.

years, but the imperial rottenness was all too evident. The exception seems to have been Kush and Nubia, where the viceroys, perhaps acting on their own, aloof from court politics, were able to uphold Egyptian control. Certainly Sudanese and Nubian troops were the backbone of this firmness. One viceroy named Huy was apparently the leading figure of that southern control and he was able to present Tutankhamun with a fine Sudanese tribute.* This tribute is depicted on the walls of Huy's tomb at Thebes in a delightful painted scene.

The scene shows a line of Sudanese in a procession carrying trays on which are heaps of gold rings, flasks of precious oils or perfumes. Over their arms lie leopard skins, while some grasp giraffe-tail switches. A group of powerful spotted bulls are represented with model heads placed on the tips of their spreading horns between which the masks of Sudanese are set—as if to depict the homage of the chiefs who own the cattle. A fine young giraffe is held by a leash by two Sudanese. This certainly must have caught the eye of Theban children. Charming is the Nubian princess in her chariot. She is shaded by a large ostrich feather fan, and drawn along the street to the palace by a pair of small oxen. The climax of the procession seems to be four beautifully attired Kushite and Nubian princes who stand handsomely to the fore. The artist painted the picture with considerable attention to the physical appearance of these Africans. He was very much aware of Negro physiognomy, for he carefully depicted the prognathism, full noses, full lips, and dark eyes of that race. He noted too the plastered hair with its definitive round cut. The ostrich feathers in the hair, the ivory or shell earrings, the bone or stone necklaces leave one with little doubt as to the African origin of these people. However the artist clearly differentiates among these Negroid people by painting some black while others are a reddish brown. One wonders whether the Nubians with their mixture of Egyptian and Hamitic blood from Arabia were lighter than the Kushites, who were more apt to be of the pure Negro stocks of West and Central Africa. Conspicuous too is the decided softening and more Egyptian appearance of the standing princes.[6]

---

* Huy also built a temple at Faras. Was this a mark of independence by a viceroy during the troublesome times after the fall of Akhenaton? In view of the power of these viceroys this does not seem unlikely.

Apparently it was customary for the sons of reigning rulers in Kush to be sent to the court at Thebes where they were raised as Egyptians. When they returned home they were obviously prepared to rule in sympathy with Egyptian ways.

Horemheb, a general in the Egyptian army, took over the throne with the co-operation of the priesthood of Amun. It does appear that Nubia, which had remained stable during the loss of the Asian possessions, provided both the troops and the revenue for a re-establishment of the empire. The number of temples, at least a dozen of which existed south of Elephantine, are representative of the thoroughly Egyptian status of the province. The protection of the Egyptian towns between the First and Second Cataracts, that is, Nubia, from the desert nomads was apparently continued successfully. Kush, being farther afield, was also well protected but not being as Egyptianized, it is more than likely that garrisons there had to be kept reinforced from Nubia. One has the feeling that the more fertile region south of the Third Cataract was a continuous lure to the Egyptians of Nubia, especially since both Kerma and Napata were flourishing trade centers. In any case the Egyptianizing of the Kushite area was a continuing process. The viceroys were well-traveled individuals whose duties might in a single year take them from administrative headquarters at Aniba or Amada near Korosko south to Semna, Kerma, and Napata, perhaps out to the Selima oasis and then by boat through Aswan to Thebes. Tutankhamun's viceroy, Huy, had depicted in his tomb his state barge, which came complete with stable for his horses.

Viceroys of Kush

	REIGN
Thure	Amenhotep I and Thutmose I
Seni	Thutmose I and II
Nehi	Hatshepsut and Thutmose III
Wesersatet	Amenhotep II
Amenophis	Thutmose IV and Amenhotep III
Mermose	Amenhotep III
Thutmose	Amenhotep IV
Huy-Amenhotep	Tutankhamun
Paser I	Ay and Horemheb (?)
Amenemopet	Seti I and Ramses II
Hekanakht	Ramses II

Paser II	Ramses II
Sethauw	Ramses II
Messuwy	Merneptah and Seti II
Seti	Siptah
Hori I	Siptah and Setinekht (?) and Ramses III(?)
Hori II	Ramses III and IV and V(?)
Wentawuat	Ramses VI and VIII
Ramessenakht	Ramses IX
Pa-nehesi	Ramses XI
Herihor	Ramses XI
Piankhy	Herihor

Ramses the Splendid

The Nineteenth Dynasty (*ca.* 1340–1200 B.C.) witnessed some revival of the Egyptian power in Asia and the continued Egyptianizing of Nubia and Kush. King Seti I (1318–1298 B.C.) was able by war and by treaty to obtain a balance of power in Syria with the Hittites. Wealth again flowed into Egyptian coffers and many new temples were constructed, including the beginning of the famed hypostyle hall at Karnak. Seti's son Ramses II was even more vigorous in his building enterprises. This ruler was especially anxious to celebrate an apparent victory over the Hittites at the battle of Kadesh. Outflanked and cut off from the main body of his army, Ramses managed by an act of personal bravery to cut his way out of the trap, losing his camp in the process. Reinforcements arrived and the embattled Pharaoh won the day. But the Hittites withdrew into the fortress of Kadesh so that the battle was indecisive. Eventually a treaty was arranged between the two countries. Ramses counted Kadesh as a complete victory and in the enormous building project he undertook at Karnak he recounts the event with much bravado. Abu Simbel, the Nubian cliff temple far south of Thebes, also has a record of this victory.

Ramses II reigned for sixty-six years (1298–1232 B.C.) —another phenomenally long reign, during which the capital was changed from Thebes in Upper Egypt to Tanis in the delta. This change was probably due to the ruler's desire to be near his Asian possessions which were now the main topic in Egypt's foreign affairs. This may also be a reflection of the peaceful condition prevailing in the African territories.

Ramses, far from neglecting Nubia and Kush, embarked on vast temple-building projects in those territories. No less than eight major temples were constructed there and the fate of some of these commands the attention of the modern world as Nubian waters rise.

As far south as the Jebel Barkal in the Napata region of the Fourth Cataract, Ramses enlarged the temple of Amun that was already there. Napata seems, even at this early period, to have been a flourishing center for the worship of Amun, probably because of a sacred allusion to the Jebel Barkal as the Throne of Amun, "Lord of the Winds." [7]

Seti I had enlarged the town at Amara West, since it was apparently an important center of trade between the Second and Third Cataracts. Ramses erected a temple there, probably also dedicated to Amun and/or to himself.

The Nubian Temples of King Ramses

Nubia is the location for six major Ramsesside temples situated from south to north at Aksha, Abu Simbel, Derr, Wadi-es-Sebua, Gerf Husein, and Beit-el-Wali. The latter is practically in the shadow of the new dam and is presently the site of intensive researches being carried on by the Oriental Institute of the University of Chicago. The temple is partly cut out of the cliff face, about halfway up the side of the western hills. The plan is to cut the temple out of the rocks and erect it on higher ground. Since the reliefs on the walls of the inner portion of the temple are painted and the colors largely preserved, it is obvious that the temple must be saved if mankind is to have this record of the past for posterity. Though the walls depict the conquests of Ramses in Asia and Africa they also tell us something of the life of the times, especially in the scenes of Nubia.

These temples of Nubia have several features in common. Initially a series of free-standing statues lead one from the banks of the river to the cliff face, into which the temple was cut. At Gerf Husein, Ramses' temple was dedicated to the god Ptah. The worshiper entered a colonnaded court via an avenue of stone rams, now mostly vanished. Probably there were colossal statues of the King against some of the pillars. On the west of this court rises the cliff wall, cut in the form of a pylon gateway. Beyond the cliff entrance is a pil-

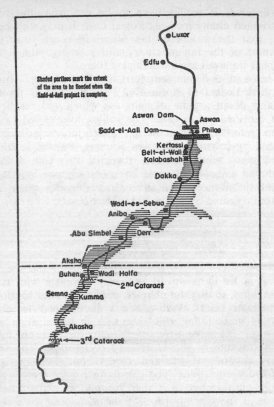

Shaded portions mark the extent
of the area to be flooded when the
Sadd-el-Aali project is complete.

lared hall with statues of Ramses against each pillar, beyond
which on either side are niches in which the King stands
as the center figure of a triad of different deities. The depths
of the temple beyond this hall contain an antechamber with
Ramses represented in the reliefs in ceremonial context with
various deities. At last, in the deepest chamber, one of three
sanctuaries, we find Ramses seated with Ptah in two forms
and Hathor, goddess of the Nile. The impression upon the
worshiper must have been very great. One moved perhaps
180 feet from the entrance of the temple court into the
inner sanctuary; moving from light to semidark, through
columned halls rich with relief, and awesome by reason of
the great statues which ranked the way—some measuring
about twenty-five feet in height. The fate of this temple is not

yet decided. It would have to be cut from the rock and resurrected elsewhere—a colossal task. It may well be, therefore, that the waters of the Nile will reach back into the darkness of the far sanctuary and submerge the four silent figures who await their worshipers there.

The Wadi-es-Sebua temple is like that of Gerf Husein but it was dedicated to Amun-Re. The approach is through the remains of an avenue of sphinxes which was reached via a now vanished pylon gate. The sphinx avenue led to another pylon gateway, still standing, which characteristically was fronted by colossal statues of Ramses. Beyond is the colonnaded court which leads to the cliff, in which is the usual columned and statued great hall. This in turn is followed by an antechamber and the sanctuaries. As with many of these temples, Wadi-es-Sebua was used as a Coptic Christian church in the years before Islam. These Christians plastered and painted holy pictures on the walls, obliterating the Egyptian material beneath. By wonderful coincidence, on either side of the central recess there are figures of Ramses II offering flowers to the gods at the head of the recess. The central figure is, however, St. Peter complete with halo and key in hand, so that the pharaoh appears to offer his flowers to a Christian saint! Wadi-es-Sebua is destined to disappear in 1964 except for the sphinxes in the avenue outside. There is little hope that the temple can be saved unless it too can be cut free and reconstructed elsewhere.

The cliff-temple of Derr is the fourth of those erected by Ramses in order from Elephantine (the First Cataract). Badly ruined, the structures that lay before the cliff entrance have now largely disappeared. The main hall is in poor condition but the antechamber and the three inner sanctuaries are in better shape. This temple was dedicated to the sun-god Re but there are numerous ruined reliefs depicting the usual wars of Ramses. The temple is apparently doomed, as its ruined condition precludes wholesale salvage, though portions of its reliefs will undoubtedly be removed. It is too bad something can't be done about the Derr temple, because its emphasis on the sun-god in the days of Amun's temples gives it a uniqueness in keeping with the other temples that are dedicated to gods other than Amun. For example, the central sanctuary was probably a storehouse for sacred boats dedicated to the sun-god. These are, of course, long vanished.

The southernmost of these Nubian temples is found just

below Buhen at Aksha. This is the smallest of the temples and is free-standing. It was dedicated to the worship of Amun and the "Living-god Ramses." It is unexcavated and is doomed to be lost unrecorded unless someone provides the means to save it—a task that should not be as difficult as that necessary for the rock-cut temples.

Abu Simbel—The Glory of Nubia

The most famous and certainly the greatest of Ramses' temples in Nubia is that of Abu Simbel. Here Ramses drew together the worship of the great gods of Egypt and—together with his own deified presence—presented on a gigantic scale the pantheon of imperial Egypt. Amun (Lord of Thebes), Ptah (Lord of Memphis), Ra (Lord of Heliopolis), and Ramses (Lord of Egypt) are given a sanctuary at Abu Simbel that ranks in its conception and sheer bulk with the greatest of the world's cathedrals and temples. Abu Simbel is oriented on the east-west axis. The rising sun sends its rays to the deepest room 180 feet back from the entrance, where are seated the four stone figures of the great gods to whom the temple is dedicated.

One approaches Abu Simbel by water. The temples are first discovered lying, it would appear, just at the water's edge, but on coming closer one finds that the shelving sand beach sets them back and somewhat higher. There are two of them; a small cliff temple on the north is dedicated to the goddess Hathor and Ramses' Queen Nefertari.

However, it is the great temple of Ramses II with its four seated colossi that commands attention. Some sixty-seven feet in height, they are higher than the famed colossi of Amenhotep III at Thebes. These statues are seated on thrones on which are depicted the Nile gods binding the two Egypts as one above rows of Asian and African prisoners. One ascends a stairway onto the terrace in front of the colossi. The mastery of the dramatic is fully demonstrated here, for the colossi, whose size has been somewhat dwarfed by the scale of the open plain to the south and the high cliffs before, now loom up in all their gigantic dimensions. The eye is forced upward along the massive limbs to the imperial but somewhat surprisingly mild countenance of the King. Above is the great cliff tamed by lines of hiero-

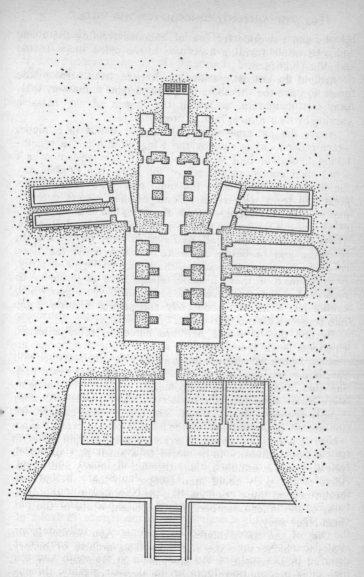

PLAN OF THE MAIN TEMPLE AT ABU SIMBEL.

glyphs and a wonderful line of baboons greeting the rising sun, the whole forming a cornice to the pylon shape of the smoothed cliff face.

Around the colossi, peeking, as it were, from between the great legs, are the members of the royal family: mother, wife, son, and daughters, softening the impact of the massive carving by their almost human presence.

Above the entrance door the sun-god stands in a niche, worshiped on either side by the King. Within is the breathtaking hypostyle hall with its square pillars against which stand eight enormous images of the King in a double row facing one another across the main aisle. The walls of this great hall teem with reliefs. Some of these depict ceremonies in which the King worships the gods; but most important of all are the scenes of the wars and campaigns of Ramses. These show in great detail an Egyptian army on the march, in camp, and in battle. Kadesh, in which battle the King saved, by his personal courage, the entrapped Egyptian army, is the climax of these historic reliefs. Here is a marvelous record of a historical event of some 3,300 years ago which cannot last if its sandstone body and painted features come into contact with the Nile water.

Beyond the hypostyle hall are numerous relief-bedecked chambers hewn from the solid rock that the ceremonies attendant in the worship of the gods be given their proper and mysterious setting. In such chambers as these one has a feeling that there is more to come. It is as if the ancients were barely scratching the mystery of these depths with their temple probes within the cliff. There is a stone support for the sacred bark in front of the statues of the central sanctuary. It is another object to evidence the Egyptian belief in the essential divinity of a world to a small part of which physical man is confined. Only through the mercy and mightiness of the gods could man escape into the real and vast realm beyond those confines, like the coming out of the darkness of the inner chambers into the bright world of the Nubian Nile valley.

One of the most interesting parts of Abu Simbel is the records which make the site a veritable archive of history. One of these records is the so-called Marriage Stele which is found on the southern side of the terrace of the main temple. The badly eroded and incomplete inscription describes the events after the battle of Kadesh when the indecisive war between the Hittites and Egyptians raged on. At last a treaty was drawn up and peace was concluded. The Hittite King Muwattali later sent his eldest daughter with an enormous dowry and a large escort to be married to the elderly Ramses. The marriage was apparently successful and the two realms dwelt in peace. The poetic and graphic power of the writing is well conveyed by the inscription and its Oriental flavor is most apparent.

> And His Majesty was delighted and the palace was in joy when he heard this marvellous event which had never before been experienced in Egypt. . . .
> When the daughter of the great king of the Hittites proceeded towards Egypt, the infantry, chariotry, and notables of His Majesty were in her following, mixed with the infantry and chariotry of the Hittites, foreign warriors and Egyptian troops alike. . . . And the great kings of all countries which they passed were puzzled, and turned back discomfited when they saw people of the land of the Hittites joined with soldiers of the king of Egypt.

Another inscription is in the nature of a "Kilroy was here" signature of World War II. Greek mercenaries of King Psammetichos II sent from their base in Elephantine into Nubia about 590 B.C. wrote in Carian script on the leg of one of the colossi:

> When King Psammetichos came to Elephantine, they wrote this, who came with Psammetichos, son of Theocles, and proceeded via Kerkis as far as the river allowed of it. Potasimto led the foreigners, Amasis the Egyptians. Archon, son of Amoibichos, and Pelekos, son of Udamos, wrote this.

John L. Burckhardt, a Swiss Orientalist, was the first traveler of recent times to visit and record Abu Simbel. In those days, 1813, the smaller temple of Nefertari was exposed but the great temple was just about completely covered by sand. Burckhardt made out the colossi, though he could not be sure whether they were sitting or standing. His narrative of Abu Simbel bears repeating:

> Having, as I supposed, seen all the antiquities of Ebsambal, I was about to ascend the sandy side of the mountain by the same way I had descended; when hav-

ing luckily turned more to the southward, I fell in with what is yet visible of four immense colossal statues cut out of the rock, at a distance of about two hundred yards from the temple; they stand in a deep recess, excavated in the mountain, but it is greatly to be regretted, that they are now almost entirely buried beneath the sands, which are blown down here in torrents. The entire head, and part of the breast and arms of one of the statues are yet above the surface; of the one next to it scarcely any part is visible, the head being broken off, and the body covered with sand to above the shoulders; of the other two, the bonnets only appear. It is difficult to determine, whether these statues are in a sitting or standing posture; their backs adhere to a portion of rock, which projects from the main body, and which may represent a part of a chair, or may be merely a column for support. They do not front the river, like those of the temple just described, but are turned with their faces due north, towards the more fertile climes of Egypt, so that the line on which they stand, forms an angle with the course of the stream. The head which is above the surface has a most expressive, youthful, countenance, approaching nearer to the Grecian model of beauty, than that of any ancient Egyptian figure I have seen; indeed, were it not for a thin oblong beard, it might well pass for a head of Pallas. This statue wears the high bonnet usually called the corn-measure, in the front of which is a projection bearing the figure of a nilometer; the same is upon the bonnets of the two others; the arms are covered with hieroglyphics, deeply cut in the sand-stone, and well executed; the statue measures seven yards across the shoulders, sixty-five to seventy feet in height; the ear is one yard and four inches in length. On the wall of the rock, in the centre of the four statues, is the figure of the hawk-headed Osiris, surmounted by a globe; beneath which, I suspect, could the sand be cleared away, a vast temple would be discovered, to the entrance of which the above colossal figures probably serve as ornaments, in the same manner as the six belonging to the neighbouring temple of Isis.[8]

In the torrid summer of 1817, the Italian, Giovanni Belzoni, who had made some discoveries at Thebes set to work to clear the sand away from the front of the temple in order to gain entrance:

We continued our operations regularly, and in the course of a few days more we perceived a rough projection from the wall, which indicated apparently that the work was unfinished, and no door to be found there. At this the hopes of some of our party began to fail; nevertheless we persevered in our exertions, and three days after we discovered a broken cornice, the next day the torus, and of course the frieze under, which made us almost sure of finding the door the next day; accordingly I erected a palisade, to keep the sand up, and to my utmost satisfaction saw the upper part of the door as the evening approached. We dug away enough sand to be able to enter that night, but supposing there might be some foul air in the cavity, we deferred this till the next morning.

Early in the morning of the 1st of August we went to the temple in high spirits, at the idea of entering a newly discovered place. We endeavoured as much as we could to enlarge the entrance; but our crew did not accompany us as usual. On the contrary, it appeared that they intended to hinder us as much as lay in their power; for when they saw, that we really had found the door, they wished to deter us from availing ourselves of it: the attempt however failed. They then pretended, that they could not stop any longer with the boat in that place, and if we did not go on board immediately, they would set off with her and leave us. On our refusal they knelt on the ground, and threw sand over their faces, saying, that they would not stop an instant. The fact was, they had promised to the Cacheffs to play some trick to interrupt our proceedings, in case we should come to the door. But even all this would not do. We soon made the passage wider, and entered the finest and most extensive excavation in Nubia, one that can stand a competition with any in Egypt, except the tomb newly discovered in Beban el Malook.

From what we could perceive at the first view, it was evidently a very large place; but our astonishment increased, when we found it to be one of the most magnificent of temples, enriched with beautiful intaglios, paintings, colossal figures, &c. We entered at first into a large pronaos, fifty-seven feet long and fifty-two wide, supported by two rows of square pillars, in a line from the front door, to the door of the sekos. Each pillar has a figure, not unlike those at Medinet Aboo, finely executed, and very little injured by time. The tops of their turbans reach the ceiling, which is about thirty feet high: the pillars are five feet and a half square. Both these and the walls are covered with beautiful hieroglyphics, the style of which is somewhat superior, or at least bolder, than that of any others in Egypt, not only in the workmanship, but also in the subjects. They exhibit battles, storming of castles, triumphs over the Ethiopians, sacrifices, &c. In some places is to be seen the same hero as at Medinet Aboo but in a different posture. Some of the columns are much injured by the close and heated atmosphere, the temperature of which was so hot, that the thermometer must have risen to above a hundred and thirty degrees.

It took twenty-two days to open it, beside six days last year. We sometimes had eighty men at work, and sometimes only our own personal exertions, the party consisting of Mr. Beechey, Captains Irby and Mangles, myself, two servants, and the crew, eleven in all, and three boys. It is situated under a rock about a hundred feet above the Nile, facing the south-east by east, and about one day and a half's journey from the second cataract in Nubia, or Wady Halfa.

The heat was so great in the interior of the temple, that it scarcely permitted us to take any drawings, as the perspiration from our hands soon rendered the paper quite wet. Accordingly, we left this operation to succeeding travellers, who may set about it with more convenience than we could, as the place will become cooler. Our stock of provision was so reduced, that the only food we had for the last six days was dhourra, boiled in water without salt, of which we had none let. The Cacheffs had given orders to the people not to sell us any kind of food whatever, hoping that we might be driven away by hunger. But there was an Abady, who lived in the village, and as he was of a different tribe, he was not so much afraid of disobeying the Cacheffs. He sometimes came at night, and brought us milk; but he was at last detected, and prevented from bringing any more.[9]

Since those pioneer days there have been many visitors to Abu Simbel. Their accounts are frequently colorful, but whatever the writing, the authors were always considerably impressed—and no wonder. It is hard to believe that this famous temple, which has fascinated so many people through the years, will probably rest in its place no more.

Several accounts are worth quoting. The first is by Dr. W. H. Yates, a distinguished member of the Royal College of Physicians in London who visited "Aboo-Simbal" in 1841.

Ascending over a hill of hot, loose, red sand, which continued pouring down, like grains of quartz or millet-seeds, from the crags above, we reached the face of the rock which forms the front of the temple: we found the entrance entirely obliterated and immediately set the two crews to work, with some of the natives, to clear away the sand, that we might enter. It was a tremendous undertaking; as fast as it was removed, a fresh quantity rolled down to supply its place: but after some time, we succeeded in making a hole at one corner, large enough to admit of our crawling in on all-fours. On each side of the door, were originally, two colossal statues of a youthful Osiris, bearing on his head the bushel or corn-measure,—the emblem of plenty; but the upper half of one has been broken off: they are in a sitting posture, the hands resting on the knees, and measure seven feet across the shoulders, and seventy feet in height, i.e. including the pedestal. The expression of the countenance is placid and benign: the lips are moderately broad, but well proportioned; the nose not exactly aquiline, yet not Grecian, but a medium between the two; the eyes, though slightly sunk, are fine and full; the cheeks are well rounded: the cheek-bones rather high: there is a beard, and the mouth and chin are in such exquisite keeping with the other features, that they impart a softness to the physiognomy which is prepossessing and attractive, and admired by all.

According to Burckhardt, the width of the entire front is 117 feet, and the height to the upper cornice, eighty-six feet six inches. Over the entrance is a representation in bas relief, of Aroeris (twenty feet in height) receiving offerings from two female figures, which have a very grotesque appearance. Above the moulding which runs along the top, is a row of monkeys eight feet high; there are figures of Isis, and the wolf, and a tablet of hieroglyphics answering to each statue. This magnificent temple penetrates to the depth of 154 feet, and contains fourteen chambers. On entering, we found ourselves in the Pronaos, a large Hall (fifty-seven feet by fifty-two) divided into three aisles by two rows of statues, which support the roof: they are thirty feet in height, and represent Osiris with his arms crossed on the breast, one hand holding the scourge, the other the crosier or sacred *"tau."* The walls are ornamented with coloured hieroglyphics in a tolerably perfect state, considering that this temple has suffered from damp. Many of the delineations described by Mr. Banks and Mr. Salt, are now no more to be seen. For instance—these gentlemen inform us, that there was a representation of a great many prisoners of different nations, (but chiefly Ethiopians, as known by their dress and colour,) being led away in chains by the conqueror. With some difficulty, we were able to discover where this had been; but nothing more—certainly there were no characteristics of the country or demeanour of the captives: for the colour was nearly all gone, and the stone itself had become so soft, that it was peeling off in great quantity. The most distinct designs are those on the walls of the south aisle, which exhibit a Hero (probably Sesostris) vanquishing his enemies: he is standing in a war chariot drawn by two spirited horses, and in the act of shooting an arrow. The figure is well executed: I was particularly struck with the noble mien and undaunted steady gaze of the warrior:—entirely free from anxiety, as if conscious of the justness of his cause, the countenance evinces all that intrepidity and collected coolness which are the attributes of true bravery. His adversaries are falling around him, and the earth is strewed with the slain, and the fallen, who are suing for mercy. At a distance is a castle, the walls crowded with people evidently thrown into confusion, and confounded by the prowess of the Hero, who everywhere seeks the thickest of the fight, and seems to "enact more wonders than a man." His opponents are white, and have black hair and black eyes, and long black beard—apparently Jews. Facing the entrance, is a small apartment leading into another, where there are four statues in a sitting posture, eight feet high: the first represents *Aroeris,* the hawk-headed deity—the second (a beardless figure) *Isis*—the third *Osiris*—and the fourth *Phthah.* In this, the *Adytum,* there is also in advance of the idols, a square stone altar, about three feet high. As several mummies were found in the anterooms, it is evident that some of them were places of burial. The walls are covered with hieroglyphics: but the colour is quite gone, and they can scarcely be deciphered. This is the only temple either in Egypt or Nubia which has suffered from damp. We first effected an entrance at night: for some time we could scarcely breathe, it was so hot and oppressive, and the air so bad: we could not endure clothing; and although we stripped to the shirt, we broke out into as profuse a perspiration as if we had been in a Turkish bath. The thermometer stood at 86°, and in the morning, when we again entered we found it 88°, the rock forms a sort of ravine or hollow, which has been filled up from time to time, with sand from the western desert, threatening to hide (perhaps for ever) this wonderful specimen of human skill—within whose gloomy portals the Scriptures lead us to infer that the grossest abominations were practised. In this overwhelming of the Egyptian temples we read a terrible lesson: and no reflecting mind can do otherwide than see in it the most awful proof of the wrath of an offended Deity—doubtless intended to convey a merciful warning to the great nations of Europe, who are now, as the Egyptians once were, at the very zenith of earthly power, wisdom and glory.[10]

Another worthwhile account is that of Amelia B. Edwards, who was a scholarly traveler, indefatigable in her efforts to understand and describe correctly the monuments of ancient Egypt. She was a pioneer in the job of translating academic knowledge into popular understanding. During her investigation of Abu Simbel she was instrumental in finding the little temple just on the south of the great edifice. This is decorated with fine reliefs commemorating the royal deified position of Ramses with the gods. Her credo is stated in her book *A Thousand Miles up the Nile:*

There are fourteen temples between Abou Simbel and Philae: to say nothing of grottoes, tombs and other ruins. As a rule, people begin to get tired of temples about this time and vote them too plentiful. Meek travelers go through them as a duty; but the greater number rebel. . . . For myself, I was never bored by them. Though they had been twice as many, I should not have wished them fewer. . . . I could have breakfasted, dined, supped on temples. My appetite for them was insatiable and grew with what it fed upon. I went over them all. I took notes of them all. I sketched them every one.[11]

Her impressions of Abu Simbel are classics of their kind,

especially as they state so clearly what most of us have difficulty saying about that wonderful temple.

It was wonderful to wake every morning close under the steep bank, and, without lifting one's head from the pillow, to see that row of giant faces so close against the sky. They showed unearthly enough by moonlight, but not half so unearthly as in the gray of dawn. At that hour, the most solemn of the twenty-four, they wore a fixed and fatal look that was little less than appalling. As the sky warmed this awful look was succeeded by a flush that mounted and deepened like the rising flush of life. For a moment they seemed to glow —to smile—to be transfigured. Then came a flash, as of thought itself. It was the first instantaneous flash of the risen sun. It lasted less than a second. It was gone almost before one could say it was there. The next moment mountain, river and sky were distinct in the steady light of day; and the colossi—mere colossi now— sat serene and stony in the open sunshine.

Every morning I waked in time to witness that daily miracle. Every morning I saw those awful brethren pass from death to life, from life to sculptured stone. I brought myself almost to believe at last that there must sooner or later come some one sunrise when the ancient charm would snap asunder and the giants must arise and speak.

The Nefertari temple won her heart:

Here the whole front is but a frame for six recesses, from each of which a colossal statue, erect and likelife, seems to be walking straight out from the heart of the mountain. These statues, three to the right and three to the left of the doorway, stand thirty feet high, and represent Rameses II and Nefertari, his queen. Mutilated as they are, the male figures are full of spirit and the female figures are full of grace. The queen wears on her head the plumes and disk of Hathor. The king is crowned with the pschent and with a fantastic helmet adorned with plumes and horns. They have their children with them; the queen her daughters, the king his sons—infants of ten feet high, whose heads just reach to the parental knee.

The walls of these six recesses, as they follow the slope of the mountain, form massive buttresses, the effect of which is wonderfully bold in light and shadow. The doorway gives the only instance of a porch that we saw in either Egypt or Nubia. The superb hieroglyphics which cover the faces of these buttresses and the front of this porch are cut half a foot deep into the rock and are so large that they can be read from the island in the middle of the river. The tale they tell—a tale retold in many varied turns of old Egyptian style upon the architraves within—is singular and interesting.

"Rameses, the Strong in Truth, the Beloved of Amen," says the outer legend, "made this divine abode for his royal wife, Nefertari, whom he loves."

The legend within, after enumerating the titles of the king, record that "his royal wife who loves him, Nefertari the beloved of Maut, constructed for him this abode in the mountain of the pure waters."

On every pillar, in every act of worship pictured on the walls, even in the sanctuary, we find the names of Rameses and Nefertari "coupled and inseparable." In this double dedication and in the unwonted tenderness of the style one seems to detect traces of some event, perhaps of some anniversary, the particulars of which are lost forever. It may have been a meeting; it may have been a parting; it may have been a prayer answered or a vow fulfilled. We see, at all events, that Rameses and Nefertari desired to leave behind them an imperishable record of the affection which united them on earth and which they hoped would reunite them in Amemti. What more do we need to know? We see that the queen was fair; that the king was in his prime. We devine the rest; and the poetry of the place, at all events, is ours. Even in these barren solitudes there is wafted to us a breath from the shores of old romance. We feel that Love once passed this way and that the ground is still hallowed where he trod.

But the wonder of Abou Simbel is the huge subject on the north side of the great hall. This is a monster battle-piece which covers an area of fifty-seven feet seven inches in length, by twenty-five feet four inches in height, and contains over eleven hundred figures. Even the heraldic cornice of cartouches and asps which runs round the rest of the ceiling is omitted on this side, so that the wall is literally filled with the picture from top to bottom.

Fully to describe this huge design would take many

pages. It is a picture-gallery in itself. It represents not a single action, but a whole campaign. It sets before us, with Homeric simplicity, the pomp and circumstance of war, the incidents of camp life and the accidents of the open field. We see the enemy's city, with its battlemented towers and triple moat; the besiegers' camp and the pavilion of the king; the march of infantry; the shock of chariots; the hand-to-hand melee; the flight of the vanquished; the triumph of the Pharaoh; the bringing in of the prisoners; the counting of the hands of the slain. A great river winds through the picture from end to end and almost surrounds the invested city. The king in his chariot pursues a crowd of fugitives along the bank. Some are crushed under his wheels; some plunge into the water and are drowned. Behind him, a moving wall of shields and spears, advances with rhythmic step the serried phalanx; while yonder, where the fight is thickest, we see chariots overturned, men dead and dying, and riderless horses making for the open. Meanwhile, the besieged send out mounted scouts and the country folk drive their cattle to the hills.

A grand frieze of chariots charging at full gallop divides the subject lengthwise and separates the Egyptian camp from the field of battle. The camp is square and inclosed, apparently, in a palisade of shields. It occupies less than one-sixth part of the picture and contains about a hundred figures. Within this narrow space the artist has brought together an astonishing variety of incidents. The horses feed in rows from a common manger, or wait their turn and impatiently paw the ground. Some are lying down. One, just unharnassed, scampers round the inclosure. Another, making off with the empty chariot at his heels, is intercepted by a couple of grooms. Other grooms bring buckets of water slung from the shoulders on wooden yokes. A wounded officer sits apart, his head resting on his hand; and an orderly comes in haste to bring him news of the battle. Another, hurt apparently in the foot, is having the wound dressed by a surgeon. Two detachments of infantry, marching out to re-inforce their comrades in action, are met at the entrance to the camp by the royal chariot returning from the field. Rameses drives before him some fugitives who are trampled down, seized and dispatched upon the spot. In one corner stands a row of objects that look like joints of meat; and near them are a small altar and a tripod brazier. Elsewhere, a couple of soldiers, with a big bowl between them, sit on their heels and dip their fingers in the mess, precisely as every fellah does to this day. Meanwhile, it is clear that Egyptian discipline was strict and that the soldier who transgressed was as abjectly subject to the rule of stick as his modern descendant. In no less than three places do we see this time-honored institution in full operation, the superior officer energetically flourishing his staff; the private taking his punishment with characteristic disrelish. In the middle of the camp, watched over by his keeper, lies Rameses' tame lion; while close against the royal pavilion a hostile spy is surprised and stabbed by the officer on guard.

Alone in the temple, Miss Edwards, sensitive to the surrounding and the mystery of the past in the present, recounted her feelings:

There is but one hour in the twenty-four at which it is possible to form any idea of the general effect of this vast subject and that is at sunrise. Then only does the pure day stream in through the doorway and temper the gloom of the side-aisles with light reflected from the sunlit floor. The broad divisions of the picture and the distribution of the masses may then be dimly seen. The details, however, require candle-light and can only be studied a few inches at a time. Even so, it is difficult to make out the upper groups without the help of a ladder. Salame, mounted on a chair and provided with two long sticks lashed together, could barely hold his little torch high enough to enable the writer to copy the inscription on the middle tower of the fortress of Kadesh.

It is fine to see the sunrise on the front of the great temple; but something still finer takes place on certain mornings of the year, in the very heart of the mountain. As the sun comes up above the eastern hill-tops, one long, level, beam strikes through the doorway, pierces the inner darkness like an arrow, penetrates to the sanctuary and falls like fire from heaven upon the altar at the feet of the gods.

It was a wonderful place to be alone in—a place in which the very darkness and silence are old and in which time himself seems to have fallen asleep. Wandering to and fro among these sculptured halls, like a shade among shadows, one seems to have left the world behind; to have done with the teachings of the present; to belong one's self to the past. The very gods assert their ancient influence over those who question them in solitude. Seen in the fast-deepening gloom of evening, they look instinct with supernatural life. There were times when I should scarcely have been surprised to hear them speak—to see them rise from their painted thrones and come down the walls. There were times when I felt I believed in them.

There was something so weird and awful about the place, and it became so much more weird and awful the farther one went in, that I rarely ventured beyond the first hall when quite alone. One afternoon, however, when it was a little earlier, and therefore a little lighter than usual, I went to the very end and sat at the feet of the gods in the sanctuary. All at once (I cannot tell why, for my thoughts just then were far away) it flashed upon me that a whole mountain hung—ready, perhaps, to cave in—above my head. Seized by a sudden panic such as one feels in dreams, I tried to run; but my feet dragged and the floor seemed to sink under them. I felt I could not have called for help, though it had been to save my life. It is unnecessary, perhaps, to add that the mountain did not cave in, and that I had my fright for nothing. It would have been a grand way of dying, all the same; and a still grander way of being buried.[12]

A final statement by Christiane Desroches-Noblecourt, Curator of the Department of Egyptian Antiquities of the Louvre, written in the Nubian issue of the *UNESCO Courier*, is perhaps the most important of all:

Protected where they stand in their hallowed bay, preserved in the rock so frail that no water can touch them without disintegrating their stones, the two temples of Abu Simbel cannot be allowed to perish. They must remain facing the rising sun whose brilliant rays each day awaken the colossal statues of the Great Rameses.[13]

The scheme presently being aired to preserve Abu Simbel would have pleased Ramses II. The most practical and certainly the best is to erect a cofferdam which would seal off the bay in which the temples are located. This involves rais-

34. BROWN QUARTZITE HEAD OF A KING, probably Ramses II, wearing the war helmet. Dynasty XIX. *(Courtesy of The Metropolitan Museum of Art, Rogers Fund, 1934)*

35. KARNAK STATUE OF RAMSES II. *(W. Fairservis)*

36. FAÇADE OF THE TEMPLE OF ABU SIMBEL (see also below).
(The American Museum of Natural History)

37. RAMSES CO-
LOSSUS AT ABU
SIMBEL.
*(The American
Museum of Natural
History)*

38. **BRONZE STATUETTE GROUP**—Triad of Gods: Osiris, Isis, and Horus. Ptolemaic Period.
(Courtesy of The Metropolitan Museum of Art, Rogers Fund, 1942)

39. **GREEN STONE STATUETTE OF ISIS AND CHILD HORUS.** Saite Period.
(Courtesy of The Metropolitan Museum of Art, Rogers Fund, 1945)

40. GODDESS HATHOR, a panel from one of the four sides of a wooden capital. Dynasty XXX.
(Courtesy of The Metropolitan Museum of Art, gift of Mrs. Lucy Drexel, 1889)

41. MAP OF THE ISLAND OF PHILAE
drawn by one of Napoleon's engineer
officers. The thick black blocks represent the pylons of the Isis temple.
(*From* Description de l'Egypte, *Paris,*
1820)

42. THE ISLAND OF PHILAE, "Pearl of the East," one hundred years before it was engulfed by the waters of the Aswan Dam. (*From* Description de l'Egypte, *Paris, 1820*)

43. VIEW OF ASWAN, EGYPT, before the dam was built.
     (The American Museum of Natural History)

44. TEMPLE OF ISIS AND LANDING PLACE, PHILAE, about
1890, before the dam was built.
(The American Museum of Natural History)

45. TEMPLES OF PHILAE, AFRICA, ASWAN. The island is
out of the water at low Nile. Compare this picture with
that showing Philae one hundred years before.
(The American Museum of Natural History)

46. THE TEMPLES ON THE ISLE OF PHILAE as the officers of Napoleon's army saw them.
(*From* Description de l'Egypte, *Paris, 1820*)

47. TEMPLE WALL—DENDEREH. Characteristic relief of the time ot Ptolemaic and Roman rule in Egypt. *(The American Museum of Natural History)*

48. MARBLE STATU-ETTE OF A DWARF, Ptol-emaic Period. *(Courtesy of The Metropolitan Museum of Art, Carnavon Collection, gift of Edward S. Harkness, 1926)*

49. THE JEBEL BARKAL SEAT OF THE WORKSHOP OF AMUN IN KUSH (old drawing by G. A. Hoskins, *ca.* 1833).
(*The American Museum of Natural History*)

50. THE PYRAMIDS OF THE MEROITIC KINGS in 1833 (drawn by G. A. Hoskins).
(The American Museum of Natural History)

ing a hundred-foot-high wall at a cost some estimate as being over thirty million dollars—certainly a paltry sum for the world's nations mutually to shoulder. An alternative plan requires the cutting out of each block of stone in which the temples are located and raising these immense masses to the top of the cliffs out of reach of the water. This seemingly incredible scheme is feasible with modern methods. It has the advantage of placing the temple full in the rising sun so that the motivation for its original orientation would not be lost. Re willing, one of these two schemes will be carried out. (See page 227.)

These temples of Ramses II string out along the Nubian Nile Valley in almost regular order. They appear wherever the valley opens out and permits some concentration of cultivation and population. Nothing is more of a testimonal to the solidity of Egyptian control south of the First Cataract than this line of temples. Each must have had a sizable religious community to support it; their representatives were certainly in appearance both at Thebes and at the Viceroy's headquarters at Aniba.* The emphasis on temples rather than forts is most striking. Aniba, Faras, Ikkur, and Buhen, for example, were flourishing commercial centers situated where once had been large military garrisons. Semna, Uronarti, Mirgissa, and Shelfak were practically abandoned, like the old army forts in America as the frontier moved westward. Even in Kush, fortifications do not seem to have been very important. This is, of course, in great contrast to the situation in Asia where every town was walled and garrisoned, and raids, campaigns, and battles were all too frequent.

The Gold of Nubia

At Kubban, at the mouth of the Wadi Allaqi, where the road to the gold mines in the Red Sea hills was, there is a stele commemorating the discovery of water in the Wadi. Up till then the desert trip into the Nubian Desert had been most difficult, for water was unobtainable anywhere along the route. The gold miners traveling there frequently died en

* The tombs of these viceroys of Aniba are generally located at Thebes. However, their palaces at this ancient capital of Nubia have so far eluded the archaeologist. Work at Aniba is urgent if they are to be found before it is too late.

route: "It was only half of them that arrived there; for they died of thirst on the road, together with the asses which they drove before them."

In such circumstances, water had to be found if the gold of Nubia was to reach the court. Apparently in consultation with the Viceroy, wells were dug until water was reached—surprisingly, only twenty feet down.[14]

Some authorities who have studied the Egyptian gold mines in Nubia have come to the conclusion that while there was never a great amount of gold available from one mine it was possible, when labor was available, perhaps by importing large numbers of slaves, to draw together the proceeds of many small mines. The gold was not fully processed in the desert, but the crushed ore was returned by donkey caravan to river stations where it was washed and smelted.[15]

Demise of the New Kingdom

The demand for gold, the need for slaves to mine it, the nearly continual war in Asia, the immense wealth of the Temples of Amun, the large number of mercenary troops, the almost independent powers of men like the viceroys of Kush, the gigantic building projects, and finally the endless reign of the aging king boded no good for Egypt's future.

After Ramses' death his son Merneptah ruled for a time and sustained the heritage bequeathed him, but after his death wrangling and power politics ensued: during this time the wealth and military strength of Nubia and Kush were often used to place a man in power. Merneptah-Siptah was one of these men who apparently overthrew the legitimate successor to Merneptah, and appointed a compatriot of his, one Seti, as Viceroy of Nubia so that his throne had a strong prop there. Seti, in turn, later took over the throne as Seti II but he shortly disappeared. Chaos insued, until Setinekht, founder of the Twentieth Dynasty (1200–1085 B.C.) and probably a descendant of the old Ramesside house, smashed rebellion and unified Egypt again. His son Ramses III was the last of the great pharaohs of Egypt's New Kingdom.

Ramses III organized Egypt and the Egyptian army in haste, for outsiders were bent on invading the Nile Valley. The first invaders were a combination of Libyans and Mediterranean seafarers. These Ramses III managed to crush with an army largely made up of mercenaries, though Nubian troops also took part. A few years later these sea people, as well as an enormous horde of nomadic peoples on land, came out of the north to attack Egypt. These people destroyed the old empires, such as the Hittites, and moved on to conquer Egypt's territories in Asia. Ramses attacked both by land and by sea in Syria and smashed his enemies in two massive blows. Another invasion by a new people out of Libya endangered the delta, and Ramses hurled his veteran troops against them and won a great victory. For the rest of his reign, Ramses had won comparative peace. Like Ramses II, the new Ramses created new temples and covered the walls with endless inscriptions recounting his victories. His hard-won wealth was dissipated into the hands of mercenary troops and the vast estates of the temples. It was impossible to create a stronger Egypt by ridding himself of the pressure groups that everywhere claimed their own at the expense of the common good.

An insatiable and insidious priesthood commanding enormous wealth, a foreign army ready to serve the master who paid most liberally, and a personal following of alien slaves whose fidelity likewise depended entirely upon the immediate gain in view,—these were the factors which Ramses III was constantly forced to manipulate and employ, each against the others. Add to these the host of royal relatives and dependents, who were perhaps of all the most dangerous element in the situation, and we shall not wonder at the outcome.[16]

The outcome was conspiracy and revolt. A hareem conspiracy involved even the commander of bowmen in Nubia. The plan was to murder the aging Ramses and seize the throne for one of the sons of one of the hareem ladies. The plot was nipped in the bud and the ensuing trial, of which there is a record, is a shameful affair, with the King being represented by foreigners and with the revelation of many "trusted" officials as traitors. At the end of the trial the last of the great kings of Egypt lived but twenty days more and, wearied, went to his tomb.

What followed was almost a century of power struggle with graft and dishonesty rampant under a group of weak and powerless pharaohs. During this time the Nubian military forces were a factor to offset the power of the High

Priests of Amun. Around 1090 B.C., Herihor, Viceroy of
Nubia, and thus commander of the military forces there,
seized control of Upper Egypt and made himself Vizier
(Prime Minister) and High Priest of Amun. In one swoop
he held both the sacred and the secular power, which eventually made him the first pharaoh of the Twenty-first Dynasty.
But the Egypt he controlled was divided. There was a strong
dynasty at Tanis in Lower Egypt, so that Herihor was certainly not "Ruler of the Two Lands." Shorn of the delta and
of Asia, the rulers of Thebes held only Nubia and Kush,
where much of the older way of life still flourished. A struggle with Tanis under King Nesubanebdad was maintained for
a time by Herihor's son Piankhy. This further weakened
both kingdoms until at last a slow but powerful Libyan invasion brought the final collapse and native Egyptian rule
virtually ended.

One cannot help but feel an element of sadness and dis-
may at the misery in which Egypt's New Kingdom and Empire found their demise. So much of pride and splendor had
marked the great days of the Eighteenth and Nineteenth
Dynasties—truly the first of the imperial splendors of man's
history. Prelude to Alexander, to Augustan Rome, to the
Moghuls, to Napoleon's France, the fabulous material accomplishments of the Thutmosids, the Amenhoteps, and the early
Ramessides dazzled men's eyes and made them think themselves indomitable. It is apparent that in its already two thousand years of civilized existence Egypt had experienced the
full round of historical evolution. The energetic rise from
simple beginnings, the first climax of almost isolated achievement in the Old Kingdom, the initial inability to control the
increasing complexities brought about by augmenting special-
izations and increased material and emotional demands, a
second climax with the rough-and-ready expedient of the
Middle Kingdom, a second failure and a humiliation, at last
a nativistic and infinitely patriotic fervor that seized upon the
technological advances of the time to build a new and greater
climax in which Egyptian civilization became an international
civilization so complex and amorphous that older and native
patterns could not grasp and hold it for long; at last, over-
surfeited and overdemanding, Egypt all but vanished before
others equally grasping. In all this, Nubia and Kush had
specific roles which have been outlined above. It will be
noted that Egypt's fall in each case was not really due to
foreign invasion but to internal collapse. Public labor, wars,

monumental building, welfare plans, religious elaborations, multiplication of laws, increased exploitation of men and resources, compromise governments, and the like all seem to have been mere patchwork that did not cover the ultimate fault—man's inability to understand himself or his society. Again we must admire the Egyptians, who had least reason of all to understand: lying temporarily at the very beginning of man's civilized existence, and yet sustaining themselves as long as they did.

Principal Monarchs of the New Kingdom

NEW KINGDOM, Dynasties XVIII-XX (1580–1085 B.C.)

Dynasty XVIII (1580–1340 B.C.)

Ahmose I	1580–1558 B.C.
Amenhotep I	1557–1530 B.C.
Thutmose I	1530–1515? B.C.
Thutmose II	1515?–1505 B.C.
Hatshepsut	1515?–1484 B.C.
Thutmose III	1504–1450 B.C.
Amenhotep II	1450–1415? B.C.
Thutmose IV	1415?–1405 B.C.
Amenhotep III	1405–1370 B.C.
Amenhotep IV (Akhenaton)	1370–1352 B.C.
Tutankhamun	1349? B.C.

Dynasty XIX (1340?–1200 B.C.)

Haremheb	1340?–1320 B.C.
Ramses I	1320–1318 B.C.
Seti I	1318–1298 B.C.
Ramses II	1298–1232 B.C.
Merneptah	1232–1224 B.C.

Dynasty XX (1200–1085 B.C.)

Setinekht	1200–1198 B.C.
Ramses III	1198–1166 B.C.

The Pharaohs
of Kush

Sudanese Nubia was a meeting ground of civilization. . . . It was the gateway through which objects and ideas passed between the ancient world and Africa, and vice versa. . . . By 1964, when the first stage of construction is scheduled to be completed, over 40 miles of Sudanese territory, will be permanently under water. And these 40 miles are the area with the country's richest store of archaeological remains, containing 47 sites and others likely to be unearthed in the course of prospection.—J. Vercoutter, Director of the Antiquities Service, Republic of the Sudan (*The UNESCO Courier*, February, 1960)

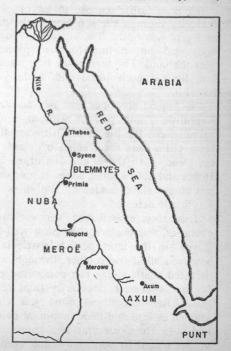

Among the more poignant myths of the past is the Egyptian one that tells of the devotion of Isis, sister and wife of Osiris. Osiris was once an earthly king who brought many useful gifts to man. His brother, Set, jealous of his accomplishments, lured Osiris into a chest. This chest was then thrown into the Nile whose current floated it to the sea. At last the chest was beached at Byblos where through some occurrence it became enclosed in a tree. When the King of Byblos built a palace he used the tree for one of its pillars. The imprisoned Osiris was thus neatly hidden from the world.

Isis, however, was tireless in her search for her husband. She wandered here and there until at last she found the chest. She obtained the position of nurse to the King's children in order to be near. She managed to free the chest from the pillar but her weeping combined with her terrible powers were too much for the royal children and two of them died through contact with her, proving the difficulty of integrating gods and mortals.

Isis bore Osiris' corpse to Egypt, where in the safety of the delta swamps her son Horus, the hawk-headed royal god of Egypt was born. But Set in his vengefulness found Osiris' body and cut in into fourteen pieces which he scattered over the land. The tormented Isis, forced to wander with her son, located each piece and tenderly buried it where she found it.

One legend describes how Isis, assisted by Horus, her sister Nephthys, Thoth god of wisdom, and Anubis god of embalming, put the pieces of Osiris together in the underworld. Here Osiris was resurrected by magic and became Lord of the Dead. Both Osiris and Isis urged Horus to avenge them. Horus and Set fought a series of epic combats in which Horus lost an eye (later healed by Hathor or Isis), and in which Set was finally defeated.

This story, embellished, and variously recounted over the centuries, was probably the most well-known myth in ancient Egypt—in the later periods particularly so. Isis' role as a bereaved all-loving mother, through whose efforts a husband defeated death and a son conquered evil, gradually achieved for her a greater popularity than for almost all the other gods. After the collapse of the New Kingdom Amun went into gradual eclipse and once dominant deities such as Ptah, Aton, and even Horus became less important. In contrast the cult of Isis waxed in popularity. She eventually was accepted by

the Romans as "Queen of Heaven" and temples for her
worship appeared by the Tiber.

Isis was above all a woman, superseding all women. She
was often identified with Nut, the sky-goddess, her own
mother; and with Hathor, cow-goddess of the Nile. She was
"Queen of all Gods, Goddesses and women." She was the
patroness of healing. It is easy to see in her a prototype for
the numerous deities of Europe and the Near East whose
motherly functions and womanly gentilities made them supreme among the divinities. The Isis cult was celebrated at
many temples in Graeco-Roman Egypt. Among these are those
of Dendereh and Edfu (the latter is the best preserved in all
Egypt). But the most celebrated, and justly so, is that of
Philae.

The Temple of Philae

The island of Philae is small, only a little over a quarter of
a mile in length and about 160 yards in width. Set somewhat
back on the east of the First Cataract, the little island, palm
dotted, rich with vegetation, and crowned with beautiful
Ptolemaic and Roman temples, was often known as the
"pearl of Egypt." Now the waters from the Aswan Dam in-
undate the island for a considerable part of the year
(December to August) and when the island is above water it
is barren except for the picturesque ruins. Though the ruins
are of hard stone and therefore remained undamaged by the
inundation, the new High Dam will cause strong currents that
are apt to bring about the collapse of the buildings. A pro-
tective dam, however, would cut the island off from the main
flow of the river in the west. Philae thus rescued from
the flood could rise once more in its own lake and in its
pre-Aswan condition as the "pearl"—if the millions of
dollars necessary to save it are forthcoming.

The temples of Philae are somewhat conventional in the
usual layout of pylon gates, colonnades, courts, and inner
sanctuaries. There are numerous reliefs, graffiti, and the like.
However, there is a lightness and graciousness to the colonnades and to the celebrated kiosk, the latter erected by the
Roman Emperor Trajan, that recalls some of the splendid
architecture of the Temple of Luxor.

Philae has caught the imagination of many travelers. The

mysterious healing rites of the Isis cult gained a magic aura
for the island. Even after the full acceptance of Christianity in the Roman Empire and the abolishment of paganism, the
Isis cult still flourished at Philae. It was not till the reign of
Justinian in the sixth century A.D. that the last chants to Isis
were heard. However, the Copts took over some of the temples
just as at Wadi-es-Sebua and made Christian chapels out of
them so that for a time at least the religious life of the island
was still a reality. But soon all memory of the ancient ceremonies disappeared and when Dominique Vivant Denon, an
officer in the invading Napoleonic army, visited the place he
found only ruins and a village of warlike Moslems. Denon
tried to understand what he saw but came up with questions
only:

> What could be the meaning of this vast number of
> sanctuaries, so contiguous to each other, and yet so
> distinct? Were they consecrated to different divinities,
> were they votive chapels, or places devoted each to
> particular ceremonies of religious worship? The inner-
> most temples contained still more mysterious sanctu-
> aries, such as monolithic temples, or tabernacles of a
> single stone, containing, perhaps, what was most pre-
> cious and most sacred to the worshippers; perhaps even
> the sacred bird, which represented the presiding
> deity of the temple; the hawk, for example, the em-
> blem of the sun, to whom the building might be conse-
> crated. On the ceilings of the same portico were painted
> astronomical pictures, the theories of the elements; on
> the walls, religious ceremonies, images, priests, and
> gods; by the side of the gates gigantic portraits of cer-
> tain sovereigns, or emblematical figures of strength or
> power, threatening a group of suppliant figures, which
> they hold with one hand by the hair of the head. Can
> these be rebellious subjects, or vanquished enemies? [1]

An essential part of Egyptian religion was the sense of
mystery. Whenever Hollywood or the novel writers get
hold of ancient Egypt as subject matter for their dollar mills,
they seem almost invariably to use the old priests as villains.
It is as if the priests really knew the religion was a farce
to be profitably used for one reason or another. While it is
true that certainly in later times aspects of the religion were
used for commercial purposes, much as Christmas is employed in the West, these acts hardly negate the moving and

profound faith possessed by the general populace and their
priestly exponents.

It is particularly the sense that the rebirth of the soul was
a mysterious phenomenon, a phenomenon of which Isis and
Osiris were concrete symbols, that gave the Isis cult much
of its popularity. The isolated temples where priests studied, mediated, and worshiped were worldly manifestations of
an individual's hope for salvation. The once isolated and safe
world of Egypt was in these late periods the pawn of international powers, a prime place of exploitation. The entity
"Egypt" did not evoke to each peasant a vision of an indomitable pharaoh, a wise noble, or a winged sun. Egypt was
more apt to mean a place of misery where taxes and oppression stole away the fruits of a man's work. In the chaos of the
times the great goddess of healing and of salvation acted for
all men who worshiped her. What matter the toil of this world
compared to the bliss to come. Professor Samuel A.B. Mercer
describes this worship in a fine, succinct account:

> The worship of Isis, and communion with her, was
> daily, and began before dawn. On festivals the main
> service took the form of a drama of divine sacrifice, the
> passion of Osiris. Priests carefully trained in mystic the-
> ology, liturgics, and symbolism, accompanied by at-
> tendants, all clad in appropriate vestments, came into
> the presence of the ancient deities, Osiris (and or) Sera-
> pis, Isis, Horus, and others, the faithful being in front of
> the sanctuary. The first great sacred act consisted in the
> exposing to the view of the assembled congregation the
> sacred image of Isis. Before the image libations of holy
> Nile water were poured out, and the faithful were
> sprinkled with it. Then the sacred fire was kindled,
> after which the high priest awakened the goddess in an
> address uttered in the sacred Egyptian language. A
> burnt offering was then presented, accompanied by
> singing and music; and finally the goddess was cere-
> moniously clothed, adorned, and adored. A second
> service took place in the afternoon, which consisted
> chiefly of prayer and meditations before the images and
> symbols of the gods and which closed with music and
> antiphonal singing. A third service, quite brief, ended
> the day. The sanctuary was purified, the statue of Isis
> was disrobed, the curtains of her sanctuary closed, and
> the goddess was left in mystic solitude till the next
> morning. In addition to these three daily services the

devotees spent long hours in the presence of the goddess.

On the two great festivals of autumn and spring, the death and resurrection of Osiris was the central thought, and it was expressed with all the symbolism, mystery, music, singing, ritual, and pageantry, so well-understood by the ancient Egyptians, all of which was calculated to stimulate the deepest religious emotions, and fan the flames of ecstatic joy. The death and resurrection of Osiris, realistically represented, created a situation of intense grief and lamentation, of joy and exultation. Such a festival ended in processions, banquets, and carnivals, which greatly appealed to the popular imagination. The resurrection of Osiris was a guarantee to the hearts of the faithful that they too would rise again to a life of immortal bliss.

To become a devotee in these mysteries, long hours and days of study and meditation had to be spent, in which he was taught to hear and see secret things, before being ready to receive from the high priest the secret and ineffable words of mystic meaning. He was then, after appropriate ablutions and fasting, robed in sacred garments, and thus was prepared for his initiation. In the course of his preparation, the neophyte received a symbolic baptism, the cleansing of his soul; by a symbolic death, the death of his soul into sin; by a symbolic re-birth, the beginning of a higher and purer life; by a symbolic life of darkness in his cell, the illumination of the mind by revealed truth; and by a symbolic transformation into an Osiris or a Re, the sanctification and deification which made him a god indeed.[2]

It is no wonder then that in ancient times men are drawn to Philae. In more recent days the lonely ruined island has provoked the comments of numerous travelers, some of them well worth quoting: Philae has motivated a fine harvest of rich feelings and thoughts from the men and women who have seen her. The name "Philae," by the way, was probably first known to history during the reign of King Nectanebos II (359–341 B.C.), an Egyptian monarch of the short-lived Thirtieth Dynasty which collapsed before Alexander and the Ptolemies. Nectanebos II started construction on Philae and it is to him that the oldest structures there owe their origin.

Denon recorded one of the early modern impressions of Philae:

The mountains, the surface of which is broken by black and ragged projections, are reflected with their gloomy aspect on the clear mirror of the stream below, which is broken and divided by sharp points of granite that roughen its channel, and form long white lines of foam wherever any of these rocks cut its smooth surface. These rough, shapeless masses, with their dark hues, form a striking contrast with the soft green of the groups of palm-trees that cluster around the irregular cliffs, and with the celestial azure of the clearest sky over the face of the earth. A picture faithfully representing these striking objects, would have the rare advantage of exhibiting a true and yet perfectly novel scenery. After passing the cataracts, the rocks grow loftier, and, on their summit, rocks of granite are heaped up, appearing to cluster together, and to hang in equipoise, on purpose to produce the most picturesque effects. Through these rough and rugged forms the eye all at once discovers the magnificent monuments of the island of Philae, which form a brilliant contrast, and one of the most singular surprises that the traveller can meet with. The Nile here makes a bend, as if to come and visit this enchanting island, where the monuments are only separated by tufts of palm-trees, or rocks that appear to be left merely to contrast the forms of nature with the magnificence of art, and to collect, in one rich spot, every thing that is most beautiful and impressive. The enthusiasm which the traveller so constantly experiences at the sight of the monuments of upper Egypt, may appear to the reader a perpetual and monotonous exaggeration; but it is, however, only the simple expression of feeling which the sublimity of their character excites, and it is from the distrust that I feel at being able to give an adequate idea of their magnificence by the pencil, that I have endeavoured to do justice to them by my expressions for the surprise and admiration with which they impress the beholder.[3]

A marvelous, though historically inaccurate, impression was rendered by that exuberant essayist-traveler of the nineteenth century, George William Curtis.

You will be grave at Philae, how serenely sunny so-
ever the day; but with a gravity graver than that of
sentiment; for it is the deadness of the death of the
land that you will feel. The ruins will be, to you, the remains of the golden age of Egypt, for hither came
Thales, Solon, Pythagoras, Herodotus, and Plato, and,
from the teachers of Moses, learned the most mystic
secrets of human thought. It is the faith of Philae that,
developed in a thousand ways, claims our mental allegiance to-day—a faith transcending its teachers, as the
sun the eyes which it enlightens. These wise men
came—the wise men of Greece, whose wisdom was Egyptian; and hither comes the mere American Howadji, and
learns, but with a difference. He feels the greatness of a
race departed. He recognizes that a man only differently
featured from himself, lived and died here two thousand
years ago.

Ptolemy and his Cleopatra walked these terraces;
sought shelter from the same sun, in the shade of these
same columns, dreamed over the calm river, at sunset, by moonlight; drained their diamond-rimmed goblet
of life and love; then, embalmed in sweet spices, were
laid dreamless in beautiful tombs. Remembering these
things, glide gently from Philae, for we shall see it no
more. Slowly, slowly southward loiters the Ibis, and
leaves its columned shores behind. Glide gently from
Philae; but it will not glide from you. Like a queen
crowned in death, among her dead people, it will smile
sadly through your memory forever.[4]

Amelia Edwards, whose spirited account of Abu Simbel
appears in another chapter, also found expression when at
Philae:

The approach by water is quite the most beautiful.
Seen from the level of a small boat, the island, with
its palms, its colonnades, its pylons, seems to rise out of
the river like a mirage. Piled rocks frame it in on either
side, and purple mountains close up the distance. As
the boat glides nearer between glistening bowlders,
those sculptured towers rise higher and ever higher
against the sky. They show no sign of ruin or of age.
All looks solid, stately, perfect. One forgets for the
moment that anything is changed. If a sound of antique chanting were to be borne along the quiet air—
if a procession of white-robed priests bearing aloft the

veiled ark of the god were to come sweeping round between the palms and the pylons—we should not think it strange.

Most travelers land at the end nearest the cataract; so coming up the principal temple from behind and seeing it in reverse order. We, however, bid our Arabs row round to the southern end, where once a stately landing-place with steps down to the river. We skirt the steep banks and pass close under the beautiful little roofless temple commonly known as Pharaoh's bed— that temple which has been so often painted, so often photographed, that every stone of it, and the platform on which it stands, and the tufted palms that cluster round about it, have been since childhood as familiar to our mind's eye as the sphinx or the pyramids. It is larger, but not one jot less beautiful than we had expected. And it is exactly like the photographs. Still, one is conscious of perceiving a shade of difference too subtle for analysis; like the difference between a familiar face and the reflection of it in a looking-glass. Anyhow, one feels that the real Pharaoh's bed will henceforth displace the photographs in that obscure mental pigeon-hole where till now one has been wont to store the well-known image; and that even the photographs have undergone some kind of change.

And now the corner is rounded; and the river widens away southward between mountains and palm-groves; and the prow touches the debris of a ruined quay. The bank is steep here. We climb, and a wonderful scene opens before our eyes. We are standing at the lower end of a court-yard leading up to the propylons of the great temple. The court-yard is irregular in shape and inclosed on either side by covered colonnades. The colonnades are of unequal lengths and set at different angles. One is simply a covered walk; the other opens up a row of small chambers, like a monastic cloister opening upon a row of cells. The roofing stones of these colonnades are in part displaced, while here and there a pillar or a capital is missing; but the twin towers of the propylon, standing out in sharp, unbroken lines against the sky and covered with colossal sculptures, are as perfect, or very nearly perfect, as in the days of the Ptolemies who built them.[5]

The Holy Island—beautiful, lifeless, a thing of the far past, with all its wealth of sculpture, paintings, history, poetry, tradition—sleeps, or seems to sleep, in the midst.

It is one of the world's famous landscapes, and it deserves its fame. Every sketcher sketches it; every traveler describes it. Yet it is just one of those places of which the objective and subjective features are so equally balanced that it bears putting neither into words nor colors. The sketcher must perforce leave out the atmosphere of association which informs his subject; and the writer's description is at best no better than a catalogue raisonné.[6]

James Henry Breasted, first ranking among American Egyptologists of the past years, wrote an interesting commentary on Philae for a stereoscope tour at the time when the Aswan Dam construction was threatening the island:

Words add little if anything to the impression left by this lovely spot. Set like a peerless gem among the wild, desolate rocks of the cataract, still softened and enriched by the swaying palms, in which every Egyptian temple should be framed, this temple and its island have preserved and still awaken more of the romance of the Nile than any other spot in Egypt. And yet as we shall see it is condemned to certain destruction.

Look long and well at this island and its temple, for it conveys a more adequate impression of how an Egyptian temple actually appeared in the days of the Pharaohs than any surviving building on the Nile.

When the addition to the dam, a contemplated increase in the height, is completed, the temples will be largely submerged. It is, therefore, only a matter of a comparatively short time, when this lovely spot will have become a mud-covered, desolate waste, with the ruins of its once picturesque temples, rising in shapeless heaps, and eventually disappearing. When this project was first suggested, it roused the indignation of the whole cultured world, and in the face of universal protests the government constrained the engineers to alter their plans so as not to totally submerge the temples. But the changes were not sufficient to save the buildings, as the engineers probably very well knew, but they pacified the public; and when we shall have grown accustomed to the pending destruction, the dam will be raised and the work of annihilation will be complete. Undoubtedly the work is a necessity, but it will not be a pleasant item for the future Englishman to read in his guide-book, that the great dam at this point, while insuring the payment of all interest on Egyptian bonds, resulted in the destruction of the temples on Philae.[7]

Lovely as Philae is, there is a sadness in its delicacy, for it represents the ultimate rays of an architectural sun that had shone with great brightness for over two millennia. Passing strange but natural to the course of human development, it was the Romans who motivated and for a time sustained the last gasp of a native tradition. The Romans had borrowed many of their architectural forms from the Greeks who in turn had learned much from Egypt, especially in those centuries after Ramses III and the Homeric Age. But in Egypt, as one clearly understands upon viewing the monuments, the Romans and their predecessors the Ptolemaic Greeks built in almost purely Egyptian style. The colonnaded courts, the pylon gates, the succession of halls and antechambers terminating in inner sanctuaries are purely Egyptian, as are the lotus capitals and the teeming but formal reliefs that bedeck almost every wall. But—and strangely perhaps, in view of what we know of Graeco-Roman accomplishments in art—one becomes conscious of a stiffness in style which is un-Egyptian. There are just too many upright figures of gods and kings standing in rows. The iconography seems lifeless. Horus' wings do not soar, the "ankh" symbol of life-giving lacks vibrance, and even Isis, so often the patroness of the temple, seems to be neither a deity whose presence astounds and awes nor a woman whose real femininity lies in an inner quality to which the physical form gives bare outline.

Kalabsha, one of the best preserved temples of this period, was built about the time of Christ in the reign of the Emperor Augustus. Like Philae the buildings have been inundated for part of the year by the flood rise caused by the Aswan Dam. Salvation depends on whether money will be forthcoming to take it down stone for stone and to re-erect it in another safer place. As the largest free-standing temple south of Philae, the removal of Kalabsha will be difficult but amply feasible—and essential.

Among the more interesting features of Kalabsha may be mentioned a Greek inscription of the third century A.D. when, presumably, temple attendance was at its flourishing maximum. The inscription warns all pig owners to keep their animals out of the holy place!

Other Ptolemaic or Graeco-Roman temples exist in Nubia, many of which were later used as Christian churches. Among these buildings are the Ptolemaic kiosk at Kertassi and the temples at Debod, Dendur, and Dakka—the later dedicated to the ibis-headed god Thoth, the great recorder. Some of these buildings were begun in pre-Ptolemaic times, but their enlargement was later. In most cases it would appear that there may have been early shrines already located at these sites—some at least dating back to New Kingdom times. It is of interest that in these later temples the imperial god Amun barely appears, whereas the more universal deities of Egypt, Isis, Hathor, Horus, Osiris, and Thoth, continually reoccur in settings of considerable splendor. This is a mark of the innate conservatism which made Nubia one of the last strongholds of the old faith. Romans stationed in this far southern frontier of the empire probably saw more of the culture of Old Egypt than did those Romans who visited the centers in Lower Egypt. In the north the rise of Greek, Latin, and Aramaic as lingua franca, and the full establishment of associated alphabetic writings, gradually confined hieroglyphic and its more cursive form, hieratic, to religious activities. Even demotic, the characteristic cursive method of writing Egyptian in Graeco-Roman times, fell into disuse. The basic cause of this decline in the use of Egyptian writings was, of course, the increased employment of Greek-speaking officials in all the important posts. However, in Nubia there is every indication that the old writing forms continued long after their eventual total eclipse in most of Egypt. It is of interest that the irrepressible Giovanni Belzoni found two small obelisks on the island of Philae and after a host of difficulties managed to ship them to England where they graced a fine estate in Dorset. The obelisks were Ptolemaic in time and on one of them the name Cleopatra was inscribed both in hieroglyphics and in Greek. Because of this dual writing a Mr. W. J. Banks was able to translate her name from hieroglyphics some six years before Champollion produced his famous translation of the Rosetta Stone.

If Philae and Kalabsha stand at one end of the span of Egypt's architectural triumph, Saqqara and Giza stand at the other. But these monuments also symbolize other things; for it is obvious that the remote and epic qualities of the classic pyramid cities of the Old Kingdom are at once symbolic of

Egypt's isolation and of her attainment of a civilization where there were answers to almost all questions. How different are the Graeco-Roman temples with their busy formality and the clear indications of dying tradition. One can feel the hypocrisy of eulogizing a Greek Ptolemy or a Roman emperor with all the divine attributes of a classic pharaoh. How empty the titles: "Son of Re," "Avenging Horus," "Beloved of Isis," for a Ptolemaic house that was all too frequently immersed in foulest intrigue during which the fate of the Egyptians was nothing compared to personal gratification. In that international world there were many questions and few answers. Accordingly men buried themselves in practices, religious and otherwise, at which the priests of the Old Kingdom would have shuddered.

The known world had gone international indeed. Civilization had spread from its places of origin and moved east and west, both as a body of copyable invention and as a motivating wind of ideas. No longer were Egyptians seeking resources beyond the bounds of their land. Matters were reversed. Instead, men and nations were seeking after Egypt. In both the Achaemenid and Roman Empires, Egypt was a source of good food supply and luxuries. Corn ships from Egypt landed at Ostia and their arrival was a matter of considerable profit to Roman businessmen. Egypt, as the gateway to Africa, helped make accessible the elephants, lions, and giraffes with which to enliven imperial circuses; and the ivory, fragrant woods, slaves—probably including dwarfs—no longer stopped at Thebes and Memphis but were moved far off to Susa, Persepolis, or Rome.

Details of the fundamental change that finally brought Egypt and its Nubia from the status of a first-class power to almost nonentity are lacking in the historical record. This is, in a way, fortunate; for their sum total reflects a multitude of failures, partial successes, betrayals, ambitions, and disunities painful to the imagination.

Kushites and Egypt

Napata in the area of the Fourth Cataract is at the northern terminus of an overland route from Merowe via the Jakdul Well. Merowe is located below the Sixth Cataract about midway between the mouth of the Atbara on the north and the

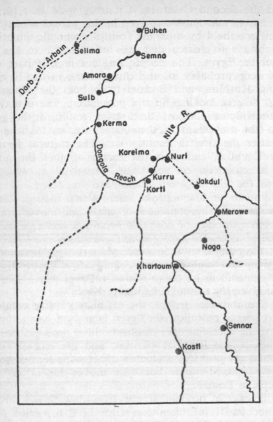

modern town of Shendi on the south. The Jakdul route by-passes the difficult river barrier at the Fifth Cataract as well as saving a considerable distance which one would have to travel following the river route.

The Napata area is also on the upstream end of the Dongola Reach, probably the most fertile stretch of the Northern Sudan. It is then an area of more than a little importance. With the collapse of the Egyptian empire many Egyptians found refuge in Nubia and Kush, the priests of Amun especially flocking to the sanctuary of Amun at Jebel Barkal.

During the Twenty-second Dynasty (950–730 B.C.) Libyan control under the Sheshonks and Osorkons probably reached into Lower Nubia, but it does not appear to have gone beyond the Second Cataract, if it truly went that far. Both Upper Nubia and Kush achieved in this period an autonomy which was upheld by both the fruitful economic situation on the highways to Africa and the isolation far to the south of troubled Egypt. The people resident in this part of the Sudan were probably most heterogeneous, with Egyptians, Nubians, Kushites, and Bedawi from both the eastern and western deserts making up the population. There may even have been some Libyans there as a result of the general west-to-east movement of these tribes known to have taken place after the twelfth century B.C. The cultural form was largely Egyptian and it is not surprising that the gods of Egypt were worshiped and their hieroglyphics used rather generally.

Initially there may have been some local autonomy, but the rulers of the Napata area gradually unified the whole region from the Second Cataract to as far south as the Fifth Cataract, where the vast grasslands began—probably the *raison d'être* for the cattle wealth of a truly African realm. Merowe in this southern area was a kind of second capital ruled by members of the Napatan royal family. The whole realm is given the name "Kingdom of Kush."

The fine Sudanese troops, the excellent cavalry created by hard experience patrolling the desert bounds of Kush, the deep economic resources of the kingdom, and a continual pressure from the numerous Egyptian elements resident made an attempt to conquer Egypt a persistent aim of the Kushite rulers—most of whose names have been lost. However, Kashta, who reigned just before 751 B.C., actually invaded and succeeded in holding Upper Egypt, driving the Libyan king, Osorkon III, into the delta.

Piankhy (751–716 B.C.), Kashta's son, was even more successful carrying the war into the delta, where he broke up the various coalitions against him and received the submission of each prince. Memphis was carried by assault and Piankhy could return to Napata as the "Beloved of Amun," "Lord of the Two Lands." He created a marvelous stele in the temple at Jebel Barkal which records his campaigns. Horses were so much a part of Kushite life that favorite steeds were frequently accorded regal burial in the cemeteries of Napata. This mobile arm of the military gives reason for the swiftness of the Kushite campaigns. Piankhy was a great lover of horses and on his stele he recorded his indignation when he visited the stables of Nimrod, Prince of Hermopolis. When he saw that they suffered hunger, he said: "I swear as Re loves me . . . it is more grievous in my heart that these horses have suffered hunger than any evil deed that you have done in the pursuit of your ambitions."

As a part of Piankhy's celebration of the conquest of Egypt he rebuilt the Jebel Barkal temple, and perhaps because there were so few artists capable of catching the old spirit in stone, he took the fine ram sculptures from the causeway before the Sulb (Soleb) temple of Amenhotep III and set them up at Jebel Barkal.

Shabaka, Piankhy's brother, ascended to the throne as a result of a peculiar Kushite system of succession in which the brothers of the king have priority over the sons. He promptly moved his capital to Thebes. One wonders what rejoicing there must have been that in this sense at least, the active vigorous pharaohs who had brought glory to Egypt were resurrected in the person of these almost completely Egyptianized Sudanese monarchs. Shabaka was not lacking in the requisite energies to crush rebelliousness wherever it appeared. Both Shabataka (Shebitku) and his younger brother Taharqa, who succeeded Shabaka on the throne in the following reigns, were active in restoring temples in Egypt and Nubia and even undertaking the building of new ones; and they appear to have brought about a considerable unity in the "Two Lands." Taharqa held his coronation at Memphis, an indication of just how hard these Kushite monarchs strove to resurrect the older Egyptian traditions. Taharqa, who was a powerful, energetic individual, recorded that in the year of his coronation there were exceptionally heavy rains in the Sudan and an extraordinary rise of the Nile flood—an event received as a symbol that the new reign would be a fortunate one. Unfortunately, it was not.

The Assyrian Foe

Among the peoples of ancient times the Assyrians hold the reputation for being the most militaristic and the most ruthless. This is probably an exaggeration, but in a world where war raged incessantly and subjugation was the lot of the weak, the Assyrians created the means of successful survival—for which we can hardly blame them. Certain it was that the land of Assyria, situated along the Upper Tigris River valley, was vulnerable to foreign invasion from many sides. The sturdy Assyrian peasantry were used to plowing while fully armed. Their techniques of agriculture may have been very ancient, going back to the Sumerians, but their war-like arts were far advanced, learned through bitter experience as new ideas and techniques were brought to them on the wings of savage invasion. Among the things learned by the Assyrians was the manufacture of weapons and scale armor in iron. In a bronze-using age the general employment of iron for warfare gave the Assyrians an enormous advantage. This advantage was enhanced by the creation of a superb military organization. Siege engineers, transport, and ordnance units were regular parts of the army on the move; an army which had its divisions with battalions of light and heavy infantry, bowmen, and spearmen. There was a heavy and light cavalry as well as units of chariotry which by sheer weight and speed resembled a modern armored outfit. Ultimate command was in the hands of the monarch but he seems to have been solidly backed by fine officers. The Assyrian soldier is depicted in the reliefs as a swarthy, muscular fellow, well armored, physically tough, and accustomed to obey.

The Assyrian army was so well organized, so experienced in all-out warfare, and so superior in equipment that the Assyrians were not only able to defend themselves but were able to conquer large areas of Western Asia. The Assyrians ruled foreign lands through the local monarch, who was made loyal by hostages and the presence of an Assyrian garrison. However, many of these rulers continued to plot against the Assyrians, thus forcing them into the almost continual necessity of being on the march to put down rebellion. Particularly noteworthy were the alliances made in Syria and Palestine between princes subject to the Assyrians and those still independent. In these actions against Assyria both Judah and Israel had a part.

The Kushite rulers of Egypt meddled in Syro-Palestinian affairs and, probably because of the ancient respect in which Egypt was held, were able to foment considerable trouble for Assyria. When Sennacherib (704–681 B.C.) fought Hezekiah of Judah and his allies in 701 B.C., there were considerable forces of Egyptian military in the Palestinian armies. The reasons for this involvement of the Kushites in Palestine are not clear. Some authorities are of the opinion that the Kushites were aware of the direct menace to Egypt that the Assyrians constituted and wished to set up buffer states. This hardly seems likely in view of the success of Kushite arms everywhere and the sense of great strength given by the truly vast territories they controlled. It would appear rather that the Kushites were not content with Egyptian conquests, but as pharoahs resurrected, they envisioned a recapture of the Asiatic possessions held during the New Kingdom. Taharqa, as crown prince, appears to have been in the Kushite army which went to the assistance of Hezekiah against Sennacherib. This was, of course, during the reign of his elder brother Shabataka. However, plague struck the Assyrian armies, probably before the walls of Jerusalem, and they were compelled to retire from Palestine before a battle between the two forces could occur.

Taharqa seems to have been made bolder by the retreat of the Assyrians and when he became sole ruler he set up his residence at Tanis in the delta in order to make it easier to carry out his Asian plots. He managed to get both Sidon and Tyre in Phoenicia to revolt. This was too much for Esarhaddon, successor to Sennacherib, and before Egypt

ASSYRIAN SOLDIER

could come to help either city he smashed the revolts. Then with great rapidity the Assyrian forces moved toward Egypt itself. The first barrier was the Sinai Desert. But this Esarhaddon crossed with the aid of camels which by now were probably becoming a conventional beast of burden as well as a cavalry mount.

Taharqa led his forces to meet Esarhaddon on the frontier at the edge of the eastern delta. His army seems to have been composed of a solid nucleus of Sudanese troops but its bulk was made up of the local militia of the various princes of the delta, who, though conquered by the Kushites, still retained a degree of autonomy. We have no details of this vital battle. Apparently the Assyrian army was too powerful for the rather heterogeneous Kushite forces. Taharqa was forced to retire rapidly to his citadel at Memphis. This may indicate that the delta princes deserted him. Left to their own devices each eagerly submitted to the Assyrians. Esarhaddon crossed to Memphis in fifteen days—a clue to the total defeat of the Egyptians. The walls of Memphis were unable to resist the siege-wise Assyrians and Memphis readily fell to their assault. Taharqa fought his way out and escaped into Upper Egypt, even though his son was captured by Esarhaddon. That monarch was apparently not ready to pursue him very far to the south, and after taking the submission of the Egyptian princes of the delta and some of Middle Egypt, he returned to Asia. In Northern Syria he set up a stele at Senjirli with an inscription recording his successful conquest of Egypt. At the top of the stele Esarhaddon holds ropes which pass through the lips of the shackled figures of Taharqa and Ba'al of Tyre.

> I slew multitudes of his men and him I smote five times with the point of my javelin. . . . Memphis, his royal city, in half a day, with armies, tunnels, assaults, I besieged, I captured, I destroyed, I devastated, I burned with fire. His queen, his harem, Esanhuret, his heir, and the rest of his sons and daughters, his property and his goods, his horses, his cattle, his sheep, in countless numbers, I carried off to Assyria. The root of Kush I tore up out of Egypt and not one therein escaped to submit to me.[8]

Taharqa had escaped, however. The Kushite forces were apparently intact and ample reinforcements available out of Africa. In less than a year Taharqa retook Memphis, drove the

Assyrians out of the delta, and received again the allegiances of the petty delta princes, who by now probably saw advantages under Kush that they had not received under Assyria.

Esarhaddon was furious at the speedy overthrow of his control in Egypt and was goaded by evidence that Taharqa was again plotting with Tyre. Perhaps apoplexy set in: in any case he died en route for Egypt. His son, Ashurbanipal, was left to continue the campaign—which he did with a vengeance. Again Taharqa attempted to stop the Assyrian forces at the delta but was badly defeated. It is more than likely that his Egyptian allies, weak in their allegiance at best and unable to work with him as a unit, deserted at a critical time. Shame to relate, when Memphis fell again and Ashurbanipal's troops marched south toward Thebes, they were accompanied by levies sent by Taharqa's former allies—the Egyptian princes of the delta. The duplicity of the time is amply illustrated by the fact that as soon as they were able, some of these very same princes were writing Taharqa to help them overthrow the Assyrians once more!

Taharqa, safe in his control of Kush, may have sought ways of creating an army better able to deal with the Assyrians. At Merowe, iron ore was available and since it was generally lacking both in Egypt and Nubia, Taharqa may have encouraged the full development of an iron industry there.[9] He also tried to secure the allegiance of some of the princes of Lower Egypt but seems to have been frustrated in this by Ashurbanipal. Taharqa died, probably worn out by his exertions, and Tanutemun (Tanwetamani) his nephew, son of Shabataka, succeeded. This king was the last of the great Kushite monarchs, even though the line was to continue to rule Kush for centuries to come. Tanutemun had a dream in which he saw a vision of two upright snakes, one on his right and the other on his left. The interpretation was obviously that Tanutemun would reconquer both the lands of Egypt. Dauntless, strengthened by Taharqa's bitter experiences with the Assyrians, Tanutemun marched north with a well-trained and -equipped army. All went well until at Memphis he was forced to do battle with an Assyrian force backed by the soldiers of some of the delta princes, who feared Assyrian recriminations otherwise. The Kushites successfully assaulted the old city and Tanutemun entered in triumph. However, when he tried to get the delta princes to acknowledge his sovereignty few indeed came to him. They seemed to have learned a lesson.

Ashurbanipal returned as angrily as his father before him. Tanutemun could not hold Memphis but retreated to Thebes where Mentuemhat, Prince of Thebes, was an old ally. The Assyrians, probably convinced that the fall of Thebes would be the ultimate lesson necessary to secure the pacification of Egypt, drove south and Thebes fell in an agony of massacre and looting. So deep an impression was made by the collapse of the old imperial capital "of a hundred gates" that the Hebrew prophet Nahum could compare the fate of Thebes with that destined for Nineveh.

Art thou better than populous Thebes (No) that was situate among the canals. . . . Egypt and Kush were her strength and it was infinite. . . . Yet was she carried away, she went into captivity: her young children also were dashed in pieces at the top of all the streets: and they cast lots for her honourable men, and all her great men were bound in chains.[10]

Tanutemun retreated into Kush. More than likely his Sudanese army had been thoroughly beaten and only the distance and the difficulties attendant on pursuing them into the desert and cataract regions of Nubia prevented an Assyrian advance into Africa. The Kushite rule in Egypt was effectively ended. Even when the Assyrians were involved in a terrible struggle for survival a few decades later the Kushites were generally unable or unwilling to return even to Upper Egypt, which now acknowledged the Saite princes of the delta as the legitimate rulers of Egypt. Yet at Napata and Merowe the Kushite monarchs still called themselves rulers of the "Two Lands," by now an empty title.

These Kushite monarchs together made up Egypt's Twenty-fifth Dynasty. Though they made every effort to demonstrate their "Egyptianness" it appears that they were still more loyal to their Sudanese home. The Napata area with its sacred and historic allusions provided a focus for their home-love. In full cognizance of their Egyptian affinities, the kings of Kush created royal tombs at Kurru in Napata.

I. E. S. Edwards, eminent British Egyptologist, has suggested that when Piankhy saw the pyramids at Giza and Saqqara he abandoned the Napata custom of erecting mastaba tombs and built a pyramid tomb.[11] This began a kingly and queenly custom practiced from then on in the centuries at Kurru and Nuri in Napata, and later at Merowe. Much of the evidence we have on the Kushite rule derives from the excavations carried on by Reisner at Kurru, Nuri, and Merowe.[12] There, pyramid tombs consist of a burial chamber or chambers lying in the bedrock which are reached by a stairway and tunnel. Above the tunnel is a chapel for the dead located on one side of a large pyramid which is directly over the burial chambers. Subsidiary graves of followers, relatives, and even horses occur in the cemetery. It was customary to bury the servants of the king with him in his tomb, perhaps in the same tradition as at Kerma in Middle Kingdom times.

A number of travelers visiting these "Ethiopian" pyramid fields have come away impressed with the ruins. But they are really rather pathetic vestiges of an old Egyptian tradition—made more so by their present ruined condition.

The loss of Egypt did not mean that the Kingdom of Kush collapsed. Quite the contrary, it had the effect of turning Kushite interest to the south. It is no coincidence that as time went on Merowe became a more important place than Napata.*

It is possible that Kushite longing for Egypt may have led to one last attempt to cross below the First Cataract. Details of this are obscure, but the Egyptians of the then reigning Saite Dynasty (the Twenty-sixth) were utilizing Greek mercenaries in their army by now (ca. 600 B.C.) and King Psammetichos II, even though threatened on the north by Babylonian armies, was able to smash the threat to his southern frontier most expeditiously. Some record of this counterattack is written at Abu Simbel (see page 149). This Greek force may have reached Napata—in any case the blow to Kushite ambitions was a severe one.[13]

Sometime after that date the center of Kushite power was shifted to Merowe and the Napatan kingdom was ruled from two centers, with the northern area gradually diminishing in importance. The kings were still buried in the Napata region (Nuri) until 308 B.C.—a proof, probably, of the holy regard with which that region was held.

The years after the fall of Assyria saw the centers of civilization shift from the Near East to Europe. The rise of Achaemenian Persia under Cyrus after 532 B.C. brought the known Orient from the borders of India to the Libyan

* There is a "Merowe" at Napata which is not the more celebrated Merowe, capital of later Kushite kingdoms.

Desert under a single rule. It was the vastest empire yet. The Achaemenids were content to restrict their possessions along the Nile to Lower Nubia, though Herodotus records an expedition to "Ethiopia" made by Cambyses. But no evidence for this expedition has yet been found.*

The wars with the Greeks occurred during the early years of the Achaemenid Empire (494–479 B.C.) and the vigorous, successful defense of Marathon, Salamis, and Platea were indicative of the ascendance of new forces in the world. Kush, however, with all the vastness of Africa accessible to it, was content simply to maintain the older Egyptian traditions. It does not even appear that the Nubian boundary on the north was a very definite one. The impression is that contact with Persian Egypt was slight and that there may very well have been other peoples intervening. These people were probably the Beja, whose homeland on the barren east had never been seriously challenged. The Kushites had to be constantly alert to their raids and the few inscriptions of the period extant record expeditions to put the Beja down.

The impression of growing weakness pervades the evidence from these times. One might wonder why it was that Kush decayed, except that ancient Egypt, which for so long had supplied a kind of cultural lifeblood, was also dying. There was no African culture at hand which by its cultural advantages might infuse a new life. Africa had accepted an older Egypt and there it stood conservatively wavering between a civilized tradition and an aboriginal way of life. Conceivably, if the Greeks had revived Egypt with a Western dynamism Kush might have revived formidably, but no such resurrection came about and the old ways staggered on, including the worship of Amun by the "Lord of the Two Lands."

Dating the Rulers of Kush

For scholars, archaeological evidence from Kush has left a tangible record that has enabled them to fill what otherwise might have been a chronological blank of many cen-

---

* Older writers on Nubia and Kush have frequently used the term "Ethiopia." This term was rarely used in ancient times and in view of the modern designation of the Abyssinian area it has generally fallen out of usage.

turies. It has been noted above that the kings of Kush were buried in pyramid tombs in the Napata region. Obviously, if one could determine the order in which these pyramids and supplementary tombs were built there, a relative chronological scheme could be worked out. The name of the monarch buried is usually to be found somewhere about his tomb, so that a list of kings could be made. G. A. Reisner gave each pyramid he found at Nuri, the royal cemetery, a number for purposes of identification. He began a systematic excavation of each tomb only to discover that they all had been looted by robbers, probably shortly after the cemetery was no longer used by the monarchy—a further indication of failing strength. However, enough remained in most of the tombs and foundation deposits to identify the original inhabitants. Thus Reisner identified the pyramids to which a monarch belonged and at the same time procured a collection of objects belonging to each pyramid, but he did not have any chronological order for his material. In an extraordinarily perceptive manner he came up with a chronological list that forms the backbone of these studies today.

Reisner noted that each pyramid represented in its contents "the work of the best craftsmen of that generation." Accordingly, since this work began in the period of Taharqa (Twenty-fifth Dynasty), each pyramid tomb collection represented both an older tradition and the influence of new ideas, styles, and methods. A craftsman might carry his work through several kings' reigns, but there would always have to be new artists as life wore on. Thus each tomb collection was a "unique group" possessing examples of the past generation as well as the new. By identifying each group, the connection to the groups which fitted just previously was obvious. Thus the relative order of the groups could be determined.[14]

The Seriation Method Used by Reisner on the Napata Tombs

Each letter stands for the style of any given cultural trait or body of traits.

Earliest Pyramid Tomb	(1) A A A A A
	(2) A A A B B
Intermediate	(3) A A B B C
	(4) A B C C D
	(5) C C D D E
Latest Pyramid Tomb	(6) C D E E F

Reisner supplemented this evidence with a study of the geographical position of the pyramids, where because of the limitations of the ground at Nuri the best sites were chosen earlier; he examined changes in the kind of construction and forms, and finally, what inscriptional evidence there was available. The result is the chronological listing of Kushite kings ranging from Taharqa (sixth century B.C.) to Nastasen (fourth century B.C.).[15]

The Early Kushite Rulers

	APPROXIMATE DATE
Analma'aye	538–533 B.C.
Amani-natake-lebte	533–513
Karkamani	513–503
Amani-astabarqa	503–478
Si'aspiqa	478–458
Nasakhma	458–453
Malewiebamani	453–423
Talakhamani	423–418
Aman-nete-yerike	418–398
Baskakeren	398–397
Harsiotef	397–362
———	362–342
Akhratan	342–328
Nastasen	328–308

During this lengthy period the administrative capital of Kush was shifted to Merowe. Arkell suggests that overgrazing of the area around the Dongola Reach must have played an important part in bringing about this shift.[16] Merowe was of course a prominent town before this shift but under its new status the place flourished as never before. Remarkable among the buildings were a fine temple of Amun and a Sun Temple—the latter remarked by Herodotus though he certainly had not seen it.

> . . . to Ethiopia he [Cambyses] decided first to send spies, ostensibly with presents to the king, but actually to collect what information they could; in particular he wanted them to find out if the so-called Table of the Sun really existed. This Table of the Sun is said to be a meadow, situated in the outskirts of the city, where a plentiful supply of boiled meat of all kinds is kept; it is the duty of the magistrates to put the meat there at

night, and during the day anybody who wishes may
come and eat it. Local legend has it that the meat appears spontaneously and is the gift of the earth.[17]

The actual temple was a great brick platform (the Table?)
on which was a sanctuary made of stone. One ascended stairs
of dark sandstone into a chamber with walls of sky-blue
tiles; on the west wall was the sun disk in all its glory; all
about the entrance to the shrine were hieroglyphic writings
in Meroitic which commemorate some Kushite victory.[18]

Again Reisner, utilizing the same techniques as at Nuri,
managed to compile a chronological list of the royal monarchs whose pyramid tombs were found in the cemeteries
at Merowe. This covers the years from about 308 B.C. to
A.D. 355—certainly a significant period in the history of the
world. Alexander's legacy after his conquest of the Persians
was the teeming world of Hellenistic science, philosophy, and
religion. It was also a politically unstable world that struggled with the growing demands of an industrial revolution
which standardization, effective transport and communication, advancing technology, and abundant slave and animal
energy was creating. The Ptolemies were instigators of much
of this activity and it would appear that some of the benefits
of new Graeco-Egyptian prosperity accrued to Meroitic Kush.
The resources of iron there, the access to the grasslands of
the south, and, of course, the natural resources of Africa
generally, made possible some revival. The Kushite borders
were pushed northward and it even appears that there was a
conflict in Nubia between Ergamenes of Kush (225–200 B.C.),
a patron of Philae, and Ptolemy V. However, this surge to the
north was short-lived and the Kushites retired beyond the
Second Cataract.

Roman Times

The control of Nubia in those days was apparently always
uncertain. For Ptolemies and Romans the maintenance of garrisons in the stretch between Aswan and the Second Cataract,
in the same fashion as the Middle Kingdom pharaohs, was
fraught with difficulties. Beja, now probably called Blemmyes, on the east, and the Kushites to the south had bases
too distant for effective retaliatory raids. The rise of Roman

power in Egypt was a matter of no little concern to the Kushites, however. Probably with the collapse of Ptolemaic rule the Meroitic rulers had seen it expedient to seize and hold strongpoints in Nubia, among these Kasr Ibrim, a high fortified post then known as Premnis. Emboldened perhaps by alliances with the Beja, by their cushion of distance, and by the fact that Roman garrisons in Egypt had been weakened generally in order to provide reinforcements elsewhere, the Kushites or Kushite enlisted forces attacked Elephantine, wrecking Roman monuments at Philae. They even carried off bronze statues of Caesar Augustus to Merowe.

A Roman army under Petronius crushed the Kushite forces in Nubia, fortified Kasr Ibrim, and with that vaunted Roman expedition moved to Napata where in a vengeful orgy he destroyed the town and the great temple of Amun at Jebel Barkal (23 B.C.). Petronius brushed aside the Meroitic queen's pleas in the process, and left a wake of destruction from the Second Cataract to the Fourth.* The Romans then withdrew to Nubia, making Kasr Ibrim the frontier marker. The Romans were not quite finished with Kush, however, for some decades later Nero sent an expedition led by two centurions deep into the Sudan to see if there was anything there of interest to Rome. Fortunately for Kush the centurions reported in the negative—probably because they had been forced to travel over the desert tracks far to the east and west outside of Meroitic control of the Nile.

In spite of the disaster to Merowe's northern territories some restoration at Napata was carried on by King Natakamani and his queen, successors to "Candace." Merowe, which of course had escaped the Romans, was apparently a very flourishing city at this time, possibly because of contact overland with the Red Sea trade. In those days the Romans were able to acquire trade goods from India via both the Persian Gulf and Red Sea routes. In recent years archaeological research has evidence that Roman trading posts were established on the Bay of Bengal. Quite possibly as far east as Burma and Thailand Roman-motivated merchants sought raw materials for Mediterranean markets. Arkell has pointed up a number of Indian traits appearing in Merowe about this time, especially at the temple of Naga, where

---

* Queens were called "Candace" in Kush, which gave rise to the title being used as a proper name for the Queen (Amanishakhete) who fought the Romans.

Egyptian artisans imported for the purpose erected a Meroitic temple to Amun. Among these traits in Merowe are multi-faced deities, elephant riding, and the use of tanks for water storage.[19] Control of the Red Sea ports was certainly not in the hands of the Meroitic kings, however. Both Nabateans in Arabia and Ethiopians of the growing kingdom of Axum to the southeast were powerful groups whose geographic and political position enabled them to tap the lucrative eastern trade.

The Lower Nubian area was generally known by the term Dodeka-schoinos. In Roman times the interest in holding the area appears to have been primarily the need to protect Upper Egypt from raids. As in Old Kingdom times Elephantine (Aswan) was really the true frontier for the Romans. There do not seem to have been any caravans coming from the south laden with ivory and dwarfs as there had been when Pepi II had reigned. Presumably that African luxury trade had shifted westward where Roman control of North Africa was firm and the caravan routes across the Sahara actively employed. Axum also flourished on a trade from Central Africa to the Red Sea, from whence African articles were sent to the Mediterranean. Merowe, Axum, the Beja (Blemmyes), and a new people, the Nobatae who may have come from the west, were all barriers too high for any mercantile advantages to the Romans. In fact, both the Blemmyes and the Nobatae appear in the third century A.D. to have seized control of the Dodeka-schoinos even though the Emperor Diocletian is stated to have voluntarily withdrawn the Roman frontier to Aswan (Syene).

Merowe, completely cut off from Egypt and increasingly so from Africa (probably by the Nobatae and almost certainly by the Axumites), completely collapsed and its royal remnants retreated westward into Kordofan and Darfur where tantalizing traditions among the living people tell of their final refuge.

Christian Nubia

Christianity rapidly infiltrated Egypt in the year during and after the fourth century. Ethiopia was converted around 350 A.D. Nubia, on the other hand, was slow to accept the new faith. This was in part due to the nomadic character of the population of Nobatae and Blemmyes (Beja) and as at Philae the fact that the land was the last refuge of the old pagan cults. The Nobatae, in fact, may have adopted some of the old customs. A number of tombs have been opened at Ballana and Qustal near Abu Simbel that belong to a group called the "X" group by archaeologists.[20] These "X" people, who may be the Nobatae, accepted much of Meroitic material culture, their tombs being decorated with Kushite-Egyptian designs. Human sacrifice was practiced in order to provide retinues for the royal dead. The quantity of Late Roman or Byzantine objects found in the tombs suggests that the influence of the Mediterranean world was waxing.

Mound graves like those of the "X" group in Nubia occur in great number in the Meroitic area as far south as Khartoum and north to Tanqasi and the mouth of the Atbara. These graves, few of which have been excavated, are generally ascribed by authorities to the Noba—a western people who may have been responsible for the final collapse of Merowe.[21] The Noba were the basis for the kingdom whose capital was at Soba near Khartoum. This kingdom, called Alodia, was long-lived. It was converted to Christianity by Longinus about 570 A.D. North of Alodia was another Christian kingdom, the little-known Mukurra centered on the Dongola Reach. From the Third Cataract to Aswan the true Nubia, the Nobatae Kingdom, converted to Christianity by Julian in 543, was ruled from its capital, Faras—now about to be flooded. Thus the old Kingdom of Kush and Merowe was divided up by new peoples and the ancient world was at an end.

It is interesting to speculate why civilization, which had at least some of its origin and certainly much of its early development along the Nile, should have moved into Europe and not into Africa. In the active days of the New Kingdom, when Egyptian viceroys encouraged the settlement and development of Kush, both the technological and philosophic skills of the Egyptian Empire were funneled into Africa. Kush itself was, for a time, a center of civilized activity. The rich natural resources of the Sudanese region, including both useful metals and fertile soil, were a securer basis for civilization than, say, the desert-prone alluvial plains of Southern Mesopotamia or the rocky valleys of Greece. Africa stood at least equal to Europe in its civilized potential during the second millennium B.C. and even later. Christianity, which many historians believe was an early exponent of progress, had a firm hold in Egypt, Nubia, Sudan, and Ethiopia by the sixth century, which is hardly later than its conversion of Northern and Western Europe. What then prevented Africa's early grasp of Western civilization? The answers are certainly complex and our studies too incomplete for certainties. One factor was the conservatism of Egyptian civilization which to the degree already described impeded dynamic change. Another was certainly the vast distances that separated High Africa from the Egyptian centers; Nubia's cataracts and deserts were effective barriers to a flourishing intercourse. Nevertheless our question remains unanswerable now. The more archaeologists work in Africa the more they become aware that considerable populations possessing flourishing cultures were seated in various fruitful regions at the time when Egypt and the Eastern Sudan were peerless exponents of a civilized way of life. Yet aside from certain ceremonial and technological traits, civilization essentially did not take hold. Why this happened is one of the enigmas in human history which Africa itself will have to answer as time rolls on.

Principal Monarchs of Late Egyptian History

Dynasty XXI (Tanite, 1085–950 B.C.)

Dynasty XXII (Libyan Dynasty; Priest Kings of Thebes, 950–730 B.C.)

Sheshonq I	950–929 B.C.
Osorkon I	929–893 B.C.
Takelot I	893–870 B.C.
Osorkon II	870–847 B.C.
Takelot II	847–823 B.C.
Sheshonq III	823–772 B.C.

Dynasty XXIII (817–715 B.C.)

Dynasty XXIV (730–715 B.C.)

Tefneket	730–720 B.C.

Dynasty XXV (Kushite, 751–656 B.C.)

Kashta	
Piankhy	751–716 B.C.
Shabaka	716–701 B.C.
Shabataka	701–690 B.C.
Taharqa	690–664 B.C.
Tanutemun	664–653 B.C.

Fall of Memphis to Esarhaddon of Assyria, 671 B.C.

Fall of Thebes to Ashurbanipal of Assyria, 663 B.C.

Dynasty XXVI (Saite Period, 663–525 B.C.)
  Psammetichos I   663–609 B.C.
  Necho   609–594 B.C.
  Psammetichos II   594–588 B.C.
  Apries   588–568 B.C.
  Amasis   568–525 B.C.

Dynasty XXVII (Persian, 525–404 B.C.)

Dynasty XXVIII (404–398 B.C.)

Dynasty XXIX (394–378 B.C.)

Dynasty XXX (378–341 B.C.)
  Nectanebos I   378–360 B.C.
  Nectanebos II   359–341 B.C.

Dynasty XXXI (Persian, 341–332 B.C.)

Dynasty XXXII (Ptolemaic Greek, 332–30 B.C.)
  Alexander the Great 332–323 B.C.
  Ptolemy I   323–283 B.C.
  Ptolemy II-XIII   285–244 B.C.
  Cleopatra (VII)   44?– 30 B.C.

Roman Rule (30 B.C.–A.D. 324)

Coptic (East Roman Rule, A.D. 324–640)

Islam and
England

*To walk around Wady Halfa is to read the whole romance
of the Sudan. . . . On us English, too, the Sudan has played its
fatal witchery, and half the tale of Halfa is our own as well
as Egypt's. On its buildings and up and down its sandy windy
streets we may trace all the stages of the first conquest, the loss,
the bitter failures to recover, the slow recommencement, the
presage of final victory.*—G. W. STEEVENS, *With Kitchener to
Khartum* (1898)

*From afar Wadi-Halfa may not seem a great center of civili-
zation. But it strikes you differently when you have traveled all*

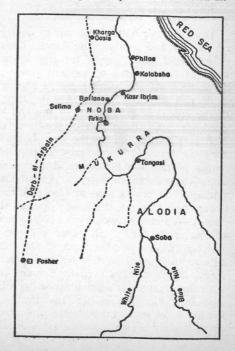

the way from the first cataract and penetrated a little way be-
yond the second. Its newly paved main street that will now
never need repair . . . the carefully tended flower-beds of the
railway station, the sight of boys running to catch the school
bus in an outlying suburb, all in different ways suggest efforts
promising rapid fruit, but which must now be started all over
again somewhere else.—The Manchester Guardian Weekly
(March 17, 1960)

ASSOUAN, Egypt, Dec. 10.—The great Nile reservoir
and dam were opened to-day in the presence of the
Khedive, the Duke and Duchess of Connaught, Lord
Cromer (the British Agent and Consul General in Egypt)
and Lady Cromer, the Ministers, and many other distinguished persons.

The opening ceremony took place in the afternoon,
when the Khedive turned a key which put the electric
machinery in motion, whereupon the sluice gates were
opened and a great body of water rushed through
them.

The Duchess of Connaught then laid the last stone of
the dam. (*New York Times*, December 11, 1902.)

Thus was symbolized the end of over two thousands years
of disunity and trouble. The Aswan Dam, with its assurance
of perennial water supply for Egypt and its firm advertise-
ment of the coming of modern times, sent a clarion call
throughout Africa, stirring native awareness of strange and
wonderful ways. In this the Aswan Dam was in the tradition
of the nobles of Elephantine of the Old Kingdom, whose appearance awed the people of Kush, or the fortresses of the
Middle Kingdom where the hard-bitten armies of Pharaoh
kept vigilance, or the mighty temples of Ramses II before
whose portals the believer and the stranger stood humble.
Like Ramses' monuments the Aswan Dam was an imperial
symbol. The proud men of Great Britain who watched the
waters boil through the newly opened sluices were heirs of
empire—an empire won by a devoted few against the hordes
of the earth. The "sun never set" on the imperial lands
which had been wrested from all the earth's continents. It is
strange that today so few really appreciate the accomplishments of those days even in Britain. In the restless world
with the great maw of civilization to fill, no people are safe
from insecurity, the real fear that their economy will collapse
leaving them impoverished, prey to stranger and alien powers. Certainly Western civilization as we know it today is not

unlike the civilizations of the past in the need for raw material. Whatever the political doctrine of the nation seeking resources for its economic machine, the results are the same —imperialism—explicitly or not. In the nineteenth century it was stated explicitly in London, Paris, Berlin, and Moscow. The hypocrisy of our time is that the powers that be try to conceal their imperial urges: in the past they were proud to state them. The splendor of Great Britain's role in empire building was that many Englishmen knew, even while the empire reached its zenith, that things could not last as they were. Even in the nineteenth century they struggled to create a civilized legacy for their subjects' future independence. What was true for India was even more so for the Sudan. Here it was a matter of bringing order out of chaos. Yet within that web of chaos were the threads of rich native traditions upon which an independent people might build a civilized entity of great significance to all Africa. History had brought many civilizations through Nubia to the Sudan. The last, and perhaps the greatest, would help the arrival of a new era.

Islam in Egypt, Nubia, and the Sudan

The rise of Islam in the seventh century A.D. changed the balance of power in the Mediterranean world. Egypt was one of the first Arab conquests, and by 640 A.D. the Moslems were threatening Nubia and the Sudan from bases in Upper Egypt. The Christian kingdoms of Nubia apparently successfully resisted and were able to prevent wholesale conquest. However, the Arab armies passed beyond the Third Cataract into the Dongola Reach and were able to put Dongola under siege. Dongola was bombarded with catapult stones and the Christian church destroyed. It appears, however, that the town held out and both sides agreed to terminate the conflict. A treaty was signed which lasted some six hundred years —remarkable longevity for treaties at any time. The treaty has survived and is worth recording for its vivid insight into the pattern of the times:

In the name of God, etc. . . . This is a treaty granted by the *amir* 'Abdulla ibn Sa'ad ibn Abu Sarh to the chief of the Nubians and to all the people of his dominions, a treaty binding on great and small among them, from the frontier of Aswan to the frontier of 'Alwa. 'Abdulla ibn Sa'ad ordains security and peace between them and the Muslims, their neighbours in the Sa'id, as well as all other Muslims and their tributaries. Ye people of Nubia, ye shall dwell in safety under the safeguard of God and his apostle, Muhammad the prophet, whom God bless and save. We will not attack you, nor wage war on you, nor make incursions against you, so long as ye abide by the terms settled between us and you. When ye enter our country, it shall be but as travellers, not as settlers, and when we enter your country it shall be but as travellers not as settlers. Ye shall protect those Muslims or their allies who come into your land and travel there, until they quit it. Ye shall give us the slaves of Muslims who seek refuge among you, and send them back to the country of Islam; and likewise the Muslim fugitive who is at war with the Muslims, him ye shall expel from your country to the realm of Islam; ye shall not espouse his cause nor prevent his capture. Ye shall put no obstacle in the way of a Muslim, but render him aid till he quit your territory. Ye shall take care of the mosque which the Muslims have built in the outskirts of your city, and hinder none from praying there; ye shall clean it, and light it, and honour it. Every year ye shall pay 360 head of slaves to the leader of the Muslims [i.e., the Khalifa], of the middle class of slaves of your country, without bodily defects, males and females, but no old men nor old women nor young children. Ye shall deliver them to the Governor of Aswan. No Muslim shall be bound to repulse an enemy from you or to attack him or hinder him, from 'Alwa to Aswan. If ye harbour a Muslim slave, or kill a Muslim or an ally, or attempt to destroy the mosque which the Muslims have built in the outskirts of your city, or withhold any of the 360 head of slaves, then this promised peace and security will be withdrawn from you, and we shall revert to hostility, until God decide between us, and He is the best of umpires. For our performance of these conditions we pledge our word, in the name of God, and our compact and faith, and belief in the name of His apostle, Muhammad, God bless and save him. And for your performance of the same ye pledge yourselves by all that ye hold most sacred in your religion, by the Messiah and by the apostles and by all whom ye revere in your creed and religion. And God is witness of these

RULER OF NOBATIA in horned headdress

things between us and you. Written by 'Amr ibn Shurahbil in Ramadan in the year 31 [May-June, 652 A.D.].[1]

Arab migrations to the Eastern Sudan and the gradual conversion to Islam of numerous peoples around and within the Nubian borders mark the story of the Sudan over the centuries when Europe was in its medieval age. The Christian kingdom of Dongola seems to have been an amalgam of the old Nobatia and Mukurra kingdoms, while Alwa to the south was still independent. In the twelfth to the fourteenth centuries the Nubians dabbled in Egyptian affairs, even presuming to raid beyond the frontier at Aswan. In the twelfth century this aroused no less a personage than the formidable Saladin, celebrated for his prowess against the crusader Richard Plantagenet, surnamed "Lion-Heart." Saladin sent two successive expeditions into Nubia: one headed by his brother. Kasr Ibrim, which as in Roman times was a key fortress in Nubia, was besieged and its garrison fell. It is said that the local church was looted, the Bishop tortured, and some seven hundred pigs slaughtered by the pig-hating Moslems. The Moslem general sent an envoy to Dongola to find out something about the country. His report is enlightening, as it reveals something of the poverty that actually pervaded this last Christian kingdom of the Sudan.

. . . a poor one, where scarcely anything is grown except a little *dura* and some small date-palms on the fruit of which the inhabitants live. The king came out of his palace naked and mounted a horse without saddle or caparisons: he had wrapped round him a robe of silk, and he had not a hair on his head. "I advanced towards him," said the ambassador, "and when I would have saluted him he burst out laughing. He appeared to understand no word of what I said, and he ordered one of his men to mark on my hand the figure of a cross. He gave me about fifty *rotls* of corn. There were no buildings at Dongola excepting the palace of the king. The rest were all huts of straw." [2]

Some of the Christian ruins in Nubia to be covered over by the impending inundation are fortifications attesting to the tempo of the times. In the fourteenth century wars and invasions had not only ended Christian political power, but Christianity itself became an increasingly minor factor in Nubia. However, Alvarez, a Christian chaplain of a Portuguese mission to Abyssinia in the 1520's, heard of Christians in Nubia at that time. These were probably remnants of the Kingdom of Alwa, whose geographic position was nearer Merowe than Nubia but whose location was generalized as Nubia by the Abyssinians.

The rise of several powerful kingdoms in the Sudan during the sixteenth and seventeenth centuries effectively separated Christian Ethiopia from Moslem Egypt. These kingdoms were largely Islamized. One of them, the Kingdom of the Fungs, had its center at Sennar on the Blue Nile and included most of the territory between the Ethiopian Highlands and Nubia. Nubia itself was partly in Fung, partly controlled by Egypt, and partly in the hands of local rulers. In the seventeenth century the Shaigia of Dongola, an indigenous people whose ancestors may have served the rulers of Kush and Merowe in their heyday, threw off Fung rule. The center of their control was the Dongola Reach—the old Kush. The Shaigia, like the Kushites of Piankhy's day, were horse lovers. In fact Dongola was a center for horse raising. Each Shaigia chief had a fortified castle which was the center for raiding operations against the caravan routes linking Egypt and the Fung. These were the days of firearms, and the marvelous Shaigia horsemen were not only able to use them to maintain their independence but to wax fat on the caravan trade. The consequence of this was, of course, the gradual collapse of the trade.

The Fung empire was ruled from Sennar by a line of strong monarchs whose horned caps were emblems of royalty derived probably from the headdresses worn by the Christian kings of Nubia. These in turn were derived from the royal crowns of Merowe when the horns were emblematic of the god Amun. Thus in the midst of Islam the old traditions still had some survival.

The Fung kingdom, effectively cut off from the north, got involved in a series of weakening wars with the Abyssinians. The Fung expanded westward, however, and for a time ruled Kordofan. West of that region, however, was the powerful kingdom of Bornu—and later of Fur—which ruled vast areas of Darfur. Wars and local disorders brought the Fung to a virtual end. In 1821, Mohammad Ali, the celebrated expeller of the Mameluke rulers of Egypt, sent a Turkish army into the Sudan under his son Ismail Pasha. The Turks found little resistance except from the Shaigai, who eventually joined them. Thus Nubia and the Sudan came under Egyptian control once more in a repeat of a historic process centuries old.[3]

Slave Trade in the Sudan

But Egyptian and Turkish excesses in the Sudan were of such scope as to shock the civilized world. The Sudan was looked upon as a source of revenue in which slaves were a chief asset. The black tribes of the south were especially valuable to the slavers and raiding accelerated as never before. In 1837, Ignatius Pallme, a Bohemian who had lived for some time in Egypt and knew Arabic, took a journey into Kordofan to determine the feasibility of commerce with more distant points in the Turko-Egyptian realm. His account of the slave trade as he saw it carried on in Kordofan remains a classic of human horror. Some of his observations bear repeating.

Pallme describes a raid in the Nuba hills where a number of agricultural tribes had their villages. The villagers resisted desperately but superior weapons defeated them:

But now, indeed, in vengeance terrific: neither aged

men nor the infirm, neither helpless women and children, nor, indeed the baby unborn are spared, every hunt is plundered, the property of the unfortunate besieged either pillaged or destroyed, and whosoever falls into the hands of the destroyer with his life is carried down into the camp as captive. When the Negroes see that resistance is no longer of avail, they frequently prefer suicide, unless prevented, to slavery; and thus it often occurs that a father rips the abdomen of his wife, then of his children, and lastly murders himself, to avoid falling alive into the hands of the enemy.

The greatest sufferings are not yet surmounted, and many of these unhappy men would prefer death inflicted by their own hands to the dreadful fate which awaits them, if they were acquainted with their lot beforehand. They now have to suffer every description of ill-treatment from their tormentors; blows with the butt-end of the musket, bayonet wounds, and stripes with the whip, are the ordinary modes of encouragement adopted to arouse the energies of those miserable beings, who, exhausted by physical or moral suffering, may happen to sink. Pity is unheard of in these transports, and as personal interest is not engaged for the preservation of one of those unhappy wretches, or to prove it an advantage, the only consideration is to render their escape impossible. The Djelabi treat their slaves with more humanity, because their personal interests are implicated, for each slave may be considered a capital to them, and they, consequently, do all in their power to preserve life, at least, and thus to avert a loss. The Turks, on the other hand, who have no considerations of this description to attend to, treat their prisoners far worse than they would beasts. As soon as they have collected from three to six hundred, or perhaps a thousand slaves, the convoy is sent with an escort of native troops, and of about fifty men, regulars, under the command of an officer to Lobeid.

To prevent flight, a *Sheba* is hung around the neck of the full-grown slaves; it consists of a young tree about six or eight feet in length, and two inches in thickness, forming a fork in front; this is bound round the neck of the victim so that the stem of the tree presents anteriorly, the fork is closed at the back of the neck by a cross-bar, and fastened *in situ* by straps cut from a raw hide; thus the slave, in order to be able to walk, is forced to take the tree in his hands, and carry it before him. No individual could, however, bear this position for any length of time; to relieve each other, therefore, the man in front takes the log of his successor on his shoulder, and this measure is repeated in succession. It amounts to an impossibility to withdraw the head, but the whole neck is always excoriated, an injury leading often to inflammatory action, which occasionally terminates in death. Boys from ten to fifteen years of age, who could not carry the sheba, are handcuffed together by wooden manacles. The instruments are applied to the right hand of the one and the left of the other, above the wrists, where they are fastened by straps; they are somewhat excavated to admit the hand, but generally fit so closely that the skin is excoriated, and malignant ulcers are the result; but even if the hand were to mortify, or drop off, no alleviation of the sufferings of the individual would ensue, for the fetters are not taken off before the arrival of the convoy at Lobeid. Some of the boys are fastened together in couples by straps applied round the upper part of their arms. It may, therefore, easily be imagined how difficult progression is rendered to these poor sufferers, and what tortures they have to endure on this march. In addition to these trials, they have to bear with most miserable fear, and further ill-treatment, should their strength fail them, or should they become too weak to proceed. Children under the age before-mentioned, women, and old men, are marched singly, and unfettered. Many a mother carries her infant, born but a few days before, at her breast, and must even take two or three of her children, who may be too young or too weak to walk alone, in her arms, or on her back. Old and infirm men who can scarcely creep along with the aid of a stick, the sick, and the wounded, are taken in the middle, between their daughters, wives or relations, and thus slowly dragged onwards, or even carried by turns. If one of these unfortunate beings happen to remain behind the ranks, he is immediately stimulated to increased activity by blows with the butt-end of the musket, or flogged on with the whip. Should even this encouragement fail, and when several of these poor wretches cannot possibly proceed any further, ten or twenty of them are bound by the hand with a rope, the one end of which is attached to the saddle-bow of a camel, and thus those who are half dead are dragged onwards; even if one of them happen to sink no mercy is shown, but the fallen man is trailed along the ground and not liberated, even should he breathe his last, before his arrival at the stated place of rest. Before the caravan halts there is no idea of offering any refreshment whatever in the way of food to the exhausted; the heartless Turk feels no compassion, knows no pity; even if a drop of water might revive a weary wretch, none is given him—no, he may perish from want.

When the caravan reaches the place of rest, those who have been dragged along are liberated; whilst the dead and the exhausted are thrown without mercy on the sand, and the latter left to their fate. No prayers, no entreaties can soften the obdurate hearts of their torturers. They do not even allow a wife to take leave of her husband, or a child to press the parting kiss upon the lips of its expiring parent. No one is permitted to approach these unfortunate wretches,—they are given over to their fate. Not even as much as a piece of bread, or a drop of water is left behind for them. The discarded wretch is given up to his doom to linger out his existence, add to which the misery of the full consciousness of certain death. In six or fourteen days, the transport reaches Lobeid, and it is no wonder, considering the inhuman treatment the captives have had to endure, that on its arrival more than one-tenth of the number is found wanting. No notice, however, is taken of this frightful loss on the road, for it is government property, and personal interest is not concerned.

In Lobeid the slaves remain together until all the transports arrive, and then the distribution takes place. The men best adapted for the purpose are drafted into the regiments as recruits, and the remainder of the full-grown slaves are delivered over to the troops, quartered in Kordofan, in liquidation of their arrears of pay, at an estimate of three hundred piasters a head; younger slaves are valued at various prices. The soldiers are compelled to re-sell them to the merchants for ready money, or for money's worth; sometimes the slave dies of over-fatigue, or excess of torture, or does not realize the full sum on account of his age or infirmities, and then the soldier suffers the loss, who, moreover, generally receives but half his pay, although he has had to wait for several months, or more frequently a whole twelvemonth for this portion of his arrears.

It is not an uncommon occurrence for a son to find his own father, or a father his son, assigned to him, or

51. PYRAMID FIELD AT NURI as seen by G. A. Hoskins in 1833.
(*The American Museum of Natural History*)

52. "FUZZY-WUZZY," Port Sudan, Africa. These people are probably descendants of the ancient Beja nomads.
(*The American Museum of Natural History*)

53. SUDANESE ARAB—a modern descendant of the Arabs who brought Islam into Africa.
(*The American Museum of Natural History*)

54.   MEDITERRANEAN ENTRANCE TO SUEZ CANAL, Port Said, Egypt. Suez at the time of the Mahdi.
(The American Museum of Natural History)

55. BEGGARA NATIVES OF KOSTI. These people were early supporters of the Mahdi and fought fiercely at such famous battles as El Teb and Omdurman. *(The American Museum of Natural History)*

56. SUAKIN, SUDAN. This port city was a meeting ground of Africa and Islamic Asia. The architecture reflects the proximity of Arabia. *(The American Museum of Natural History)*

57. BAZAAR SCENE, TOKAR, Red Sea Hills, Sudan
(The American Museum of Natural History)

58. SUAKIN, AFRICA. Key to the Sudan during the nineteenth century. This famous port city is now largely abandoned.
(The American Museum of Natural History)

59. SUAKIN, SUDAN. This was the key port on the Red Sea during the wars of the Mahdia. (*H. E. Anthony, American Museum of Natural History*)

60. CAMEL CORPS AT JEBEL MOYA, SUDAN. The camel corps was one of the key branches of the Anglo-Sudanese military. It had rapidity of movement and great endurance, prerequisites to direct warfare.
(The American Museum of Natural History)

61. VISIT TO JEBEL MOYA of Lord Kitchener and His Excellency the Governor-general Sir Reginald Wingate and their staffs. Tallest figure in foreground is Kitchener. An unusual and rare picture of the conqueror of the Sudan and Wingate, the friend of Gordon and Slatin.
(The American Museum of Natural History)

62. "FUZZY-WUZZY" TRIBESMEN, Tokar. Backbone of the Mahdist armies in 1884-1898.
(*H. E. Anthony, American Museum
of Natural History*)

for a brother to become the possessor of his brother; but he is forced in defiance of the feelings of nature to sell him, in order to share the proceeds with a comrade who is co-proprietor of the slave with him. Officers and privates are obliged to receive these slaves at a certain valuation in lieu of money, and generally sell them at a loss to the Djelabi. The remainder is disposed of by public auction, in the market-place, to the highest bidder.

I was unfortunately, during some few days, an eye-witness of the misery these poor prisoners endured. No pen can describe the cruelties these miserable men were made to suffer, in addition to the mental torment consequent on their loss of freedom; for laden with the heavy sheba round their necks, or bound together with tight straps or handcuffs, the poor Negroes were driven on like cattle, but treated with far less care or forbearance. The greater number of them, covered with the wounds they had received in battle, or excoriated by the sheba, or the straps, and handcuffs, were put to yet severer trials on the road, and, if too exhausted to keep pace with the transport, the most cruel punishment awaited them; the piercing cry of complaint of these unfortunate beings, and the tears and sobs of the children who had either lost their parents in the capture of the village, or were too tired to follow their exhausted mothers, would have melted a heart of stone to pity. On these ruthless executioners, however, even this scene of misery produces no effect; they march with unconcern by the side of the prisoners, and are only anxious to further the progress of the convoy, by urging on those who may be so weak that they cannot follow the rest with blows and stripes. As they dragged every-one away with them whom they found living, there was, of course, a large number of lame, blind, and old men, and persons afflicted with other infirmities, among the complement of slaves, who were sure to perish on the road, or who would be of no value on their arrival in Lobeid. But, even this circumstance was not deemed worthy of consideration; without mercy all were driven from their homes, and delivered up to their fate; for the sole object is, to furnish the number of slaves demanded by the government. Every morning, at about ten o'clock, a halt was ordered, whereupon the prisoners were formed according to their age into divisions, to receive their rations, consisting of boiled dokn. Salt was out of the question, and the dokn so hard that the fullgrown men experienced difficulty in masticating it. Children, who are too weak in the jaw to reduce the grain, swallow it as they would pills, and are frequently put to the most excruciating agony in consequence; for, not being able to digest the food, their bodies swell, and they suffer from flatulence and spasm. I have seen mothers chewing the victuals for their children, and then offering it to them. In forming these detachments according to age, children who anxiously cling to their parents are torn by force from their arms, that they may eat alone. The condition of sick and wounded was not considered; their wounds were not even dressed, and they received the same allowance; many of them threw themselves on the sand, and, refusing all food, preferred to rest their weary limbs. When one of these poor wretches was so debilitated that it became a matter of doubt whether he could be dragged on any further, or when he was drawing his last breath, he was thrown, like a piece of wood, aside, either to languish in despair, or to be torn to pieces by the wild beasts. Bread is unheard of on these marches, although they have every convenience for baking; this would be too great a luxury, however, for the poor slaves, who must content themselves with food not even good enough for cattle.

As soon as the signal for the march was given, the slaves were forced to join their detachments, and, in case of delay for one minute only, the whip and butt-end of the musket were again at work. Old men and infirm women, bent down with the weight of years and care, who could scarcely creep along, suffered like treatment, and when too weak to move on were left to perish on the sand. Children were not allowed to take leave of their nearest relatives; a tear and a look of sorrow was the only tribute they could pay to the unfortunate beings delivered over to their doom. To prevent a father or a mother from perishing in this miserable manner, their wives or daughters, who were unfettered, would take one of these wretches between two of them, who, passing his arms round the neck of both, was thus dragged on, or even at times carried. Children above six years of age, or even at the age of four, were forced to walk; they also generally succumb to the fatigues of the march, and are then carried by their mothers or sisters. I have seen a mother with an infant on one arm, and a child of two years of age on the other, at last charge herself with a grown boy on her back, until she sank herself exhausted under this triple load.

An hour before sunset a halt was again ordered, and rations of boiled dokn were once more served. But in the night the misery of the slaves reached its very climax. In the month of January, when the changes of temperature are ordinarily very perceptible, and the thermometer falls below 4 ° Reaumur [41 ° Fahrenheit], the cold is felt as severely as when at 4° or 5° below 0 ° Reaumur [23 ° to 20 ° Fahrenheit], in the northern parts of Germany. Imagine, now, the poor Negroes, in a state of absolute nudity, without the means of covering themselves, and debilitated by hunger and fatigue, when some idea may be formed of the sufferings they had to endure; fires were certainly lighted but the scanty supply of wood rendered it impossible to defend these poor wretches from the effects of cold. The shrieks and sobs of the children, the cries of the wounded, and the groans of the sick, were perfectly horrifying, and in the morning an infant was once found dead and stiff with the cold at its mother's breast. It is true that the Negroes have no covering in their own villages beyond a girdle or a piece of linen passed round their loins, but then they lie at night in their huts, or cover themselves with the skins of animals, none of which they can find on their march. Those who wore the sheba could not sleep at night for pain, as it so severely compresses the neck that it impedes every movement, and thus not one man was free from suffering. A woman far advanced in pregnancy was delivered in the night without assistance. I gave the poor mother a skirt, in which she wrapped her infant, and thus safely carried it to Lobeid, and in compassion for her weak state I lent her my ass to ride. I am unequal to the task of narrating all the horrors I witnessed during the few days I attached myself to the convoy; no words are sufficiently expressive to describe the sufferings of the slaves, and no tongue can tell the painful sensations of a man of feeling who witnesses these atrocities.[4]

Accounts of this kind aroused tremendous indignation in Europe, especially in England. Representations to Mohammad Ali were made by various governments and reforms were promised but not carried out. The trade was too lucrative. Notable is the fact that the Nubians of Dongola were foremost among the slave traders. After Mohammad Ali's death a law was passed in 1857 abolishing the slave trade, but again profit made the law ineffective. The attention aroused by the slave trade, the economic possibilities of Africa rapidly being grasped by Europeans, and the lure of geographical exploration, particularly to discover the sources of the Nile, brought a number of fascinating and hardy Europeans on to the scene. The famous explorers Speke, Grant, and Burton, the engineer John Petherick, and the explorer-soldier Sir Samuel Baker are noteworthy among these. English interest in Egypt and the Sudan led to a greater participation in Egyptian affairs. Petherick, in fact, was first British Consul in Khartoum. This post he used as an instrument for reporting on affairs in the Sudan, especially the corruption of the Egyptian officials. He undertook projects to prosecute the slave traders and by so doing earned the enmity of local governors. The Egyptians added to his unpopularity so that he eventually left his post. Nevertheless he pointed up the difficulties of bringing reform.

Sir Samuel Baker, excerpts from whose writings are quoted in this book, made numerous travels of exploration in Africa in company with his beautiful Hungarian wife, from 1861 to 1865. These travels led to the discovery of the Albert, Nyanza, and Murchison Falls. Baker was both opposed and helped by the slave and ivory traders in this period. On his return to the Sudan in 1869, he was a representative of the Egyptian Government empowered to bring the equatorial provinces of the Sudan under administrative control. This brought him into direct conflict with the slavers, and only his implacable steadfastness and indomitable courage enabled him to accomplish what he did. His administration effectively reduced slave trading as long as he was there, but after he left the Sudan the old corruption returned.[5]

Among the colorful figures who roamed the shores of the White Nile during the nineteenth century there was none more colorful or more daring than the beautiful Alexandrine Tinne, daughter of a Dutch merchant. Her mother was of the Dutch nobility, Baroness van Steengracht Capellen. Miss Tinne was accomplished in many languages and noted for her horsemanship. As the legend goes, she was disappointed in love when quite young and forthwith buried her emotions in undertaking long journeys into Africa. After a few of these carried out in the better-known regions, she determined to enter the far country west of the Bahr-el-Ghazal. In 1863 Miss Tinne, in company with her mother, aunt, lady's-maids, and two German scientists, went by chartered vessels from Khartoum far into the interior. Much geographical knowledge was acquired, but her mother and one of the Germans died in the field and the returning expedition barely reached Khartoum. Undaunted, Miss Tinne continued her travels, visiting much of North Africa. However, in her mind was the determination to reach the unexplored Upper Nile regions. She worked out a plan to go across the Sahara by caravan to Lake Chad and thence to the Upper Nile. Unfortunately rumors that she had vast treasures with her reached the ears of the Toureg of the Central Sahara. When she reached their territory she was promptly set upon. Her Dutch companions were killed and she received two blows from a saber. One of these cut into her neck but her hair saved her by cushioning the blow. The other practically cut off her right hand. The girl was left lying on the sand in the full sunlight for some seven hours, when she finally died at the age of thirty-three.

Miss Tinne was remarkable in an age of remarkable Europeans. In a full sense she is representative of the high courage and determination which opened Africa to the West. Western Europe was now the new juggler of civilization. Industrialization was creating a demand unprecedented in the history of civilization. Whereas men in the eighteenth century had been thinking of single countries as sources for raw materials or potential markets, now whole continents of peoples and land were sought with an imperial avariciousness surpassing Alexander and Rome. Egypt and the Sudan were no longer required for themselves alone but for their strategic importance as a way to India, East Asia, and Central Africa. What happened on the shores of the Nile could affect London, Calcutta, and Hong Kong in one fell swoop. Global strategy reared its awesome head, but even so the old combination of Egypt, Nubia, and the Sudan still played major roles in the new civilizations.

Gordon and the Mahdi

In the midst of the high adventure of the time Charles "Chinese" Gordon stands out. As many have remarked, he was fully representative of the Victorian soldier. Brave, principled, impetuous, born to an aristocratic code, he was religious, capable of great gentility, and a natural leader of men. It is a wonder with a heritage of such men that the modern phenomenon of the "teddy boy" could ever come about. For certainly Gordon, with all his virtues and all his faults, was a model fit for any high-minded youth. But then Americans have fine models in their heritage and juveniles languish just the same.

Gordon's story has often been repeated and should be read by anyone with a thirst for adventure. Trained as a military engineer, he saw service in the Crimea and Asia Minor. In the early 1860's he was in China, where he gained great fame as the commander of European and Chinese forces fighting the Taipings. In 1874, after a brief service in England and Eastern Europe, he succeeded Sir Samuel Baker as governor of the equatorial provinces under the Khedive of Egypt, the quasi-independent ruler who more and more came under the influence of London. Gordon set up administrative posts at various strategic points in the provinces from which he could operate against the slave trade. So well organized was his administration that the slave trade was effectively lessened. As a result of his success and under pressure for greater reforms in the oppressed Sudan the Khedive appointed Gordon Governor-General of the Sudan.

The slave traders tried every means possible to upset Gordon's administration. Their efforts, plus the long grievances against the Egyptian government for oppressive taxation, arbitrary justice, and the like, kept the Sudan in a turmoil of dissatisfaction and in places actual revolt. Gordon acted as best he could to bring about reform. His own efforts and those of his lieutenants, one of whom was Rudolph Slatin, an officer in the Austro-Hugarian army, were successful in putting down the open revolts and in bringing order. Gordon became a kind of legend in the Sudan, noted for his swiftness to punish revolt and for his justice to all who reached him. Border trouble with Ethiopia was to have been settled by a peace treaty. Gordon was sent by the Khedive as envoy but the King of Ethiopia took him prisoner and sent him back to the Red Sea port of Massawa. Gordon, tired out by his efforts in the Sudan, resigned from the governorship and returned to England in 1879. This was a more severe blow to the Sudan than was known at the time. Try as they might to improve matters, the officials left by Gordon found corruption too deep-seated and hatred for Egyptian rule undiminished.

The Suez Canal, among other important factors, made control of Egypt increasingly necessary for Britain and France. The Turkish influence in Egypt was almost negligible now and the Khedive Ismail, who tried to modernize Egypt, got himself into heavy debt. Heavy taxes and local corruption brought revolts against his rule and opposition to Europeans who were blamed for the impoverished condition of the country. In 1882, matters reached such a peak that a British army had to be landed to suppress the hostile Egyptians. Victory for the British at Tell-el-Kebir placed the country in their hands—an event not particularly welcomed in London. Reforms were absolutely necessary if there was to be any stability, and the British chose to bring these about by giving proper advice to Khedival authority. One of the pressing problems was the Sudan. In the days of Mohammad Ali that region had been a source of considerable revenue. Decades of corruption had sapped the wealth and impoverished the people. The upkeep of the Egyptian administration and the far-scattered garrisons was expensive and by now the cause of a considerable bite into an already thin Egyptian treasury. It was obvious to the British that the Sudan should be abandoned. This decision was enhanced by the open revolt which had spread all over that country.

At Dongola a religious figure, Mohammad Ahmad, emotionally preached against the corruption of the "Turks" (all foreigners) from his headquarters on Abba Island. As we have seen on other pages, Dongola was a strategic area for thousands of years: the richest stretch in the Northern Sudan, crossroads for many caravan routes, the control of Dongola was critical in history. Mohammad Ahmad, called "the Mahdi" (the Guide) quickly gained popularity among the Dongolese; trips into Kordofan under the guidance of his lieutenant, the tribe-wise Abdullahi Mohammad or "Khalifa," gained him important support.

The tribes were receptive and as the Mahdi became more and more eloquent his adherents waxed in number. In the beginning of the year 1883, the Mahdist forces were strong enough to seize El Obeid, nerve center of Kordofan. Aroused to the danger in the Sudan, the Egyptian-British government decided to act by sending an army of some ten thousand Egyptians under Colonel William Hicks. Hicks avoided the troublesome Nubian route and instead sailed his forces to Suakin on the Red Sea. From there he marched overland to Khartoum. Forced by policy to act in spite of his better judgment, Hicks invaded Kordofan with only nine European officers and poorly trained Egyptian troops. The Mahdist forces attacked savagely near El Obeid and Hicks and most of his men, worn out by the desert march, perished. This was the proof of the Mahdi's invincibility needed to really rouse the country. On the Red Sea coast another Sudanese force, under the slave dealer Osman Digna, smashed another Egyptian army at El Teb under General Baker.

Only a British force under General Graham managed to stop the Mahdists in a second battle at El Teb, and in so doing, hold Suakin.

Thus the decision to retire from the Sudan was precipitated by the success of the Mahdists. However, Egyptian garrisons were widely scattered and their numerous families had to be evacuated and at once. In this situation Gordon was recalled to Egypt by the British Government and from Cairo sent to the Sudan with orders to get the Egyptians out and, if possible, suppress the revolt. Gordon, undaunted by the personal danger of using the desert route from Korosko, went overland through Nubia to Khartoum, capital of the Sudan since 1830.

Gordon was in a position of immense danger, further enhanced by the withdrawal of most of the British troops from Suakin. Berber, on the Nile just below the junction of the Atbara River, was the terminus of the route from Suakin. For Gordon this was the key to the Sudan. He telegraphed to London that a British force be used to keep that route open but London, uncertain about its involvement in Sudanese affairs, refused. The withdrawal of the British forces at Suakin was followed by the surrender of the Egyptian garrison at Berber in May, 1884. Gordon and his weak forces at Khartoum were cut off from the outside world by an advancing Mahdist (sometimes called Dervish) army. In March, 1884, Khartoum had gone under siege and Gordon with but one British aide was compelled to fight for his very life. The splendor of his action was that, deserted by all, he yet remained with the people he had come to succor. Thus the code of the English gentleman was stronger even than life itself.

Gladstone's government had been reluctant all along to involve Great Britain too deeply in Egyptian affairs. The peril to both the Suez route and to British prestige by Egyptian actions had caused the British government to use troops to put down Egyptian rebellion. By so doing they were forced to take an active part in Egyptian problems whether they liked it or not. The Sudan was certainly one of these problems. However, Gladstone and many of his party saw the Sudanese revolt as the proper rebellion of a people against Egyptian oppression, whether represented by the slave traders or the corrupt officials. Besides, whatever deficits were incurred in the Egyptian treasury because of the Sudanese, Great Britain had to make up.

Whatever the logical reasons for British noninvolvement in the Sudan the fact was that the British were the new masters of Egypt. For thousands of years Egypt and the Northern Sudan had been linked. Great Britain had a responsibility that all history could not let her deny. And there was Gordon. Public opinion was fanned to white heat by the vision of this lone British soldier fighting hopelessly in the midst of the far Sudan. Political opponents of Gladstone used the issue to undermine him. Frederick Burnaby, soldier, adventurer, and ardent Tory, who had fought at El Teb, was among those eloquently demanding help for Gordon. His words are typical of the time.

Every moment is precious and our Ministers, apeing the Pharisees, thank God they are not like other men who wish to save Gordon; they have deceived him, betrayed him and thrown him over; now they wish to let him die to save the expense of an expedition for his release. Mr Gladstone once said that he could not stand the blood-guiltiness in the Soudan. Are the deeds of butchery to be consummated by the sacrifice of the noblest Christian soldier this country has ever seen? Is he to be one more victim to Midlothian? Is the blood of that gallant fellow to lie at our people's door? Now is the time for action, let all English men and women, irrespective of party, and who love their country's honour, combine, lest Gordon's blood should be on their heads and their children's. Ask yourself this question, "Is Mr

Gladstone's Government to live or Gordon to die?" [6]

At last it was decided to undertake a rescue. Lord Wolseley, who had served in Egypt and Canada, was given command. Wolseley, remembering his Canadian experiences and well aware of the difficulty of passing the Nubian cataracts, engaged a corps of Canadian Voyageurs and ordered whaleboats built in England. The immediate goal was Korti in the Dongola Reach just below the old Napata area. Steamers and whaleboats were forced past the Second and Third Cataracts in a massive effort in which Nubians and Egyptians pulling on steel hawsers played the significant role just as they must have in the days when the viceroys of Kush brought their laden barges up the Nile. The expedition left Cairo in October. A message was received from Gordon written on November 4: "At Metamma, awaiting your orders, are five steamers with nine guns. We can hold out forty days with ease: after that it will be difficult."

But moving the troops with all their stores was time-consuming. The delays earlier caused by government had made every movement critical now. It was the season of low Nile—the worst time for river travel. Fighting the river current, the complications of bringing together a fighting force now strung out from Aswan to Korti, the difficulty of amalgamating all the different peoples who made up the expedition into a unity—all served to impede. But by Christmas the chosen base at Korti was swelled with the concentration of a great army.

On December 31, a desperately tired native messenger reached Korti from Khartoum: "We are besieged on all three sides, Omdurman, Halfayah and Khojoli. Fighting goes on day and night. . . . Our troops are suffering from lack of provisions. The food we have is little, some grain and biscuit. We want you to come quickly. You should come by Metemma and Berber. Make by these two roads."

Wolseley ordered his camel corps and units of cavalry to strike across the desert to Metemma at once while the main column followed around the great bend of the Nile. But it turned out that they were short of camels. This meant it would be necessary to set up a base at the Jakdul Wells in the midst of the desert. It was not until January 15 that the desert forces were able to leave Jakdul. The next wells were at Abu Klea and there the Mahdist forces, some eleven thousand of them, rose out of the desert and attacked the

British square. A desperate battle ensued in which that same
Burnaby, who had spoken so eloquently for Gordon's relief,
was killed by a spear in the throat.

As he died a young English soldier held his hand and
with tears running down his cheeks cried out to an officer:
"Oh! sir; here is the bravest man in England, dying and no
one to help him." [7]

The desert column eventually won through to Metemma
and reached Gordon's surviving steamers on January 21.

After an inexplicable delay an advance force embarked in
two steamers and sailed off to Khartoum. The men of the
Sussex regiment donned red uniforms so that Gordon, seeing
them, would recognize the symbols of England and take
courage that help was near.

On January 28, the steamers came in sight of Khartoum at
last. How eyes were strained to catch the signs that Gordon
and his men still held out! But the flag was gone and only
rifle fire from the Mahdists on the shore greeted them. On
January 25, the Mahdi, taking advantage of the low Nile and
a river-damaged section of the defenses, had assaulted the
city just before dawn. The defense collapsed and thousands
of the fanatic enemy poured into Khartoum. The main goal
was the Palace, where was Gordon, the last representative
of a past they hated.

The guardian of Khartoum, realizing the end had come,
had put on his full-dress white uniform. He came to the
head of the palace stairs where he faced the attack alone.
He was immediately speared, hauled down the steps, his
head severed and sent to the Mahdi, while his body was
stabbed a thousand times over by the wild Mahdists.

Rudolph Slatin, who had been the governor of Darfur
and captured by the Mahdi, was a prisoner in chains in the
Mahdi's camp at Omdurman. With a touch of fiendish pleasure the fall of Khartoum was announced to him as a former
officer who had served Gordon.

The sun was now rising red over the horizon; what
would this day bring forth? Excited and agitated, I
awaited the result with intense impatience. Soon shouts
of rejoicing and victory were heard in the distance,
and my guards ran off to find out the news. In a few
minutes they were back again, excitedly relating how
Khartum had been taken by storm, and was now in the
hands of the Mahdists. Was it possible the news was

false? I crawled out of my tent and scanned the camp; a great crowd had collected before the quarters of the Mahdi and Khalifa, which were not far off; then there was a movement in the direction of my tent, and I could see plainly they were coming towards me. In front marched three Black soldiers; one named Shatta, formerly belonging to Ahmed Bey Dafalla's slave body-guard, carried in his hands a bloody cloth in which something was wrapped up, and behind him followed a crowd of people weeping. The slaves had now approached my tent, and stood before me with insulting gestures; Shatta undid the cloth and showed me the head of General Gordon!

The blood rushed to my head, and my heart seemed to stop beating; but with a tremendous effort of self-control I gazed silently at this ghastly spectacle. His blue eyes were half-opened; the mouth was perfectly natural; the hair of his head and his short whiskers were almost quite white.

"Is not this the head of your uncle, the unbeliever?" said Shatta, holding the head up before me.

"What of it?" said I quietly. "A brave soldier, who fell at his post. Happy is he to have fallen; his sufferings are over."

"Ha, ha!" said Shatta, "so you still praise the unbeliever; but you will soon see the result"; and, leaving me, he went off to the Mahdi, bearing his terrible token of victory; behind him followed the crowd, still weeping.[8]

The British relief forces had no other choice than retirement from the Sudan, leaving Khartoum to the horrors of a Mahdist army. The problem was the future. Again the British Government hesitated. The military wanted to hold Dongola and Suakin. These were the critical areas whose possession would effectively confine the Mahdi. A railroad was planned from Suakin to Berber. Again Gladstone changed his mind and Dongola was evacuated, leaving only Suakin under the Khedive. The Mahdi died and his lieutenant, the Khalifa, succeeded.

Defeat of the Mahdists

The Khalifa envisioned the conquest of Egypt much as had the ancient rulers of Kush. The retreat of the British and Egyptians from Dongola made concentrations of Sudanese forces near the frontier possible. Only through the utmost effort on the part of the British and Egyptians was the invasion threat offset. It is of interest that the Mahdist defeats were all in Nubia. The first, in December, 1885, was at Ginnis, between Dongola and Wadi Halfa. The second attempt by the Mahdists was led by Emir Wad-el-Negumi, the best soldier in the Khalifa's forces. To avoid the natural barrier of the Nubian Nile, Wad-el-Negumi chose to advance in the wastes of the western desert with his goal Aswan if possible. But a combined British-Egyptian force intercepted him when his subordinates tried to strike the Nile Valley near Kasr Ibrim. At Toski the Emir was killed, along with twelve hundred of his men.

These defeats stopped major threats to Egypt from the Sudan even though petty raids continued. How very much like the patterns of the past was this: ancient Egyptians, Ptolemaic Greeks, Romans, Moslem Arabs, and now British and Egyptians operating out of the Aswan area or from bases in Nubia to prevent raids on the lands farther north.

The peremptory law of the Khalifa, the constant wars, the displacement of tribes, the impoverishment of the people, actual starvation because too few men were available for cultivation, and a host of other miseries made life in Mahdist Sudan a harsh matter. The raids on Egypt and the possible encroachment of European powers on Sudanese territory in the "scramble for Africa" pointed up the necessity for settling the Sudan question once and for all. Gordon's death was still unavenged and among many Victorian gentlemen this was a matter that stood out above all others. At last the decision was made to reoccupy the Sudan. Sir Herbert Kitchener was appointed Sirdar, commander of the combined forces under the Khedive. Now there was a railroad built to Wadi Halfa. In 1896, another battle at Firket, not far from Akasha where one of Ramses II's temples stands, smashed the Khalifa's frontier faces. Sudanese battalions now were used in the combined forces and formed some of the best of the troops, much as the Medjai had in ancient Egypt.

Kitchener had the advantage of a co-operative British government and his plan for pushing the railroad from Wadi Halfa to Abu Hamed across the desert, thus completely avoiding the Dongola Stretch, was readily approved, as were his requests for equipment and reinforcements. His army was well trained, thoroughly equipped, and battle wise; and all the valor of the Khalifa's "fuzzy-wuzzies" had no effect. The results were terrible. On the Atbara in April, 1898, a major battle was fought. The end result was 81 killed and 493 wounded for Kitchener's forces and at least 3,000 dead for the Mahdist, with wounded unknown, and no one knows how many lost in the desert in their desperate flight. The fanatical fury of their resistance is best symbolized by a little ten-year-old Sudanese boy standing by his dead father trying to shoot an elephant gun at the British foe.

At Omdurman the final page to the miserable story of the Mahdist period was written. We who live so much later cannot conceive of the gravity of that day, September 2, 1898, within sight of the walls of Khartoum. For all the wrongs of the Khalifa his people were fanatically loyal to the Mahdist ideal that death in battle would give them, in another life, some portion of the glory of God. Against the machine which was Kitchener's army the burnoused Arab and the naked Sudanese were prepared to hurl their antique weapons and home-made bullets, believing hippopotamus hide shields and amulets would protect them if it were God's will. Proud horsemen, nomadic camel riders, bush spearmen, white-bearded holy men rallied by drum and the green-and-black flags, shouted, and with all their might ran at the Maxim guns and repeating rifles that were held by the disciplined soldiers of Europe. It was, indeed, the last charge of ancient Africa—of a way of life whose record we have been tracing until this day. There could be only one result. The war correspondent Steevens described it:

> And the Dervishes? The honour of the fight must still go with the men who died. Our men were perfect, but the Dervishes were superb—beyond perfection. It was their largest, best, and bravest army that ever fought against us for Mahdism, and it died worthily of the huge empire that Mahdism won and kept so long.

Their riflemen, mangled by every kind of death and torment that man can devise, clung round the black flag and the green, emptying their poor, rotten, home-made cartridges dauntlessly. Their spearmen charged death at every minute hopelessly. Their horsemen led each attack, riding into the bullets till nothing was left but three horses trotting up to our line, heads down, saying, "For goodness' sake, let us in out of this." Not one rush, or two, or ten—but rush on rush, company on company, never stopping, though all their view that was not unshaken enemy was the bodies of the men who had rushed before them. A dusky line got up and stormed forward: it bent, broke up, fell apart, and disappeared. Before the smoke had cleared, another line was bending and storming forward in the same track.

It was over. The avenging squadrons of the Egyptian cavalry swept over the field. The Khalifa and the Sheikh-el-Din had galloped back to Omdurman. Ali Wad Helu was borne away on an angareb with a bullet through his thigh-bone. Yakub lay dead under his brother's banner. From the green army there now came only death-enamoured desperadoes, strolling one by one towards the rifles, pausing to shake a spear, turning aside to recognise a corpse, then, caught by a sudden jet of fury, bounding forward, checking, sinking limply to the ground. Now under the black flag in a ring of bodies stood only three men, facing the three thousand of the Third Brigade. They folded their arms about the staff and gazed steadily forward. Two fell. The last dervish stood up and filled his chest; he shouted the name of his God and hurled his spear. Then he stood quite still, waiting. It took him full; he quivered, gave at the knees, and toppled with his head on his arms and his face towards the legions of his conquerors.[9]

The impact of this desperate period on both Africa and Europe was very great. It resolved once and for all Great Britain's role in the Nile Valley. Not three days after Omdurman, word came to Kitchener that a small French force under a Major Marchand had reached Fashoda on the White Nile just below the mouth of the Sobat River. The French planned to build a fort there and thus claim a part of the Nile Valley in the Southern Sudan. This attempt might have succeeded except for Kitchener's victory and his subsequent ability to move troops to Fashoda. Diplomatic exchanges finally resolved the British and French spheres in this part of Africa. One thing was now certain, the British had been instrumental in finishing Mahdism; now they were responsible to the Sudanese for a new administration. The Sudan could not be left to Egypt alone—nor could it be abandoned to the chaos which it had known for so long.

The answer lay in an active participation in the Sudan by trained British officials until such time as the Sudanese could be trained to accept the responsibility of their own affairs. The next fifty years were proud ones for both British and Sudanese. The handful of devoted young men who made up the Sudan Civil Service under the governor-general were of that same breed as Baker and Gordon. They learned languages and customs; they administered justice and battled for good will on all levels. The pacification of the Sudan, the administration of the tribes, and the general improvement of the country were carried out under the stress of continual heat, killing disease, and living conditions which would have broken the unenthusiastic. The host of almanacs, gazetteers, scientific reports, agricultural digests, which poured from the Sudan are indicative of the success of the battle for understanding Sudanese problems. The Aswan Dam, which did so much for Egypt, was but one of several dams that controlled the flood of the Nile. Foremost in development was the Gezira, the rich triangle formed by the junction of the two Niles. Proper irrigation made this one of the richest agricultural regions in Africa.

For all the faults of British imperialism, the Republic of the Sudan which they left is a far cry from the torn land which they first controlled in 1898. It is a strange course of events which led British interests from Egypt to the Sudan but it is in keeping with the past. The railroad to Abu Hamed and now to Khartoum, the cement and tin officials' houses in the towns, the piers and warehouses at Port Sudan, take their place with the Middle Kingdom forts, the great temples of Ramses, the pyramids of Merowe, the ruined Christian churches, the doomed Mosques—to mark a period in the history of civilization. Wadi Halfa along with Abu Simbel, Kasr Ibrim, and Buhen will disappear beneath the Nile waters backed up by the new dam. But there will always be some trace of the past in Nubia, for human cultures have a way of giving immortality to themselves by leaving some trace in the customs and the blood of the living.

Principal Dates and Events of the Later History of the Sudan

ca. 350 A.D.	Fall of Merowe
ca. 550	Conversion of Nubia to Christianity
641	First Moslem invasion of the Sudan
1484–1790?	Fung Kingdom
1820–1821	Conquest of the Sudan by Mohammad Ali of Egypt
1882–1883	British take over in Egypt
September 13, 1882	Battle of Tel-el-Keber
1884–1898	Mahdia
January 26, 1885	Fall of Khartoum and death of Gordon
September 2, 1898	Battle of Omdurman
1899–1956	British administer the Sudan

Epilogue

As of this writing considerable progress has been made in the documentation of the endangered sites of Egyptian Nubia. In 1955, the Documentation Centre on Ancient Egypt, an international body with headquarters in Cairo, began the process of thoroughly recording the doomed ruins. Their emblem is the goddess Maat, patroness of truth, i.e., precision and balance. By means of photography, supplemented by drawing and casting, the great temples of Abu Simbel were completely recorded. In process are recording surveys of Wadi-es-Sebua, Debad, Kalabsha, and the chapels of Abu Oda and Jebel Chams. The Oriental Institute of the University of Chicago has had an epigraphic team at Luxor whose concentration has been upon the Ramesside temple of Medinet Habu. Now the team is utilizing its experienced skills at Beit-el-Wali.

The science of photogrammetry has provided invaluable aid for the accurate recording of the monuments. This is a wonderful process of stereoscopic photography which by a system of contours gives the exact dimension of an object. By means of a pantograver a frieze in relief, for example, can be traced in plaster and an exact reproduction of the original created, accurate to a fiftieth of an inch.

Aerial photographs of the Nile Valley give a basis for a photogrammetric contour map which is invaluable for archeological surveying.

Thus with all the means available, a handful of devoted men are toiling, often in uncomfortable situations, to record a doomed world. Their results will form a magnificent archive, available through microfilm, which will assure the preservation of a portion of man's story no matter how high the waters may go.

At this writing there are twenty-four temples of various periods that can be cut out of the rock and transported to high ground. Three of these have been raised by the government of the United Arab Republic in 1960–1961, and that government will take care of still others. The large remainder, however, depends upon the efforts of foreign governments and institutions. The dam to protect Philae will cost probably about $5,500,000, while the raising of the other temples will run to between $9,000,000 and $10,000,000.

Abu Simbel, however, is another matter. Ramses' colossal conception may be the doom of his great temple. The sandstone from which it is carved is porous and should a two-hundred-foot-high dam be erected as a coffer protecting the temples, pumps would have to be continually maintained to prevent the water from damaging the carvings. Just how effective pumping would be to prevent slow water permeation is conjectural. Thus the cofferdam may be only arresting destruction for a time.

An alternative plan is to cut the temples out of the rock as two great blocks, as mentioned earlier. Once this is done each block would be encased in a box made up of concrete and steel framing. The large temple block would weigh 250,000 tons—an extraordinarily heavy mass. Hydraulic lifts in great number would be placed under each block and in a series of stages the temples would be raised the two hundred feet or so necessary to clear the waters. The area would be landscaped and the temples still in correct orientation would be saved. This scheme has been proposed by Professor Pietro Gazzola, an Italian archaeologist, and the method has been worked out by a team of Italian engineers.[1]

The blocks out of which the temples were carved may have a number of cracks which would worsen under the stress of the lifting process. The detection of these inherent weaknesses and their reinforcement by means of concrete and steel are major problems. The fact that such cracks do exist and that the temple blocks are hollow creates a load-distribution problem. The equalization of the load on the jacks so that each lift is level requires a control apparatus of great complexity. The estimate is that each lift will be some 30 cm., after which prefabricated beams will be introduced under the foundation and the jacks lowered. New supports for the jacks must then be built before the next lift can take place. However, the structure thus raised under the temples creates the new foundations and insures the maintainance of the Ramesside monuments by the shores of the new Nile flood.

This latter scheme is breathtaking in scope and if carried out would certainly be worthy of the founder of Abu Simbel. However, the tab is some $60,000,000, or about five-sixths of the entire sum needed for the salvage of Egyptian Nubia.

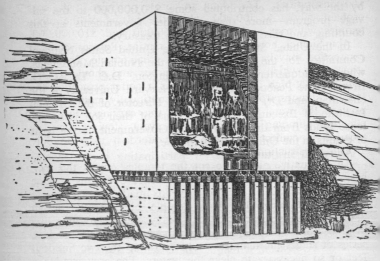

ARTIST'S DRAWING of one conception as to how one of the Abu Simbel temples might be raised. See *New Scientist*, April 1961, for further details.

Obviously only an international effort could raise this sum —actually no more than the cost of a moderate-sized battleship.

The Republic of the Sudan has a far more difficult problem because there are not only temples, like the fine one at Buhen, but hundreds of archaeólogical sites to excavate. The Middle Kingdom brick fortresses will vanish practically with the first floods. Their potential for history can only be guessed at, but it must be enormous if the work of Emery at Buhen is any criterion (see page 109). Sudanese Nubia is in the greatest danger because many institutions are more willing to work in Egyptian Nubia, since the recompense is greater. However, in contrast the Sudanese material may be of greater importance to history. Thus the tragedy of archaeological salvage unrolls.

At present there are more than fifteen expeditions in Nubia hard at work. International bodies have been set up to co-operate with the local authorities. There is the UNESCO consultative committee which is composed of experts who advise the United Arab Republic. The U.A.R., by the way, has contributed some $10,000,000 to the salvage program—more than all other governments at this counting, and this out of a slender treasury.

In the United States there is the United States National Committee for the Preservation of the Nubian Monuments, whose headquarters are in Washington, D.C. Dr. J. O. Brew of the Peabody Museum of Harvard University is the chairman, and Dr. John A. Wilson, Director of the Oriental Institute, is Executive Secretary. Part of their job is to pry loose funds from the United States Government on the basis of credits in the United Arab Republic.

American institutions so far participating in the salvage program are the Oriental Institute of the University of Chicago (at Beit-el-Wali and the Aswan region); Brown University (at Kasr Ibrim and Buhen); Yale and the University of Pennsylvania (at Ermenna and Toshka).

For those interested in contributing funds or equipment it is advisable to contact the above institutions or to write Dr. John A. Wilson, Director, The Oriental Institute, University of Chicago, Chicago 37, Illinois.

APPENDIX I

The Dam Statistics

ASWAN DAM (EL KHAZZAN)

Built first 1899–1902.

100 feet high; stored 980 million cubic meters of water; formed an artificial lake 140 miles upstream.

Raised 16 feet between 1907–1912; stored 2,400 million cubic meters of water; reservoir backed upstream 185 miles.

Raised 30 feet between 1929–1934; stored 5,000 million cubic meters of water; reservoir backed upstream 225 miles to Wadi Halfa.

Is about 1¼ miles long.

HIGH DAM (SADD-EL-AALI)

Will be 225 feet high and 2½–3 miles in length; store 130,000 million cubic meters; reservoir will back upstream 300 miles. It is expected that it will permit the cultivation of some 2,500,000 acres of desert land, or half again of Egypt's arable land.

16 turbines will provide 2,000,000 horsepower; with the Aswan output Egypt will have above 15,000 million kilowatt-hours a year.

APPENDIX II

The First Salvage Program in 1907

The building of the Aswan Dam completed in 1902 flooded some portion of the Nile Valley above the First Cataract, including the island of Philae. However, it was really not until a proposal was made in 1907 to raise the height of the dam that growing fears for the ancient remains in Nubia came to a climax. Accordingly funds were set aside by the Egyptian Government to survey, record, and where possible excavate in the endangered area, which extended some 250 kilometers upstream from Aswan. That this was done then in highly successful fashion bodes well for the present archaeological campaign. The survey was under the direction of Dr. G. A. Reisner, and a description of how the work was carried on was written by H. G. Lyons in the introduction to the first volume of publication of the material. It is well worth quoting since it gives a good idea of what is involved in these salvage studies:

The whole reach was to be surveyed, and all evidence of former human habitation was to be collected and recorded in order to preserve as accurate and complete an account as possible of the existing vestiges of early life and culture, which must inevitably perish when submerged. The region extended from the head of the First Cataract for some 250 kilometres to about the village of Derr, shortly upstream of which point the level of the new reservoir will coincide with the ordinary flood-level of the river, and consequently beyond this, no change in condition will be caused. Up to the level of 106 metres above sea-level, the banks of the river and its

233

flood-plains have been annually saturated since the first filling of the reservoir at the beginning of 1903; so it was only necessary to investigate the sides of the valley and the flood-plains of the river above this and up to the level of 115 metres above sea-level, or to a height of two metres above the final level of the water of the enlarged reservoir. The task was a formidable one, and had to be carried out on a comprehensive scale, in order, once and for all, to search the whole of this belt of country on either bank throughout the entire reach which was to be affected. The plan adopted was to provide for a complete survey of the valley and of the desert on either side for a short distance from the river; to prepare accurate plans of each locality where an ancient site or cemetery was found; and to plot special large-scale plans of each cemetery in order to show the location and orientation of each grave. The scales employed were usually 1 : 10,000, 1 : 2,500, and 1 : 250 or 1 : 100; others were utilized at times when special circumstances rendered it advisable. This series of accurate plans, admirably adopted to illustrate the region investigated, will be of great assistance in following the detailed descriptions of each locality; the work was controlled, wherever possible, by the triangulation (Second and Third Order) which had been carried out some years previously in the course of executing the Cadastral Survey of the cultivable lands of Egypt.

This topographical basis was utilized by the archaeological staff whose work commenced by having the belt of country between the levels of 106 and 115 metres examined by trained diggers, who noted all places where there appeared to be ancient settlements or cemeteries. These were then carefully excavated under the skilled supervision of Dr. G. A. Reisner, of Harvard University, who for several years has been excavating in Egypt, and has an especially intimate acquaintance with the earliest civilization of the country. Under his direction each site was carefully exposed, each interment was photographed, every object was registered and full records kept, in order that as much information as possible should be preserved in addition to the collection of objects found. Dr. Reisner's intimate acquaintance with early Egyptian art and civilization was especially valuable in the study of this new region, for it enabled him to date each interment, and thereby provide a firm basis for anthropological studies; for a thorough study of such a region involved not only the collection of objects and the reconstruction of the culture of the people who had once inhabited the valley, but also the determination of their race and ethnological affinities.[1]

Notes

Chapter 1

1. Bailey Willis, *East African Plateaus and Rift Valleys* (Washington, D.C.: Carnegie Institute, 1936), p. 165.
2. Sir Samuel W. Baker, *The Albert Nyanza* (London: 1866), p. 337.
3. Baker, *Ismailia* (London: 1874), pp. 92-96.
4. G. W. Steevens, *With Kitchener to Khartum* (New York: Dodd, Mead, 1898), pp. 198-200.
5. E. E. Evans-Pritchard, *The Nuer* (Oxford: 1940), pp. 64-65.
6. Maj. R. E. Cheesman, *Lake Tana and the Blue Nile* (London: Macmillan, 1936), p. 72.
7. Frederick C. Denison, *Records of the Nile Voyageurs* (Toronto: Champlain Society, 1959), p. 24.
8. Baker, *The Nile Tributaries of Abyssinia* (London: 1867), pp. 6-8.
9. After J. Putnam Marble, in F. E. Zeuner, *Dating the Past* (4th ed.; London: Methuen, 1958), p. 336.

Chapter 2

1. K. S. Sandford and W. J. Arkell, "Paleolithic Man and the Nile Valley in Nubia and Upper Egypt," *Oriental Institute Publications*, XVII (Chicago: 1933), xv (Introduction).
2. A. J. Arkell, in J. D. Tothill (ed.), *Agriculture in the Sudan* (London: 1948), p. 10.
3. See J. Desmond Clark, *The Prehistory of Southern Africa* (Baltimore, Md.: Pelican Books, 1959), esp. pp. 58-73.
4. For a recent description of what may have occurred see R. J. Braidwood, "The Agricultural Revolution," *Scientific American* (September, 1960), pp. 131 ff.

5. G. P. Murdock, *Africa* (New York: McGraw-Hill, 1959), pp. 66-67.

6. Note Arkell's discussion of western connection in *Shaheinab* (Oxford: 1953), pp. 104-105, 112 ff.

7. Arkell formerly identified the Khartoum Neolithic as the "Gouge Culture," but he has abandoned this term. *Ibid.,* pp. 102 ff.

8. *Ibid.,* p. 105.

9. *Ibid.,* p. 104.

10. *Ibid.,* p. 107.

11. C. B. McBurney, *The Stone Age of Northern Africa* (Baltimore, Md.: Pelican Books, 1960), p. 244.

Chapter 3

1. James Henry Breasted, *Ancient Records of Egypt* (Chicago: 1906), I, paragraph 146.

2. W. S. Smith, *The Art and Architecture of Ancient Egypt* (Baltimore: Pelican History of Art, 1958), p. 20.

3. J. Mayer and T. Prideaux, *Never to Die* (New York: Viking, 1938), pp. 57-58.

Chapter 4

1. A. H. Gardiner, *The Admonitions of an Egyptian Sage* (Leipzig: 1909), p. 12.

2. G. P. Murdock, *Africa* (New York: McGraw-Hill, 1959), p. 159.

3. A. J. Arkell, *A History of the Sudan* (London, 1955), p. 49; *Early Khartoum* (Oxford: 1949), p. 14.

4. G. A. Reisner, "Excavations at Kerma," *Harvard African Studies* (Peabody Museum, Harvard University, Cambridge, Mass.: 1923), V. 5.

5. H. E. Winlock, *The Rise and Fall of the Middle Kingdom in Thebes* (New York: Macmillan, 1947), pp. 27, 43.

6. James H. Breasted, *A History of Egypt* (2d ed.; New York: Scribner's, 1959), p. 157.

7. Somers Clarke, "Ancient Egyptian Frontier Fortresses," *Journal of Egyptian Archaeology,* III (1916), 158.

8. Gardiner, "An Ancient List of the Fortresses of Nubia," *Journal of Egyptian Archaeology,* III (1916), 192.

9. List after Arkell, *op. cit.,* pp. 62-64.

10. Reisner, "Excavations at Semna and Uronarti," *Sudan Notes and Records,* XII (1929), 154.

11. W. B. Emery, "A Preliminary Report on the Excavations of the Egyptian Exploration Society at Buhen," *Kush,* VII (1959), 7 ff.

12. Emery in *Illustrated London News,* September 12, 1959, pp. 249-251.

13. For example, read John A. Wilson, *The Culture of Ancient Egypt* (Chicago: University of Chicago Press, 1956), pp. 56-58.

14. H. C. Jackson, *Sudan Days and Ways* (London: Macmillan, 1954), pp. 195-196.

15. Reisner, "Excavations at Kerma," V, 77-79.

16. Breasted, *op. cit.*, p. 166.

17. W. Vycichl, "Notes on the Story of the Shipwrecked Sailor," *Kush,* V (1957), 70 ff.

Chapter 5

1. J. H. Breasted, *A History of Egypt* (New York: Scribner's, 1909), p. 277.

2. For an account of Egyptian views on Kush and the surrounding lands, see Ernest Zyhlarz, "The Countries of the Ethiopian Empire of Kush . . ." *Kush,* VI (1958), 7 ff.

3. Breasted, *op. cit.*, p. 331.

4. M. S. Giorgini, "Soleb," *Kush,* VI (1958), 82-98 (Campaign of 1957-1958); VII (1959), 154-170 (Campaign of 1958-1959).

5. E. A. Wallis Budge, *The Egyptian Sudan* (Philadelphia: Lippincott, 1907), I, 446-448.

6. Nina M. Davies, *Ancient Egyptian Paintings* (Chicago: 1936), Vol. II, Plates 79-81.

7. A. J. Arkell, *A History of the Sudan* (London, 1955), p. 112.

8. J. L. Burckhardt, *Travels in Nubia* (London: 1819), pp. 90-91.

9. G. Belzoni, *Researches and Operations in Egypt, Nubia, etc.* (London: 1820), pp. 211-212, 214.

10. W. H. Yates, *Modern History and Condition of Egypt* (London: 1843), II, 463-467.

11. Amelia B. Edwards, *A Thousand Miles up the Nile* (2d ed.; New York: A. L. Burt, 1888), p. 324.

12. *Ibid.*, pp. 268-277.

13. *UNESCO Courier,* February, 1960, p. 14.

14. Breasted, *op. cit.*, pp. 421-422.

15. A full account of the gold of Nubia and Kush is in J. Vercoutter, "The Gold of Kush," *Kush,* VII (1959), 120-153.

16. Breasted, *op. cit.*, p. 497.

Chapter 6

1. Dominique Vivant Denon, *Travels in Upper and Lower Egypt* (New York: 1803), II, 95-96.

2. Samuel A. B. Mercer, *The Religion of Ancient Egypt* (London: Luzac, 1949), pp. 376-377.

3. Denon, *op. cit.*, II, 82-83.

4. G. W. Curtis, *Nile Notes of a Howadji* (New York: 1856), pp. 204-205.

5. Amelia B. Edwards, *A Thousand Miles up the Nile* (2d ed.; New York: A. L. Burt, 1888), pp. 132-133.

6. *Ibid.*, p. 210.

7. James H. Breasted, *Egypt Through the Stereoscope* (New York: Underwood & Underwood, 1908), pp. 321-322, 327.

8. D. D. Luckenbill, *Ancient Records of Assyria and Babylonia* (Chicago: University of Chicago Press, 1926), II, 227.

9. A. J. Arkell, *A History of the Sudan* (London: 1955), p. 130.

10. Nahum, 3:8-10.

11. I. E. S. Edwards, *The Pyramids of Egypt* (Harmondsworth: Pelican Books, 1952), p. 201.

12. G. A. Reisner, "Preliminary Report on the Harvard-Boston Excavations at Nuri," *Harvard African Studies,* II (Cambridge, Mass.: 1918), 1-64.

13. Arkell, "An Egyptian Invasion of the Sudan in 591 B.C." (note on Sauneron and Yoyotte's article), *Kush,* III (1955), 93-94.

14. Reisner, *op. cit.*, pp. 19 ff.

15. Reisner, *ibid.*; Dows Dunham and M. F. L. Macdam, "Names and Relationships of the Royal Family of Napata," *Journal of Egyptian Archaeology,* XXXV (1949), 149. See p. 199 for list.

16. Arkell, *History of the Sudan*, pp. 148-149.

17. Herodotus, III, 17, 18.

18. John Garstang and others, *Meroe* (Oxford: 1911), pp. 25-27.

19. Arkell, *History of the Sudan*, pp. 165-167.

20. W. B. Emery, *Nubian Treasure* (London: 1948).

21. P. L. Shinnie, "The Fall of Merowe," *Kush,* III (1955), 82-85.

Chapter 7

1. H. A. MacMichael, *A History of the Arabs in the Sudan* (Cambridge: Cambridge University Press, 1922), I, 157-158.

2. *Ibid.*, I, 176.

3. The best book on the Fung is O. G. S. Crawford, *The Fung Kingdom of Sennar* (Gloucester: 1951).

4. Ignatius Pallme, *Travels in Kordofan* (London: J. Madden, 1834), p. 314.

5. Baker's works were published in numerous editions during the nineteenth century. They are well worth anyone's reading. See Bibliography, page 252.

6. Michael Alexander, *The True Blue* (London: Hart-Davis, 1957), p. 173.

7. *Ibid.*, p. 203.

8. Rudolph C. Slatin, *Fire and Sword in the Sudan* (London: Edward Arnold, 1898), pp. 206-207.

9. G. W. Steevens, *With Kitchener to Khartum* (New York: Dodd, Mead, 1898), p. 282-283.

Epilogue

1. Professor Gustavo Colonnetti, "Lifting the Abu Simbel Temples," *New Scientist*, No. 232, April 27, 1961, pp. 162-64.

Appendix II

1. H. G. Lyons, in G. A. Reisner, *The Archaeological Survey of Nubia, Report for 1907-08* (Cairo: 1910), iii-iv.

1. Professor Charles Glanman, "Before the Anti-Stink Law," *New York Scientist*, No. 232, April 22, 1961, pp. 182-99.

Appendix III

1. H. D. Crane et al., "... ..., ... , ... Journal ... Society, Vol. 23 (?: 33, 1918) ibid.

GLOSSARY

A ... measurement ... the ... of ... belongs to the carbon-14 ... found in atmospheric ... you the age of the ... that the carbon-14 ... decreases at a known rate ... the initial amount disappears, the remaining amount is also halved in another period of ... example. The amount of carbon in the ... ... found that the Egyptologist and is measured in the laboratory and this gives an approximate date.

CAESIUM

A scintillation ... used in color used commonly in argon ... ... film.

Glossary

ACHAEMENIDS

Pertaining to the ruling house of Persia which dominated much of the Near East from the sixth to the fourth centuries B.C.

ACHEULIAN

The climax of the handax development in Lower and Middle Paleolithic context.

AMRATIAN

The earliest of the predynastic cultures of Upper Egypt (ca. 4000 to 3600 or 3400 B.C.).

AUSTRALOPITHECINAE

Name for a group of primate forms of Early Pleistocene time found in South Africa.

BADARIAN

The name given to a prehistoric culture found around Badari in Middle Egypt.

CAPSIAN

A Mesolithic blade-tool industry of North Africa.

CARBON-14 DATING

A method of measuring the rate of radioactivity in the carbon-14 atom found in all organic matter. On the death of the living organism the carbon 14 begins to decrease at a definite rate; in about 5750 years half the integral amount disappears. The remaining amount is also halved in another period of 5750 years. The amount of carbon 14 in the organic matter that the archaeologists find is measured in the laboratory and this gives its approximate date.

CARNELIAN

A semiprecious stone, red in color, used commonly in ancient jewelry, inlay, and the like.

CHELLEAN, ABBEVILLIAN

Names used to designate the handax industries of the Lower Paleolithic.

CIVILIZATION

As used in the context of this volume, it refers to urbanization and the complexity of culture resulting from or influenced by urbanized communities.

DEMOTIC

A simplified method of writing hieratic commonly used in late Egyptian times.

DYNASTY

A succession of rulers usually of the same line. The Egyptian dynastic system was determined by Manetho, a Graeco-Egyptian priest, in 280 B.C.

ERG

A desert region composed of shifting sand.

GERZEAN

The earliest of the predynastic cultures of Lower Egypt. It eventually spread to Upper Egypt where it amalgamated the Amratian to produce the late predynastic culture (ca. 3600-3200 B.C.).

GRAFFITI

Ancient scribbling: writing, pictures, or symbols.

HANDAX

A tool of the Lower Paleolithic. It consists usually of a flint core chipped on both faces into a triangular or oval form. It is sometimes called a coup de poing.

HIERATIC

A cursive method of writing hieroglyphics.

HYPOSTYLE

A hall whose roof rests on rows of columns.

KIOSK

A kind of pavilion with open sides, the roof of which is supported by delicate columns of fretwork.

LAPIS LAZULI

A semiprecious mineral, rich blue in color, greatly prized in ancient times.

LEVALLOISIAN

A flake-tool industry of the Middle Paleolithic characterized by the preparation of the striking platform of the core.

MAGMA

Molten material under the earth's surface from which igneous rock derives.

MALACHITE

A copper carbonate which is green in color. In ancient times it was ground and used as a pigment in cosmetics, paint, and the like.

MASTABA

A funerary building commonly used in the earlier dynasties of Egypt. It was usually rectangular and flat-topped and contained a chapel and covered a burial chamber.

MESOLITHIC

The Middle Stone Age; a transitional period including some of the most advanced hunting cultures.

NEOLITHIC

In the older archaeological terminology, a term for the New Stone Age, the latest of the stone ages before the advent of the general usage of metal.

OROGENY

The process of mountain building.

PALAEOLITHIC

The Old Stone Age. This was the period of man's earliest cultures, those of the hunters of the Ice Age. It probably involves a time span of 500,000 or more years.

PAPYRUS

A tall marsh-dwelling plant native to the Nile Valley and adjacent areas. Its pith was used in ancient times for the preparation of papyrus paper.

PLEISTOCENE

The earlier of the two epochs of the Quaternary period, sometimes used synonymously with "Ice Age."

PLIOCENE

The latest of the epochs of the Tertiary period.

PROCONSUL

An early primate form found on Rusinga Island in Kenya.

PYLON

A gateway with sloping sides suggesting a truncated pyramid. This was commonly used in ancient Egypt from New Kingdom times.

QUATERNARY PERIOD

The geological period from the end of the Tertiary period to the present time, sometimes called the Age of Man. It consists of the Pleistocene and Holocene epochs.

STELE (STELA)

A slab of stone bearing an inscription usually commemorating a deceased person or celebrating an event of importance.

SUDD

A term referring to a dense mass of floating vegetation as known along the White Nile in the Southern Sudan.

SUTTEE

A now obsolete practice of India in which the living wife was cremated along with her deceased husband as an act of wifely devotion.

TERTIARY PERIOD

A system of geological time following the so-called Age of Reptiles and before the Quaternary: it consists of the Palaeocene, Eocene, Oligocene, Miocene, and Pliocene epochs.

TOTEM

The symbol of the relationship of human social or economic groups to animal, floral, or other groups usually thought to have supernatural or unusual qualities.

TUFA

A formation resulting from mineral deposits from springs. The formation consists of porous rock.

UNGULATES

The large group of hoofed mammals.

USHABTI

In Egyptian funerary practices, a mummiform model of a servant placed in the tomb of the lord and magically endowed to perform tasks for him in the "other world."

WADI

An Arabic word referring to the usually dry channel of a river or stream as known in desert country.

WATTLE AND DAUB

An ancient method of making a wall by means of sticks woven together (wattle) and then plastered with mud (daub).

Metric Table

10 millimeters (mm.)	= 1 centimeter (cm.)	= 0.3937 in.
10 centimeters	= 1 decimeter (dm.)	= 3.937 in.
10 decimeters	= 1 meter (m.)	= 39.37 in. or 3.28 ft.
10 meters	= 1 decameter (dkm.)	= 393.7 in.
10 decameters	= 1 hectometer (hm.)	= 328 ft. 1 in.
10 hectometers	= 1 kilometer (km.)	= 0.62137 mi.
10 kilometers	= 1 myriameter (mym.)	= 6.2137 mi.

Bibliography

This work has depended heavily upon a number of outstanding publications which are highly recommended to all who would know more about Egypt, Nubia, and the Sudan. Particularly important are A. J. Arkell's *History of the Sudan to 1821*, James Henry Breasted's *Ancient Records of Egypt* (for all translated Egyptian passages except as noted), and *A History of Egypt*, John A. Wilson's *The Culture of Ancient Egypt*, and the studies of G. A. Reisner and Dows Dunham. There are innumerable articles of importance to the study of the history, archaeology, and ethnology of the Sudan in the journal *Sudan Notes and Records* and the newer *Kush*, the journal of the Sudan Antiquities Department. In the latter the articles of J. Vercoutter, present Director of the Sudan Antiquities Service, are worthy of note.

For more recent times there are the individual exploration accounts of the eighteenth and nineteenth centuries which are summarized by Sir Harry Johnston. Sir Samuel Baker's books and that of the Swiss, Burckhardt, are particularly interesting. There are a great many publications on the Mahdia. These are contained in numerous bibliographies in books and articles dealing with the Sudan. Sir Winston Churchill's *The River War* is especially noteworthy. The studies of Sir Harold MacMichael are truly outstanding as are those of O. G. S. Crawford, P. L. Shinnie, and H. C. Jackson.

This bibliography is by no means comprehensive but will serve as an introduction to remarkable people and remarkable accomplishments. It is this writer's hope that the reader will want to delve further if for nothing else than to understand how very much has been left out of this account.

Books

ALDRED, C. *Old Kingdom Art in Ancient Egypt*: Transatlantic Arts, New York, 1949.

ALEXANDER, M. *The True Blue, The Life and Adventures of Col. Fred Burnaby—1842–85*. London: Hart-Davis, 1957.

ARKELL, A. J. *Early Khartoum*. Oxford, 1949.

———. *A History of the Sudan to 1821*. London, 1955.

———. *Shaheinab*. Oxford, 1953.

BAEDEKER, K. *Egypt and the Sudan* (antiquities sections written by George Steindorff). Leipzig, 1914, 1923.

BAKER, S. W. *The Albert Nyanza*. London, 1866.

———. *Ismailia*. London, 1874.

———. *The Nile Tributaries of Abyssinia*. London, 1867.

BELZONI, G. *Researches and Operations in Egypt, Nubia, etc.* London, 1820.

BREASTED, JAMES H. *Ancient Records of Egypt*. 5 vols. Chicago, 1906.

———. *The Dawn of Conscience*. New York: Scribner's, 1950.

———. *Egypt Through the Stereoscope*. New York: Underwood & Underwood, 1908.

———. *A History of Egypt*. 1909; 2d ed., New York: Scribner's, 1959.

BRUCE, JAMES. *Travels to Discover the Source of the Nile*. 6 vols. Edinburgh, 1790.

BUDGE, E. A. WALLIS. *The Egyptian Sudan*. 2 vols. Philadelphia: Lippincott, 1907.

BURCKHARDT, J. L. *Travels in Nubia*. London, 1819.

CAILLIAUD, F. *Voyage à Meroe et au fleuve blanc*. 4 vols. Paris, 1826–27.

CATON-THOMPSON, G. *Kharga Oasis in Prehistory*. London, 1952.

CATON-THOMPSON, G., and GARDNER, E. W. *The Desert Fayum*. London, 1934.

CHEESMAN, R. E. *Lake Tana and the Blue Nile*. London: Macmillan, 1936.

CHURCHILL, W. *The River War*. 2 vols. London, 1901.

CLARK, J. DESMOND. *The Prehistory of Southern Africa*. Baltimore, Md.: Pelican Books A458, 1959.

COLE, SONIA. *The Prehistory of East Africa*. Baltimore, Md.: Pelican Books A316, 1954.

CRAWFORD, O. G. S. *The Fung Kingdom of Sennar*. Gloucester, 1951.

CROSSLAND, C. *Desert and Water Gardens of the Red Sea*. Cambridge: Cambridge University Press, 1913.

CURTIS, G. W. *Nile Notes of a Howadji*. New York, 1856.

DAVIES, NINA M. *Ancient Egyptian Paintings*. 3 vols. Chicago, 1936.

DENISON, F. C. *Records of the Nile Voyageurs, 1884–1885*. Introduction by C. P. Stacey. Toronto: Champlain Society, 1959.

DENON, DOMINIQUE VIVANT. *Travels in Upper and Lower Egypt*. 2 vols. Translated by Arthur Aikin. New York, 1803.

DUNHAM, DOWS. *Royal Cemeteries of Kush, I: El Kurru*. Boston, 1950.

EDWARDS, AMELIA B. *A Thousand Miles up the Nile* (2d ed.). New York: A. L. Burt, 1888.

EDWARDS, I. E. S. *The Pyramids of Egypt*. Harmondsworth: Pelican Books, 1952.

EMERY, W. B. *Nubian Treasure*. London, 1948.

EVANS-PRITCHARD, E. E. *The Nuer.* Oxford, 1940.

FISHER, W. B. *The Middle East.* New York: Dutton, 1952.

GARDINER, A. H. *The Admonitions of an Egyptian Sage.* Leipzig, 1909.

GARSTANG, J., SAYCE, A. H., and GRIFFITH, F. L. *Meroe, the City of the Ethiopians.* Oxford, 1911.

GORDON, COL. CHARLES. *Colonel Gordon in Central Africa, 1874–1879.* From original letters and documents, Ed. G. B. Hill. London: Thomas de la Rue, 1884.

HERODOTUS. *The Histories.* Translated by A. de Selincourt. Baltimore, Md.: Penguin Classics, 1954.

HOSKINS, G. A. *Travels in Ethiopia.* One of the first nineteenth-century descriptions of Merowe. London: Longman, Rees, 1835.

HURST, H. E. *The Nile.* London: Constable, 1952.

JACKSON, H. C. *Sudan Days and Ways.* London: Macmillan, 1954.

JOHNSTON, SIR H. *The Nile Quest.* London: Lawrence and Bullen. 1903.

LEPSIUS, C. R. *Discoveries in Egypt, Ethiopia and the Peninsula of Sinai* (2d ed.). London, 1853.

LHOTE, H. *The Search for the Tassili Frescoes.* New York: Dutton, 1959.

LUCKENBILL, D. D. *Ancient Records of Assyria and Babylonia.* 2 vols. Chicago: University of Chicago Press, 1926.

MACMICHAEL, H. A. *History of the Arabs in the Sudan.* 2 vols. Cambridge: Cambridge University Press, 1922.

————. *The Sudan.* London: Ernest Benn, 1954.

————. *The Tribes of Northern and Central Kordofan.* Cambridge: Cambridge University Press, 1912.

MAYER, J., and PRIDEAUX, T. *Never to Die.* New York: Viking, 1938.

MCBURNEY, C. B. *The Stone Age of Northern Africa.* Baltimore, Md.: Pelican Books A342, 1960.

MERCER, S. A. B. *The Religion of Ancient Egypt.* London: Luzac, 1949.

MURDOCK, G. P. *Africa, Its Peoples, and Their Culture History.* New York: McGraw-Hill, 1959.

PALLME, IGNATIUS. *Travels in Kordofan.* London: J. Madden, 1844.

PAUL, A. *A History of the Beja Tribes of the Sudan.* Cambridge: Cambridge University Press, 1954.

RANDALL-MACIVER, D., and WOOLLEY, C. L. *Buhen.* 2 vols. Philadelphia, 1911.

REISNER, G. A. *The Archaeological Survey of Nubia, Report for 1907–08.* Cairo, 1910. Subsequent reports were issued by C. M. Firth: for 1909–10, Cairo, 1915; for 1910–11, Cairo, 1927.

SELIGMAN, C. G., and SELIGMAN, B. Z. *Pagan Tribes of the Nilotic Sudan.* London, 1932.

SLATIN, RUDOLPH C. *Fire and Sword in the Sudan.* Translated by Col. F. R. Wingate. London: Edward Arnold, 1898.

SMITH, W. STEVENSON. *Ancient Egypt as Represented in the Museum of Fine Arts* (2d ed.). Boston, 1946.

————. *The Art and Architecture of Ancient Egypt.* Baltimore, Md.: The Pelican History of Art (Penguin Books), 1958.

STEEVENS, G. W. *With Kitchener to Khartum.* New York: Dodd, Mead, 1898.

STEINDORFF, G., and SEELE, K. C. *When Egypt Ruled the East.* Chicago: University of Chicago Press, 1942.

Sudan Almanac. Compiled in the Sudan Agency Cairo War Office. London, 1936 (issued yearly).

TOTHILL, J. D. (ed.). *Agriculture in the Sudan.* London, 1948.

WILLIS, BAILEY. *East African Plateaus and Rift Valleys.* Washington, D.C.: Carnegie Institute of Washington (1936), No. 470.

WILSON, JOHN A. *The Culture of Ancient Egypt,* (First published as

The Burden of Egypt.) Chicago: Phoenix Books of the University of Chicago Press, 1956.

WINLOCK, H. E. *The Rise and Fall of the Middle Kingdom in Thebes.* New York: Macmillan, 1947.

YATES, W. H. *Modern History and Condition of Egypt.* 2 vols. London, 1843.

Articles

BRAIDWOOD, R. J. "The Agricultural Revolution," *Scientific American* (September, 1960), pp. 131 ff.

BUTT, A. "The Nilotes of the Anglo-Egyptian Sudan and Uganda," in *Ethnographic Survey of Africa*, ed. Daryll Forde, East Central Africa, Part IV (London: International African Institute, 1952).

CLARKE, SOMERS. "Ancient Egyptian Frontier Fortresses," *Journal of Egyptian Archaeology*, III (1916), 155-179.

DUNHAM, DOWS. "Outline of the Ancient History of the Sudan, V," *Sudan Notes and Records*, XXVIII (1947), 1-10.

DUNHAM, DOWS, and MACDAM, M. F. L. "Names and Relationships of the Royal Family of Napata," *Journal of Egyptian Archaeology*, XXXV (1949), 1939-149.

EMERY, W. B. "A Master-Work of Egyptian Military Architecture of 3900 Years Ago," *Illustrated London News* (September 12, 1959), pp. 232-233, 249-251.

――――. "A Preliminary Report on the Excavations of the Egyptian Exploration Society at Buhen 1957–8," *Kush*, VII (1959), 7 ff.

EVANS-PRITCHARD, E. E. "The Divine Kingship of the Shilluk of the Nilotic Sudan," The Frazier Lecture 1948 (Cambridge, 1948).

GARDINER, A. H. "An Ancient List of the Fortresses of Nubia," *Journal of Egyptian Archaeology*, III (1916), 184-192.

GIORGINI, M. S. "Soleb, Campaign of 1957–1958," *Kush*, VI (1958), 82-98.

――――. "Soleb, Campaign of 1958–1959, *Kush*, VII (1959), 154-170.

KIRWAN, L. P. "Note on the Topography of the Christian Nubian Kingdoms," *Journal of Egyptian Archaeology*, XXI (1935), 57-62.

REISNER, G. A. "Discovery of the Tombs of the Egyptian XXVth Dynasty at El-Kurruw in Dongola Province," *Sudan Notes and Records*, II (1919), 237-254.

――――. "Excavations at Kerma," *Harvard African Studies* (Cambridge, Mass., 1923), Parts 1-3; VI, Parts 4-5.

――――. "Excavations at Semna and Uronarti," *Sudan Notes and Records*, XII (1929), 154.

――――. "The Meroitic Kingdom of Ethiopia: A Chronological Outline," *Journal of Egyptian Archaeology*, IX (1923), 34-77, 157-160.

――――. "Outline of the Ancient History of the Sudan, IV," *Sudan Notes and Records*, II (1919), 35-67.

――――. "Preliminary Report on the Harvard-Boston Excavations at Nuri, etc.," *Harvard African Studies*, II (Cambridge, Mass., 1918), 1-64.

――――. "Uronarti," *Sudan Notes and Records*, XIV (1931), 1-14.

――――. "The Viceroys of Ethiopia," *Journal of Egyptian Archaeology*, VI (1920), 28-55, 73-88.

SANDFORD, K. S., and ARKELL, A. W. "Paleolithic Man and the Nile

Valley in Nubia and Upper Egypt," *Oriental Institute Publications*, XVII (Chicago: University of Chicago Press, 1933).

SHINNIE, P. L. "The Fall of Merowe," *Kush*, III (1955).

UNITED NATIONS. "Save the Treasures of Nubia," *UNESCO Courier*, (February, 1960), No. 2.

VERCOUTTER, J. "Excavations at Sai 1955–7," *Kush*, VI (1958), 144 ff.
———. "The Gold of Kush," *Kush*, VII (1959), 120-153.

VYCICHL, W. "Notes on the Story of the Shipwrecked Sailor," *Kush*, V (1957), 70 ff.

WINLOCK, H. E. "The Egyptian Expedition of the Metropolitan Museum of Art, Season 1918–1920," Part II of the *Bulletin of the Metropolitan Museum of Art*, reprinted separately (1921).

ZYHLARZ, ERNEST. "The Countries of the Ethiopian Empire of Kush and Egyptian Old Ethiopia in the New Kingdom," *Kush*, VI (1958), 7 ff.

Index

MENTOR Books on History and Politics

☐ **THE USES OF THE PAST by Herbert J. Muller.** The civilizations of the past, how they flourished, why they fell, and their meaning for the present crisis of civilization.
(#MY1042—$1.25)

☐ **ISLAM IN MODERN HISTORY by Wilfred Cantwell Smith.** A noted scholar discusses the impact of Mohammedanism on Middle Eastern political life today.
(#MY1108—$1.25)

☐ **THE WORLD OF ROME by Michael Grant.** A brilliant survey of the conquest and culture of the Romans from 133 B.C. to A.D. 217. Profusely illustrated with photographs, line drawings and maps. (#MY956—$1.25)

☐ **THE GREEK EXPERIENCE by C. M. Bowra.** An extraordinary study of Greek culture, its achievements and philosophy. 48 pages of photos. (#MY1064—$1.25)

☐ **THE ANVIL OF CIVILIZATION by Leonard Cottrell.** This fascinating history of the ancient Mediterranean civilizations reveals the long-buried secrets of the early Egyptians, Hittites, Sumerians, Assyrians, Babylonians, Greeks and Jews, brought to light by archaeological discoveries. (#MY951—$1.25)

MENTOR Books on History and Archaeology

☐ **THE ISLAND CIVILIZATIONS OF POLYNESIA by Robert C. Suggs.** An anthropologist reveals the origin and culture of primitive peoples of the South Seas.
(#MQ889—95¢)

☐ **REALM OF THE INCAS by Victor W. von Hagen.** The history, culture, religion, and social and economic life of a fascinating Indian race that achieved a fabulous empire before Columbus discovered America. Copiously illustrated. (#MY1154—$1.25)

☐ **THE AZTEC: MAN AND TRIBE by Victor W. von Hagen.** A noted authority on ancient Latin-America tells the history, daily life, religion, and art of the nation that ruled Mexico before Columbus. Profusely illustrated.
(#MQ1089—95¢)

☐ **WORLD OF THE MAYA by Victor W. von Hagen.** A history of the mysterious Mayas and their resplendent civilization that blossomed in the jungles of Central America.
(#MY940—$1.25)

☐ **THE NATURE OF THE NON-WESTERN WORLD by Vera Micheles Dean.** A noted expert on foreign affairs throws new light on the conflict between East and West as she probes the beliefs, traditions and emotions that motivate the people of the non-Western nations.
(#MY1039—$1.25)

☐ **CULTURAL PATTERNS AND TECHNICAL CHANGE Edited by Margaret Mead.** An exciting voyage to distant lands where the century-old methods of ancient people give way to the most modern machines and techniques mankind has devised. (#MY909—$1.25)

THE NEW AMERICAN LIBRARY, INC.,
P.O. Box 999, Bergenfield, New Jersey 07621

Please send me the MENTOR BOOKS I have checked above. I am enclosing $_____(check or money order—no currency or C.O.D.'s). Please include the list price plus 15¢ a copy to cover handling and mailing costs. (Prices and numbers are subject to change without notice.)

Name_____

Address_____

City_____State_____Zip Code_____
Allow at least 3 weeks for delivery

NILE — RIVER OF LIFE

Flowing through northern Africa into the Mediterranean, the great seasonal-flooding Nile nurtured one of mankind's oldest civilizations. Along its banks still stand awe-inspiring monuments, testimony to the timeless achievements of the people who flourished in its fertile valley.

A noted archaeologist and anthropologist describes the stone records of many lost civilizations as he plots the historical course of the river from the empires of the pharaohs in Egypt to the British Empire in the Sudan. His urgent plea is that the great monuments of Nubia, imposing records of man's ancient past, be saved from the waters of the dam now being built by the United Arab Republic.

WALTER A. FAIRSERVIS, Jr. is the Director of Washington State Museum, University of Washington, and former Research Associate in the Department of Anthropology of the American Museum of Natural History. He is an archaeologist with field experience in the Middle and Far East. His books include *The Origins of Oriental Civilization* and *India*. (The former is available in a Mentor edition.) He is also the author of numerous archaeological reports, and a frequent contributor to scientific journals.